Praise for *From Baldrige to the Bottom Line*

David Hutton has produced another management winner!
—Charles Aubrey II, Vice President, Quality Operations
American Express

This is the first book I have found that clearly and effectively provides a roadmap beyond assessment to the next crucial level: business improvement.
—Tony Glaudé, Staff Director Business Improvement
Bell Atlantic

Hutton's book helps fill a critical gap: it sets out a proven methodology for driving organizational improvement that is simple, effective, and works in government.
—Dr. Larry J. Taylor, Quality Management Advisor
Natural Resources Canada

This is crucial information for all educational leaders and decision makers.
—Christine Collins, Supervisor, Quality Academy
Pinellas County Schools

. . . provides an experience-based, client-tested roadmap for the assessment process. I commend it to your active interest and successful application.
—Robert C. Camp, Principal
Best Practice Institute

David's approach contains benefits of all of the things that we have learned about quality and the use of the assessment process at Xerox.
—Richard J. Leo, Vice President, General Manager XBS
Xerox Corporation

. . . provides a compelling reason for organizations to use the self-assessment process as their compass no matter where they are on the quality journey.
—Dan Corbett, President
National Quality Institute

From Baldrige to the Bottom Line

Also available from ASQ Quality Press

The Change Agents Handbook: A Survival Guide for Quality Improvement Champions
David W. Hutton

Managing Change: Practical Strategies for Competitive Advantage
Kari Tuominen

Root Cause Analysis: Simplified Tools and Techniques
Bjorn Andersen

Critical SHIFT: The Future of Quality in Organizational Performance
Lori L. Silverman with Annabeth L. Propst

The Toolbox for the Mind: Finding and Implementing Creative Solutions in the Workplace
D. Keith Denton

Quality Problem Solving
Gerald F. Smith

Mapping Work Processes
Dianne Galloway

101 Good Ideas: How to Improve Just About Any Process
Karen Bemowski and Brad Stratton, editors

The Certified Quality Manager Handbook
ASQ-Quality Management Division

To request a complimentary catalog of ASQ Quality Press publications, call 800-248-1946, or visit our website at qualitypress.asq.org.

From Baldrige to the Bottom Line

A Road Map for Organizational Change and Improvement

David W. Hutton

ASQ Quality Press
Milwaukee, Wisconsin

Library of Congress Cataloging-in-Publication Data

Hutton, David W., 1947-
    From Baldrige to the bottom line : a road map for organizational change and
improvement / David W. Hutton.
        p. cm.
    Includes bibliographical references and index.
    ISBN 0-87389-473-1
      1. Total quality management. I. Title.

    HD62.15 .H887 2000
    658.4'013--dc21   99-057709

10 9 8 7 6 5 4 3 2 1

ISBN 0-87389-473-1

Acquisitions Editor: Ken Zielske
Project Editor: Annemieke Koudstaal
Production Administrator: Shawn Dohogne
Special Marketing Representative: David Luth

ASQ Mission: The American Society for Quality advances individual and organizational performance excellence worldwide by providing opportunities for learning, quality improvement, and knowledge exchange.

Attention: Bookstores, Wholesalers, Schools and Corporations:
ASQ Quality Press books, videotapes, audiotapes, and software are available at quantity discounts with bulk purchases for business, educational, or instructional use. For information, please contact ASQ Quality Press at 800-248-1946, or write to ASQ Quality Press, P.O. Box 3005, Milwaukee, WI 53201-3005.

To place orders or to request a free copy of the ASQ Quality Press Publications Catalog, including ASQ membership information, call 800-248-1946. Visit our web site at www.asq.org. or qualitypress.asq.org.

Printed in the United States of America

 Printed on acid-free paper

American Society for Quality

ASQ

Quality Press
611 East Wisconsin Avenue
Milwaukee, Wisconsin 53202
Call toll free 800-248-1946
www.asq.org
qualitypress.asq.org
standardsgroup.asq.org

*To my wife, Aggi
and my daughters,
Sarah and Alex.
You are the sunshine of my life.*

Contents

About This Book

This book describes a powerful, proven methodology for driving organizational change and improvement: the assessment process. This process provides a "roadmap" for any organization to develop a high-performance management system and thus improve its "bottom line"—whether this means better financial results or the fulfillment of a mandate.

From Baldrige to the Bottom Line addresses the needs of a wide audience—from senior leaders and managers to educators and facilitators in the trenches. The early chapters provide information that the leaders need up front to get the process started: fundamental concepts, strategy issues, and how to plan for an assessment. Later chapters provide detailed implementation guidance, tools, and techniques, as well as case studies of five role model organizations. A companion website provides a wealth of additional information that complements the book.

Anyone, at any level, who is interested or involved in the assessment process will find valuable information in each chapter.

- *If you have never heard of a Baldrige-based assessment before* (perhaps you thought that a *Baldrige* might be some kind of farming implement), you'll find this book an easy read: it starts from the basic principles and continues up to advanced issues that keep the experts on their toes.
- *If your organization is already using Baldrige* (or one of its many counterparts), this book will help you to get even more out of your assessment process by making it more effective, more

streamlined, and more enduring. If your organization has run into snags in using the assessment process, this book will help you to see why—and figure out how to put things right.

- *If you are an expert in this area*—perhaps you have served as an examiner for Baldrige or a similar award program—most of this book will resonate strongly with your own experience. However, it may also challenge some of your thinking about what constitutes best practice *outside* an awards program, when the primary goal is to create an improvement plan and translate this into improved performance.

- *If your organization performs management system audits,* this book will reveal rich new possibilities for self-examination and diagnosis. Unlike the traditional compliance audit, the assessment process is designed to engage people in a positive fashion, help build support for change, reveal high-leverage opportunities for improvement, and thus contribute directly to the goals of the organization.

What the Book Covers

The following chapters describe the four phases of establishing an assessment-driven improvement cycle:

1. The *preparation* phase—to make sure you know exactly what you are doing before you get started
2. The *assessment process*—a structured examination of the organization's management methods
3. The *improvement steps* that must follow after an assessment—planning, implementation and monitoring—in order to translate the assessment findings into improved performance
4. The *ongoing cycle* that is needed to keep the improvement "wheel" turning. (See Exhibit I.1.)

Finally, there are five *case studies.* These are the stories of five outstanding organizations that have integrated assessment into their way of doing business:

- *Xerox Corporation:* One of the original pioneers of quality improvement and a role model. Xerox is a world-class com-

Exhibit I.1. *Turning the improvement wheel.*

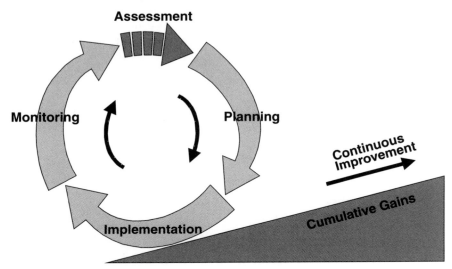

pany that has won not just the Baldrige Award (twice), but virtually every other similar award on the planet. So why is Xerox still performing assessments of every business unit every year?

- *TELUS Mobility:* A Canadian mobile phone service provider that is a model for how to achieve profitable growth by focusing on the customer. Why did TELUS start using assessment when it had only 50 employees?
- *Medrad's* products help radiologists obtain clearer X-ray, CT and MR images. Medrad created the market for such products, grew this market into a major industry, and still dominates it. Medrad has never had a serious crisis, has never been anything but successful and growing. Why did Medrad management decide that conducting assessments would enable them to do better?
- *Cargill:* The multinational agribusiness giant. Cargill operates as a loose federation of largely autonomous business units. Why is this thrifty firm encouraging its business units to spend money on assessments?

- *Pinellas County School District:* One of the largest, most diverse school districts in North America, Pinellas is recording dramatic improvements in student achievement. What does this have to do with Baldrige and the assessment process?

These case studies provide a window into the real-life experience of these high-performing organizations and how they use this methodology to drive change and improvement.

How This Book Differs from Others

"From Baldrige to the Bottom Line" has a very precise focus, which complements the other resources and literature available in this field. It concentrates on:

- The assessment *process* rather than the *criteria* (which describe what the assessment should look for).
  There are other books that describe the Baldrige criteria in much greater depth, and training is essential to properly understand these criteria. This book focuses on the assessment *process*—because assessment is not a "one size fits all" methodology, and expert tailoring of the process can make the difference between success and failure.
- Assessment as a method of *planning for improvement* rather than an *awards examination process.*
  There are many valuable uses for Baldrige-like criteria, but this book focuses on assessment as a systematic, dependable way of launching highly focused improvement efforts. The process of adjudicating awards has many similarities to the assessment process—and it can also be used to support planning for improvement—but these are different processes with different primary goals.
- How to use assessment as a *catalyst for organizational change.*
  Organizational change is usually difficult and time-consuming, and when many people don't buy in, progress grinds to a halt. This book is not just about the mechanics of the assessment process. It shows how to use assessment to engage people and bring them on board. It explains how to create an

understanding of the need for improvement, and a commitment to shared improvement goals.

The Companion Website

If you have access to the Internet, you can obtain additional information from a companion website that complements this book. This electronic material has some features that the convenient printed volume in your hand does not:

- It contains *additional sections and case studies* that couldn't go in the print version without making it a very large, expensive tome.
- It includes *reference information* that is subject to change, such as lists of awards and assessment criteria available around the world. This information is kept up to date on the website.
- It lists *recommended reading* on related subjects, such as managing change and quality management.
- It provides guidance on *how to get in touch with other leading organizations* that are using this process, such as those featured in the case studies, or the winners of Baldrige and similar awards.
- It *answers questions* that other readers have asked—perhaps questions that have occurred to you, too.
- It has *links to other online resources,* which are abundant on the Internet.
- Finally, it provides an easy way of *contacting the author,* to ask questions or to comment on this book.

The aim of this package—the book plus the companion website—is to provide a virtual consultant-in-a-box. Of course this material cannot be a substitute for real live helpers and proper training; you will still need help from competent colleagues, moral support from friends, and probably guidance from an experienced process expert. But the book gives you a huge head start in learning about the assessment process, as well as a valuable reference text. And the website provides a way of obtaining even more information and staying up to date.

If you decide to proceed with the assessment process, or if you have more questions after reading the book, the website should be your next port of call. You will see the symbol ᵂᵂᵂ whenever there is reference to materials on the companion website, which is located at:

> **www.dhutton.com/roadmap**

Important Note: The website contains a restricted area—the *Readers Lounge*—that is reserved for readers of this book. In order to gain access to the Lounge, you should have the book at hand when you visit the website for the first time.

Many capable people generously contributed their knowledge during the making of this book. The result is a distillation of more than a decade of collective experience and experimentation. So whether you are a seasoned assessor or just learning about this methodology for the first time, you will find plenty to make you think. If you are involved in the assessment process in any role, this book will help you to be more effective. If you have no intention of ever being involved in an assessment, it might change your mind.

Read and enjoy!

David W. Hutton

Introduction

*"It is always safe to assume, not that the old way is wrong,
but that there may be a better way."*

Henry F. Harrower

What do the following successful and well-known organizations have in common: AlliedSignal, Chevron, Federal Express, IBM, Intel, Motorola, Procter & Gamble, Xerox Corporation?

All of these companies are using a special type of organizational assessment process to improve performance, and have been doing so for a number of years. Some pioneers, like Xerox, have been conducting this type of assessment for more than a decade and have built it into their annual planning cycle. And these companies are just the tip of the iceberg. Many others have been early adopters—and have also become outstanding performers.

Who Can Benefit from the Assessment Process

Assessment isn't just for leading-edge pioneers or for multinationals with deep pockets. This process is being used successfully by organizations of all types, by government departments, the military, health care, educational establishments, and not-for-profit institutions. It also works well for smaller entities, for divisions or departments within a larger enterprise or modest owner-managed businesses. And it doesn't matter whether your organization is just learning about continuous improvement or is already a world-class performer. Whatever level your organization has reached, this process will enable you to see the next steps required to achieve further improvement.

If you would like to have at your disposal a proven, systematic method of improving the performance of your organization year after year, you should be learning more about this assessment process. (See Exhibit I.2.)

Exhibit I.2.   *Motives for using assessment.*

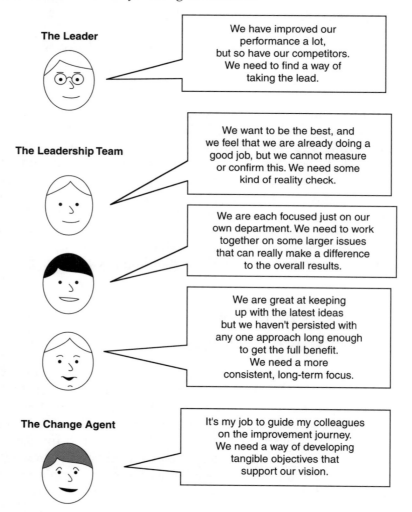

What Is the Link Between Assessment and High Performance?

The assessment process is the outcome of a kind of Trojan Horse strategy devised during the 1980s to help reeducate an entire generation of management. The Malcolm Baldrige National Quality Award was established through the efforts of a handful of dedicated people, leaders in industry and management experts, who could see that U.S. management practices were lagging seriously, leaving many industries vulnerable to foreign competition. In 1987 these people succeeded in getting this award signed into law by an act of Congress.

The purpose of the Baldrige program is to recognize companies that are successfully practicing the most effective management methods. Baldrige has been spectacularly successful in identifying companies whose high performance is sustainable because their results are due to good management rather than good luck. A recent study (described in Chapter 1) examined more than 600 winners of Baldrige-like awards over a 10-year period. The researchers discovered that on average these companies are *growing more than twice as fast* as their peers and are *more than twice as profitable.*

Assessment is not a quick fix—it works best as a long-term strategy for driving cumulative improvement. That's the bad news. The good news is that it is a highly effective approach that contributes to significantly improved bottom-line results.

Since its inception, Baldrige has also become one of the most enduring, widely emulated, and successful systems for recognizing achievement since the revival of the Olympic games. Virtually every industrialized country in the world now has a similar awards program. And like the Olympics, these programs have helped to stimulate an extensive "farm system" that draws in novices and helps them to learn and to progress to higher levels. The average citizen may never have heard of it, but to the top companies and the highest-performing institutions, the Baldrige Awards (and its counterparts in other countries) are the Olympic gold medals for management.

By putting high-performing companies in the spotlight as role models for others to study, the Baldrige program and its counterparts have had an enormous influence on thinking about management practices—and not just in the U.S. The top Japanese companies, who in the '80s hosted so many western visitors eager to learn *their* methods, are now visiting the west to study Baldrige winners.

And best of all, Baldrige has spawned a new management tool—the assessment process—that is a natural choice for organizations striving for higher levels of performance.

The Assessment Criteria

The Baldrige program has a comprehensive, rigorous method of examining potential award winners. It uses a tool called the assessment *criteria* (also called the *management model*) to guide these investigations. The assessment process used by high-performing organizations today is derived from this type of in-depth award examination process, and it makes use of the same comprehensive criteria.

The criteria are essentially descriptions of the components of an effective management system: one in which the leaders strive for outstanding performance by aligning the whole organization—plans, people, and processes—with customer needs. There are minor differences between the criteria used by various awards programs around the world, but they all cover similar ground, including the following areas:

- how the leaders provide purpose and direction to the organization
- how the organization develops strategy and plans in order to stay in business
- how the organization discovers what its customers require and their view of what they have been receiving
- how the organization selects and analyzes information and measurements, to understand its performance and the factors that drive this performance
- how the organization harnesses the talents of its people and develops their knowledge and skills

- how work processes are analyzed and improved, to eliminate error and waste, to improve speed and efficiency, and to enable employees to meet customer requirements consistently
- the overall results achieved, and how these have been caused by the strategies and the methods used.

A key benefit of these criteria is that they provide a *system* view of the organization. This is a very important and powerful concept. A system view reveals the linkages between methods and results. It clarifies the causes of good or poor performance. So when the assessment is complete, people find that they are in close agreement regarding what needs to be done in order to improve performance. We will explain this "system thinking" in more detail later.

What an Assessment Cycle Looks Like

Although it is known simply as *assessment,* this approach is more specialized and larger in scope than the name implies. Assessment is the basis of a complete "closed loop" cycle for driving continuous improvement and change throughout an organization. The assessment methodology and tools have been developed over more than a decade and are well proven. And although assessment is not yet a standard practice, most people who have used it believe that it should be. "*Everyone* should do this," they say. Perhaps so, but not every leadership team has what it takes to pull it off. When you have learned more, you will be able to judge for yourself whether it is feasible within your organization.

The assessment-based improvement cycle (See Exhibit I.3.) includes the following steps:

1. *Engaging the leaders,* so that they understand and buy into this methodology, see how it will meet their needs, and are clear about their roles in the process.
2. *Preparing an assessment team,* by training them in the assessment process techniques and the model.
3. *Gathering data* through interviews and key documents, to examine how the organization currently operates—"how we do business."

Exhibit I.3. *The assessment-based improvement cycle.*

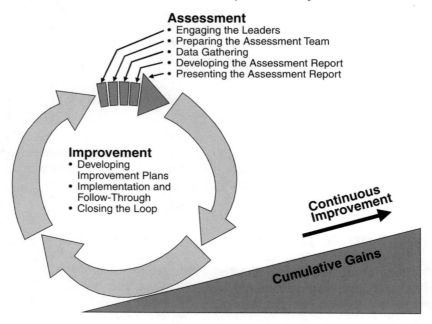

4. Analyzing the data and *developing a report* on the strengths and opportunities for improvement discovered, numerical scores and recommendations for action.
5. *Presenting the report* to the leaders, so that they can understand and accept the findings and take ownership of them.
6. *Developing improvement plans.* This step includes positively identifying the "vital few" priorities for improvement and developing plans to address them. These plans are for highly targeted, purposeful changes to "the way we do business."
7. *Implementation and follow-through*—to ensure that the plans are executed properly and the desired results achieved.

Done properly, these steps will lead to sustainable improvements in the organization's performance.

But there is no need to stop there. The most effective way to use the assessment methodology is to continue the cycle by repeating the process regularly—perhaps on an annual basis—and integrating it into the business planning cycle. We call this *closing the loop.*

Each new cycle reveals how effective the previous actions have been and identifies a new set of vital few priorities that build upon what has already been accomplished. This approach safeguards the breakthroughs or incremental gains previously made, builds momentum, and thus achieves cumulative improvements in performance. Since the improvements are cumulative, there is a snowball effect on performance, like compound interest on an investment—the gains may seem modest at first, but they accumulate in a way that is hard to beat in the long term.

How Assessment Differs from Other Examination Processes

This process may at first sight resemble many other methods of audit or examination. But we will see that it is significantly different in philosophy and a leap forward in technique.

The criteria provides a structure and a unique evaluation logic that make for a better process. Guided by the criteria, the assessment process itself is highly structured and systematic. It is rigorous without being nitpicking, and it provides a comprehensive perspective without requiring exhaustive detail.

The assessment process focuses attention on the effectiveness of the methods being used, not on the performance of individuals. For this reason, people do not find it a threatening process—rather, it is a journey of self-discovery and a positive learning experience for everyone involved. In this way, it also serves as a powerful vehicle for change.

When the assessment is repeated to examine the effect of previous improvement actions, it becomes part of a closed-loop cycle, which leads to greater predictability. Successive assessment cycles lead to a better understanding of how the organization functions and a greater ability to plan and accomplish further improvements.

Above all, this is a *system-oriented* approach. The criteria enables people to see the organization in a way that transcends the hierarchy of divisions and departments. This new perspective opens the door to a whole range of valuable improvement opportunities that cannot even be seen (let alone acted on) from within traditional departmental silos.

What Your Organization Can Gain from Assessment

You will find this process especially valuable if your organization needs to:

- establish a more focused set of priorities for improvement and align people's efforts with these priorities throughout the organization
- ensure that scarce resources are being applied effectively—to achieve strategically important goals, to combat aggressive competitors, or to respond to other external threats
- go beyond the limitations of compliance audits as a means of self-examination and diagnosis
- establish metrics to evaluate the effects of change and to quantify progress
- create an environment that fosters and encourages change, so that people are willing—even anxious—to propose ideas for change and improvement
- consolidate past gains and achieve further breakthroughs in performance

If your organization's needs are like these, then the assessment process is a tool that you can use with confidence to help improve the "bottom line."

• • • • •

Information Structure

The Book

Preparation
1. The Assessment
   Process as a
   Strategy
2. Assessment
   Process Design
3. Setting the Stage

Assessment
4. Engaging the Leaders
5. Preparing the Assessment Team
6. Data Gathering
7. Developing the Assessment Report
8. Presenting the Assessment Report

Improvement
9. Developing
   Improvement Plans
10. Implementation and
    Follow Through
11. Closing the Loop

Case Studies
- Xerox
- TELUS Mobility
- Medrad
- Cargil
- Pinellas County
  School District

www.dhutton.com/roadmap

The Companion Website
- Additional sections
- Additional case studies
- Recommended reading
- Other online resources
- Common reader questions
- Contacting leading organizations
- Contacting the author

Acknowledgments

"From Baldrige to the Bottom Line: A Road Map for Organizational Change and Improvement" is heavily based on practical experience—but not just my own. Many people generously shared information and their own learnings about the assessment process. Many also acted as reviewers and provided invaluable help at various stages in the creative process. Some spent countless hours critiquing successive versions of the manuscript until we got it right. Many thanks to:

Dennis Arter, Chuck Aubrey, Vincent Bange, Dennis Beecroft, Bob Camp, Bill Campbell, Christine Collins, Lynn Cook, Dan Corbett, Brian Cox, Paul DeBaylo, Martin Doyle, Jack Evans, Dianne Faglon, Paul Fini, Phil Forve, Ramses Girgis, Tony Glaudé, Cille Harris, Ron Higgins, Debbie Hopen, Rita Mulroney Leitch, Dick Leo, Bill Lipski, Anne Manha, Maria Mikelenas-McLoughlin, David McClaskey, Bob McGrath, Lorne McLean, Bob Osterhoff, Janet Peargin, Terry Regel, Sue Rohan, J. P. Russell, Patty Schachter, Ed Shecter, Richard Skruber, Bob Stearns, Larry Taylor, Patricia Taylor, Lori Topp, Kim Tretheway, Harry Truderung, Brian Voss, Ed Walker, and Brian Young.

Also, hats off to Gabrielle Bissonnette, the human dynamo who runs our office so efficiently, thus allowing me to stay focused on my work—serving clients and writing.

Chapter 1

The Assessment Process as a Strategy

"Opportunity is missed by most people because it is dressed in overalls and looks like work."
Thomas Edison

The first step in understanding the assessment process is to grasp the fundamental concepts that underpin this methodology, and the basic flow of a typical assessment. It is also important to understand a few simple ground rules that are vital to success in any type of assessment.

CHAPTER CONTENTS

- The case for assessment
- Management system concepts
- The assessment criteria
- The assessment process in a nutshell
- Ground rules for success

• • • • •

1

THE CASE FOR ASSESSMENT
Follow the Leaders

The introduction mentioned some well-known companies that are using the assessment process. Here are a few more: AMP, Baxter, Corning, Eastman Chemical, Hewlett-Packard, Honeywell, Johnson & Johnson, and Texas Instruments. There are many others not as well known. A few of these are: Cargill, a privately owned $50 billion agribusiness multinational; TELUS Mobility, a Canadian provider of wireless services; Solectron, an international electronics design and manufacturing services firm (and a two-time Baldrige winner); and Medrad, a Pittsburgh-based supplier of medical devices. And let's not forget Pinellas County School District –a pioneer and a role model for continuous improvement in the U.S. education system.

When so many high-performing enterprises begin to adopt a new technique—and to stick with it—then it is smart for others to pay close attention. Perhaps some previously untried innovation is becoming a common practice; a tool you ignore at your peril because your competitors will use it to gain an advantage. The leaders of these early adopter organizations see the assessment process as just such a tool.

But what proof is there that this approach will help create bottom-line results? The jury is in, and the verdict is clear: developing an effective management system—as defined by Baldrige or similar criteria—significantly improves organizational performance.

The Bottom-Line Payoff

In the past, any discussion of quality management or management systems was dogged by a lack of quantitative evidence. There were lots of great stories. Many companies have turned themselves around after a crisis and prospered by adopting a systematic, company-wide quality improvement strategy. Some excellent books have been written about these experiences, and these are often inspiring and compelling sagas. But skeptics naturally demand quantitative evidence, and proponents want hard evidence to prove their case.

This evidence is now available, in the form of studies of award-winning companies. The reason for studying award winners is that they are known quantities—unlike many of the companies that we hear stories about. These are companies whose management systems have been scrutinized and validated by experts. Any company that wins a national quality award has definitely succeeded in creating an effective management system, as defined by the criteria—it is not just "telling a good story."

The Awards Examination Process

Here is what an applicant has to go through in order to win an award. First, the company has to describe its management system in extensive detail in a written application—typically up to 50 pages for a national award—including a wide range of results data.

Each application is evaluated by a team of trained examiners, who write a consensus feedback report. In the Baldrige process each application may receive 100 to 150 hours of scrutiny by the examiners at this stage.

If the application is considered outstanding, the company then has to accept a site visit: several days of intense scrutiny, by a team of on-site examiners. Using the award criteria as their guide, the examiners investigate the company's entire management system, to determine what really happens, whether it is effective, and whether it produces the results claimed. They interview people at all levels and study key documents and data. Finally, they document their evaluation of the company.

The site visit team reports are used to select the winners, and only the most outstanding applicants receive awards.

Two important studies are available that examine the long-term performance of award-winning companies: the Baldrige Index and the "Winners 600."

The Baldrige Index   The *Baldrige Index*[1] measures the performance of a (hypothetical) investment fund that purchases $1000 worth of the stock of each company that wins the Baldrige award. The portfolio, which in 1999 included 26 publicly traded Baldrige winners, grew in value by 425 percent during the period 1988–1997, compared with growth of 173 percent for the same funds invested in the S&P 500 Index. In other words, over this 10-year period the Baldrige Index performed *2.5 times better.* And this is in spite of a few highly publicized cases in which a Baldrige winner has run into financial difficulties.

The Award Winners 600   Another study,[2] which we will call the *Award Winners 600,* examines a larger number of companies using a broader range of performance metrics. This study includes not only Baldrige winners but the recipients of similar, less stringent quality awards: state awards (mostly modeled on Baldrige), and awards presented by large companies to their suppliers. It examines various performance measures derived from an analysis of these companies' audited annual reports. Each winner is tracked for two consecutive five-year periods: before and after the company established its management system which led to an award. The study compared all of these winners with a control group of similar companies operating in the same sectors during the same time frame.

Exhibit 1.1 illustrates an important finding from this study: there was no difference in performance between the award winners and the control group during the first five-year period. *The two groups were indistinguishable—until the winners had developed their management systems.* Then the winners' performance took off.

Exhibit 1.2 shows how specific performance measures differed between the award winners and the control group during the second five-year period.

Exhibit 1.1.   *Results of developing an effective management system.*

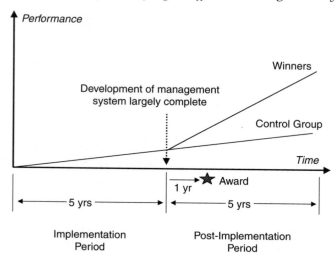

Exhibit 1.2.   *Average percentage change in performance measures.*

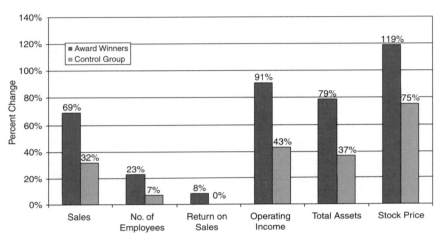

Companies in the control group improved their results significantly—but not nearly as much as the winners. The differences are striking. For example, sales for the control group companies rose 32 percent—but sales for the award winners rose 69 percent, more than twice as much. The award winners took on 23 percent more employees, compared with 7 percent for the control group, to support their faster growth. It is noteworthy that the award winners were not "buying" market share by selling at reduced margins: in fact their return on sales increased by 8 percent, compared with no change for the control group.

Driven by the increased volume of sales and the increased return on sales, the operating income of award winners increased by 91 percent, compared with 43 percent for the control group. With the benefit of more operating income, the award winners' assets increased by 79 percent compared with 37 percent. Not surprisingly, the market began to value these companies more highly—their stock price increased by 119 percent over the five-year interval compared with 75 percent.

This study does *not* indicate that every award-winning company outperformed its opposite number in the control group, or that all of the winners were highly successful (in fact a few of them ran into serious difficulties). But collectively the award winners perform *significantly* better than the control group.

• • • • •

These studies are based upon reliable, fact-based methodologies. They provide compelling evidence that having an effective management system is a great competitive advantage. It may not be a *guarantee* of success, but it does improve the odds very significantly.

All of these companies have management systems of the type defined by the Baldrige criteria. The assessment process is valuable because it provides a systematic way of charting a course that will lead toward this type of high-performance management system. It even uses the same instrument—the criteria that awards examiners use to examine high-performing organizations.

MANAGEMENT SYSTEM CONCEPTS

In order to understand what these award winners have been doing, and what the criteria are all about, it is necessary to understand the idea of a *management system*. What is a management system? It is really just "a way of doing business"—but rather well-defined and consistently applied. And it is based upon a set of principles that are the foundations of this management philosophy.

The Management Principles

High-performing, award-winning organizations all have their own distinctive ways of doing business, which may be very different from one organization to the next. However all of them display, to a remarkable degree, these characteristics:

- **A strong customer focus.** Their first priority is to serve their target customers, and they see this as a means of achieving their financial and other business goals.
- **Effective leadership.** Their leaders are effective in setting the direction and communicating through their behavior a consistent set of values and expectations.

- **Employee participation and development.** These organizations help their people to develop their full potential and to make full use of their talents and energy.
- **A process-oriented, prevention-based strategy.** They systematically design their products and services—and the processes used to perform the work—to make it easy for people to do a good job, to eliminate error and waste, and thus to *prevent* problems before they can occur.
- **Continuous improvement and learning.** They support continuous learning by their people, and they pursue a constant search for methods of improving performance.
- **Management by fact.** Their people are skilled in the use of rational methods of planning, decision-making and problem solving—supported by ready access to sources of reliable data.
- **Cooperation, teamwork, and partnering.** They strive for win-win relationships where possible—for example, teamwork and cooperation between employees and departments, and a collaborative approach to working with key suppliers as well as other partners and allies.
- **Long-range view of the future.** They plan for long-term success as well as short-term results, and they refuse to mortgage their future for short-term gain.
- **Fast response.** They recognize that reducing cycle times to achieve fast response adds value to almost any product or service and often leads to simplified processes and reduced costs.
- **Public responsibility and citizenship.** They go beyond the minimum standards required by the law and are proactive in striving to be responsible and contribute to society.
- **Results orientation.** They aim to achieve excellent results that are sustainable and that serve the needs of all of their stakeholders: investors, customers, employees, and business partners.

How do we know that all these award-winning companies have these characteristics? Because the awards criteria look for these characteristics.[3] These characteristics are in fact the "core values" or "basic principles" that underpin this approach to management. We will call them the *management principles*, and it is these that provide the foundation for an effective *management system*.

The Need for a Management System

Many people will look at this list of principles and observe that most of them seem very much like common sense. Agreed. But how many organizations actually operate in this way? These principles may be common sense, but they are definitely not common practice!

Why is this? It cannot be because people don't *want* to work in this way. In organizations that function according to these principles, people love their jobs—the work environment is exciting, motivating, and productive.

But organizations don't automatically function like this. For example, consider the need for a customer focus. Organizational hierarchies all have a tendency to degenerate into inward-looking bureaucracies that neglect their customers. This is because in a power-oriented hierarchy, people have to focus on pleasing their *boss* first and foremost in order to stay out of trouble. It takes constant management effort—and a structured, disciplined approach—to maintain a focus on pleasing the *customer*.

It's similar with decision-making. Decision-making in organizations tends to degenerate into a politicized deal-making process, dominated by internal power struggles and special interests. Countering this tendency is a huge challenge: it requires reliable measurement and information systems, an open atmosphere in which problems are not hidden out of fear, and people trained in the discipline of seeking out relevant information and processing it in a systematic fashion.

This sort of disciplined, organized approach is the basis of what we call a management system. Without this, most work is done in a way that depends on the whim of whoever is around at the time. Events become unpredictable, and the destructive effects of hierarchy and narrow self-interest begin to take over.

Key Point
Organizations that are unable to develop an effective management system are doomed forever to live in the "Dilbert Zone," where fear, unproductive behavior and wasted effort are the norm.

Let's consider what it takes for an organization to develop just one of the useful characteristics that we described—a strong customer focus.

It is easy to understand why companies that do a great job of satisfying customers can reap all kinds of benefits, such as greater customer loyalty and more repeat business, the ability to command a higher selling price or to increase sales without costly giveaways and discounts, and lower costs for complaints and claims. So becoming more customer focused is a great strategy—especially in competitive markets or where customer needs change rapidly. It is also a great strategy for institutions whose survival depends upon their perceived relevance to the needs of their clients.

However, becoming customer focused cannot be achieved simply by reminding everyone that the customer is important, by training employees to be more polite, or even by measuring or paying people based on customer satisfaction. A number of specific mechanisms are also required. Here are a few of them:

1. A *market segmentation* process: a way of clustering target customers into groups with similar needs—and identifying new groups when customers with different needs are emerging
2. A *customer listening* system: a systematic way of obtaining information about customers, collecting and integrating this information from various sources, and analyzing it to determine customer needs and priorities
3. A *translation process,* to convert these customer requirements into product specifications and service standards that reflect customer priorities
4. Methods of *designing the production and delivery processes* to meet these customer-derived specifications and standards
5. *Measurement and monitoring* systems to ensure that these specifications and standards are actually achieved day by day
6. A *feedback* system to determine how well the whole management system has worked from the customers' point of view. Are the products and services actually meeting customers' needs? How well do these products and services stack up against those of competitors?

The Need for a System as Well as Attitude

The employees of a store were receiving intensive training in how to satisfy customers through attentiveness, responsiveness, and courtesy. After completing the class, a clerk from the auto parts counter commented, "that was very interesting, but you know, it's pretty hard to pull this off when you **don't have the right part.**"

What are the chances of achieving high customer satisfaction if these mechanisms are not all in place? Not very high! Ask the customers (or the employees) of organizations that have tried to become more customer-oriented just by repeating slogans about the importance of customers, or by giving frontline employees "smile training."

Key Point

An organized system of management is required to translate "common sense" management principles into common practice in an organization. Slogans and good intentions on their own won't do it.

This is why we need the assessment criteria.

THE ASSESSMENT CRITERIA

Once management has decided that a more systematic approach to doing business is required, the criteria provide a valuable framework to help accomplish this.

This framework defines the essential, universal components of a management system. It defines a number of *subsystems,* which are required to create an effective management system.

These subsystems typically look something like this:

1. *Leadership:* the methods used by the leaders to set the direction and goals and to communicate these to everyone
2. *Information management:* the system used to capture, manage, and analyze information about performance in order to support planning, decision-making and problem solving
3. *Strategy and planning:* the process used to develop strategy and supporting plans, and how these plans are implemented

4. *Customer focus:* the mechanisms used to understand customer needs and perceptions and to manage customer relationships

5. *Human resources:* the practices used to ensure that employees' potential is developed and their talents and energies aligned with the organization's goals

6. *Process management:* the techniques used to organize and streamline important work processes in order to remove error and waste, reduce cycle times, and meet customer requirements consistently. This includes helping key suppliers to improve their processes

7. *Results:* the broad classes of outcomes that an organization should be measuring in order to obtain a balanced view of its overall performance

The criteria do not prescribe exactly how each of these subsystems should work—every organization needs to develop its own approach—but they do call for a systematic, organized approach to each one.

Exhibit 1.3 represents the structure of one of the most widely used sets of criteria—those of the Malcolm Baldrige National Quality Award.

Exhibit 1.3.   *The Baldrige criteria.*[4]

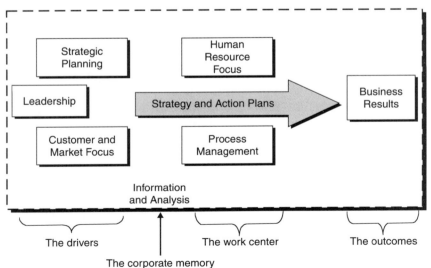

This type of framework provides a powerful tool for understanding how an organization's current management system works. It reveals the connections required between different subsystems and the cause-effect relationship between management methods and organizational performance.

To Baldrige or Not to Baldrige . . .

There are now dozens of similar awards programs around the world at a national, state/provincial, and local level. Their criteria cover much the same ground, though there are differences in structure and in complexity. This book is intended to be "nondenominational" as far as award criteria are concerned: you should find the content equally accessible whether you are using the Australian Quality Award criteria in Sydney, the Canada Awards for Excellence criteria in Ottawa, or the European Quality Award framework in London.

However, the Baldrige program has earned a unique stature, and it is more widely emulated than any other similar program. So for convenience and simplicity we will use *something like Baldrige* as our proxy for *all* similar awards criteria, and use *Baldrige-like* terminology throughout.

How the Criteria Reveal Interdependencies

The criteria clarify the linkages between the management subsystems—interconnections that must work properly for the system to work as a whole.

For example, information about customer requirements is needed in many parts of the system: in planning for new products and services; for setting operational performance targets; when refining or redesigning work processes; in selecting and training people who will have contact with customers.

This is rather like making sure that an automobile's engine is connected to the transmission, which is also connected to the wheels.

Key Point
If any piece of the system is missing, broken, or not connected properly, this will have consequences throughout the system, and the performance of the entire system will suffer.

This is a discouraging observation for people who are looking for instant packaged solutions. It means that you need to *understand* your management system as a whole before you can correctly identify what parts to work on. However, there is also a powerful upside. Once you have this understanding large gains can often be obtained by small changes in just the right place—by repairing small but vital parts of the system, or by making important connections.

For example, picture an organization that is gathering a lot of valuable customer information but isn't making good use of it. Simply by organizing this information better and making it available where it's needed, this company can begin to see a number of benefits. These might include: more targeted sales and marketing efforts; better decisions related to new product and service features; more focused action to eliminate the main causes of customer complaints; and improved customer loyalty. This is a big payback for relatively little effort: just organizing and sharing information that had already been collected!

The Human Body as a System

The human body is an extremely sophisticated system with more than a dozen subsystems: the nervous system, cardiovascular system, skeletal system, immune system, and so on. Each of these subsystems has a clearly defined purpose, several component parts, and feedback loops that control its operation. All of the subsystems work together seamlessly to maintain our health. However, none of these subsystems can exist on its own—they are all intertwined. And a problem in any one of them affects the others, and ultimately the entire body. For example, suppose that a problem in the digestive system prevents certain important minerals or vitamins from being absorbed. This will in turn affect other parts of the body: the nervous system, perhaps the skeleton, perhaps the immune system. . . .

An organization is similar to the body: it has various subsystems that must function properly, and they must all work together, otherwise the health of the entire organization is affected.

How the Criteria Clarify Cause and Effect

When organizations experience poor or static performance, a common, instinctive response by the leaders is to change the people assigned to key positions and/or to change the reporting structure.

These actions often carry a heavy price tag in terms of disruption and distraction from running the business—but that's not the main drawback. The main problem is that these actions rarely have any lasting impact on "how we do business around here."

Key Point
Restructuring and re-staffing only change the players. In order to change the way that work is done, the system must be changed.

By focusing on how we do business, rather than on individual performance, the criteria provide a more powerful way of understanding organizational performance and identifying levers for improvement.

Although deceptively simple, the criteria are powerful diagnostic tools. Like X-ray glasses, they provide a new way of looking at an organization and understanding what's really going on.

We can understand the diagnostic power of the criteria by considering what happens when some part of the management system is weak, missing, or disconnected. Exhibit 1.4 builds on the customer focus example given earlier, to illustrate how weaknesses in specific parts of the management system tend to have specific, predictable results.

When only the results are examined, all kinds of explanations and excuses can be put forward to explain what is going on. However, when an assessment reveals specific strengths and gaps in the management system, the causes—and possible solutions—often become much more obvious.

If these underlying process problems are not addressed, the same pattern of failure will likely repeat itself again and again. Even if a talented new manager does manage to put in place some fixes, these are likely to be lost when this individual moves on— unless they are somehow entrenched as "how we do business."

Key Point
Anyone who has learned to see the organization as a system can never again feel satisfied with "improvement" initiatives that simply change staffing and the organization chart but do not tackle the system itself.

Exhibit 1.4. *How the management system causes results.*

Management System Weakness	Typical Consequences
A. Ineffective methods for determining customer and market needs	New products and services often don't gain market acceptance, although they perform as specified and are competitively priced and strongly marketed. They just don't quite "hit the mark" for customers.
B. Ineffective methods of managing design and production processes	New product/service features are just what customers want, but prove disappointing in use—they often perform badly or don't work as expected. "Great features—if only they worked," say customers.
C. Ineffective methods for managing customer relationships	Although the products are well priced, perform well, and have features that attract customers, customer loyalty is poor. Many customers switch to the competition just to avoid the hassle of dealing with the company.
A, B, and **C** combined	The organization has low customer satisfaction and loyalty. Its margins are poor because its offerings are not really attractive at any price. Its sales are in decline because customers are leaving faster than new ones can be acquired. Major investments in new products, heavy discounting, and aggressive marketing all prove to be costly and ineffective because they do not address the underlying problems.

THE ASSESSMENT PROCESS IN A NUTSHELL

So much for the assessment criteria. But how do we use this framework to create an effective management system? The assessment *process* is our vehicle for doing so. There are many ways to conduct an assessment. In this chapter we will briefly describe one type of assessment to show how the process typically flows (see Exhibit 1.5).

Exhibit 1.5.   *Typical assessment cycle.*

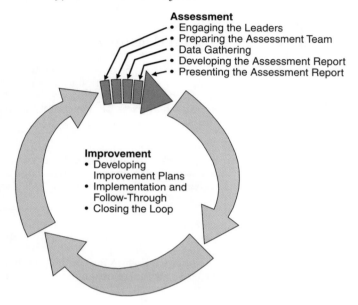

Assessment
- Engaging the Leaders
- Preparing the Assessment Team
- Data Gathering
- Developing the Assessment Report
- Presenting the Assessment Report

Improvement
- Developing Improvement Plans
- Implementation and Follow-Through
- Closing the Loop

Engaging the Leaders

If the use of assessments is to become a long-term strategy rather than a passing program, an essential first step is to engage the leadership team and ensure that they are well prepared to lead the process. It is vital to ensure right from the start that these key decision-makers buy in, since the process will involve an investment of their time and energy—not just to complete the assessment, but to ensure that the resulting improvement plans are implemented.

The involvement of the leadership team begins when one of the leaders (the *sponsor*) develops an interest in this process. This individual searches for more information from a variety of sources—articles, books, conferences, and the Internet. The sponsor will usually seek out an experienced assessment specialist to provide advice and guidance and to take part in key steps during the process. We will call this individual the *process expert*. Armed with all this new-found knowledge, the sponsor now carefully considers the organization's needs and the options available, such as the type of assessment process to use, the criteria, and the timing.

Once the sponsor has decided to continue, the next step is an *executive briefing*—a workshop for the entire leadership team, typically lasting about four to six hours. This session is designed to inform and engage this group and to prepare them to lead the assessment process.

A key element of the workshop is an assessment by the leaders of their own collective approach to the leadership of the organization. This gives the leaders a personal experience of the assessment process and allows them to immediately identify opportunities for improvement. This exercise often becomes an absorbing discussion, because the structure of the criteria allows the leaders to explore these issues in a way that is new to them and enlightening.

After this session, there is a consensus among the leaders that a full assessment should be conducted, with input from a cross section of the organization. The final portion of the workshop is a review of the practicalities: timing, cost, who to involve, and so on. The sponsor offers recommendations and guidance on these issues and sets out the pros and cons. One of the key decision areas is how to establish the data gathering team, who to assign to this task, and how much time to allow. The leaders also decide how to communicate to the rest of this organization about the process that is about to unfold.

This workshop is not simply a presentation, aimed at obtaining passive approval. It is designed to provide a true appreciation of how the process works (through personal experience), to enable the leaders to take ownership of the process, and to secure an *informed* commitment to act on the assessment findings.

On completion of the workshop, the leaders leave with the dates blocked off in their calendars and with a sense of anticipation. This has been an energizing experience, and many are intrigued by what they have learned. A few are heading straight for the offices of the people whom they want to enlist as assessment team members. The feeling of most people is "This is going to be very interesting!"

Preparing the Assessment Team

The first step is to assemble an assessment team, which usually includes someone from each of the main departments and functions. This team is trained and prepared for its task by the process expert. The training workshop covers the criteria, the evaluation process, data gathering, and interview techniques. Finally, the team develops its plan for the data gathering phase.

Data Gathering

The purpose of this phase is to understand the "current reality" by systematically gathering information about how the organization operates at present, guided by the assessment criteria. This is not a "checklist" exercise (*"we're doing this—check, we're not doing that—check . . ."*). It is systematic, but it is also a process of self-discovery, a quest for understanding and insight into how the organization actually functions.

The assessment team conducts a series of carefully planned interviews of a cross section of the organization, including people at all levels. It also reviews some key documents—plans, policies, and reports—that shed light on current practices and how well they are working.

Carrying out this intense work under a tight schedule, the assessment team members get to know each other well and become a close-knit group. And they learn a *lot*. By the end of this process, the team has usually acquired more knowledge about how the organization actually operates than any other group of people has ever had before. It is also a strong team—because the leaders have assigned some of their most capable people.

Key Point
Smart leaders recognize the value of assessment experience as an excellent development opportunity, and they assign some of their best up-and-coming people.

This team will later become a resource to support the implementation of the recommendations. Even if the team members are not directly involved in implementation, they will act as a "conscience" for the leaders, to ensure that the follow-through is not allowed to falter. These are trusted and influential people who have developed a clear vision of what needs to be done, and they want to see their hard work translated into useful action.

During these early stages, the assessment has already had some impact on the organization. Everyone has been told that the data gathering is under way, and many people are curious about the process. Those who are interviewed find it a positive experience. Leaders find the interviews thought-provoking, while frontline people appreciate the opportunity to offer their perspective and input. In some organizations, people will say "This is the *first* time since I started working here that *anyone* has asked me what I think—thank you!"

As the data gathering proceeds, there is a sense of anticipation in the air. What will the report say, when will we see it, and what will happen as a result? Some people say "nothing will change—as usual," while others note that the process seems well organized and there appears to be a game plan for the next steps.

Developing the Assessment Report

By the time the data gathering is complete, many people have been interviewed and a great deal of valuable data have been collected. The task now is to interpret what has been discovered—to turn the data into information. The assessment process uses a highly effective evaluation process for doing this.

For each element in the criteria, the team develops a fact-based consensus regarding the organization's strengths and opportunities for improvement. This is done using a structured evaluation process that requires the team to consider three dimensions:

1. The soundness and appropriateness of the *approach.*
   This refers to the methods used, such as whether these are systematic, whether they include appropriate tools and techniques, and whether they draw upon relevant factual data.
2. The completeness of *deployment.*
   This refers to the *implementation* of the methods described, such as whether they are used consistently and in every part of the organization.
3. The *results* obtained.
   This refers to improving trends and/or excellent levels of performance, which result from the methods used.

The assessment report (often called a *feedback report*) sets out these strengths and opportunities for improvement, following the structure of the criteria. The team also assigns a rating to each element, using a scoring system that has been shown to give surprisingly consistent results in the hands of trained assessors. These ratings help to quantify the findings and confirm that some parts of the management system are much stronger than others. The assessment report also includes the team's recommendations regarding the top priorities for improvement.

Because the evaluation process focuses on observable facts, achieving a consensus is relatively easy once all the relevant data have been shared. If a different team were to repeat the assessment, the final report would look essentially the same, with similar strengths and opportunities, and similar scores, because this is a repeatable process.

As the report begins to take its final shape, the team starts to think more about how the leaders will react to some of the findings. The team members are usually surprised at how many opportunities for improvement they have discovered. There are some sobering observations to be shared, and based on their past experience some team members are nervous about how the leaders will receive this information. They wonder: Will this report be an eye-opener that leads to a leap forward for the organization—or will it be badly received, with negative consequences for the team members?

So there is some fine-tuning of the wording of some findings to ensure accuracy without giving offense. However, everyone wants to get the key messages across undiluted, and the discussion turns toward a review of the evidence. What examples can the team give to support their key points and to make these come alive for the leaders? What did the team see and hear that makes them so certain about these points? The key is to focus on the facts, which are undeniable.

Finally, they feel adequately prepared. They are ready to deliver their message.

Presenting the Assessment Report

This session starts with some scene setting and a review of what the team has done—such as statistics on the number of interviews and the coverage achieved. These demonstrate that the team has followed the process and done its job thoroughly.

Then the team starts to work through its report, explaining the key points carefully, and taking the time to respond properly to questions.

There are always lively discussions of certain findings, and some challenges by the leaders. But contrary to the team's fears, these are mainly attempts to clarify and understand what the team has learned, rather than to deny the findings or to "shoot the messenger." If some leaders are baffled by a particular finding, all of the team members can offer supporting examples of what they saw and heard —and other leaders who have already grasped the point may also join in the discussion. The process expert plays a key role in facilitating this entire process and helps to manage the tone of the debate.

Some of the findings are not a complete surprise to the leaders, but help bring dimly understood issues into a sharper focus. Other findings are revelations to the leadership team because they offer a new perspective—yet they are clear and irrefutable once the evidence has been properly explained. Some of the findings may be wake-up calls, challenging long-standing beliefs and assumptions about the organization.

After three or four hours, the discussion is complete. For the leaders, there is a real payoff in accepting this self-portrait of the organization—warts and all—because this brings them closer to solutions. For example, the findings may shed light on the causes of some recurrent problem that has defied all previous efforts to fix it. Once these findings are understood, the path toward a solution becomes clearer.

When the leaders have accepted the findings, their focus quickly shifts to "what should we *do* about it?" They are clearly impatient to get into action. This is a sign of progress.

The presentation ends with the assessment team's view of the priorities for improvement—not as a prescription, but as an input to the decision-making process that is to follow. This input gives the leaders some food for thought, and it helps them to prepare for the next step, which is a planning workshop. As pre-work for this workshop, the leaders agree to reflect on the report and to each reflect on what he or she would choose as the top five priorities for improvement.

Finally, the senior leader thanks the team for their hard work, and the meeting is over.

With the most difficult part of their mission successfully accomplished, the assessment team members gather round to share their surprise (and relief) at how well it went—and then head off to celebrate.

• • • • •

Although it is over in a few hours, this session is in many ways the most critical step in the entire assessment process. It is the "moment of truth" when the leadership team finds out whether it is ready to embark on this particular journey. At its best, this session is a powerful eye-opener and a call to action, providing insights that help the leaders clarify what they need to focus on. As the president of a major oil company said of the assessment, "*It gave us a picture of ourselves so clear that we could not ignore the message.*" It is also an experience that they will want to repeat sometime, to find out how much progress has been achieved.

Developing Improvement Plans

The next step is to create the improvement plan and to set the stage for action, using a planning workshop. The participants in this workshop are typically the leadership team, the assessment team, and the process expert. This combination of people makes best use of the knowledge and expertise available and helps to ensure that the plans are sound, practical—and aimed squarely at the right issues.

The goals of the workshop are:

- to identify the highest-leverage opportunities for improving performance (the "vital few")
- to develop an initial project plan for each of the vital few
- to agree on the next steps, including communications and follow-through.

The first part of this workshop demonstrates the power of the assessment process as a tool for creating consensus. A simple technique such as an Affinity Diagram[5] is used to capture everyone's top priorities for improvement and to display these in a graphical manner for all to see. This exercise reveals a strong clustering of ideas—everyone has independently come to very similar conclusions about what needs to be done! Each cluster—there are typically five or six of them—represents an issue that the participants view as a high priority to tackle. These are the "vital few" priorities for improvement.

The discovery that everyone's views are so closely aligned is a revelation, and it provides a strong reinforcement that these conclusions are on the right track. This is not an accident; it is the predictable outcome of a well-conducted assessment. This is the "bull's eye" that we have been shooting for from the very start, even though we did not know what specific issues would bubble to the top in this way.

Key Point
*Given the **same information** regarding the current state, **any** group of rational people will come to essentially the **same** **conclusions** about what needs to be done.*

These "vital few" priorities—and the action plans that will flow from them—are the key deliverables from the assessment process.

Having selected and agreed upon the vital few, the leaders decide which of them will be responsible for each one, and the workshop participants break into small groups to develop initial project plans, using a planning template.

When the small groups have completed their task, the entire group reassembles and these initial project plans are shared and discussed. This discussion reinforces common goals, allows overlaps or potential conflicts to be resolved, and leads to some initial decisions, such as those regarding staffing and time frames.

The final topics for the workshop relate to implementation. If the organization has a track record of poor follow-through, this will need to be acknowledged at this point—it may have been mentioned in the assessment report—and some countermeasures must be agreed upon. Having done so much work to get this far, no one wants to leave implementation to chance.

Finally, everyone leaves with their thoughts concentrated on their piece of the task that lies ahead. The stage is now set for focused, effective action. When they are asked by their colleagues back at the office, *"How did it go?"* the participants' response is, *"We're off and running!"*

Implementation and Follow-Through

At this point it may seem that success is reasonably assured. There is an improvement plan that is sound and a critical mass of influential people who understand the plan and are committed to seeing it executed. And there is a senior person—a project sponsor—responsible for the success of each improvement project. All that remains is to follow through diligently and the results will follow. Right? Wrong!

It is so easy for plans like these to be derailed by crises and distractions. During the planning workshop the leaders recognized this, and they agreed on some actions to make implementation as "fail-proof" as possible:

- building the improvement project goals into the personal objectives of each of the project sponsors
- integrating the improvement plan into the business plan
- establishing at least one measurement of success for each project
- conducting reviews of progress—including these measurements—at regular intervals
- communicating to all employees the key findings and the actions to be taken.

With these safeguards in place, progress continues throughout the year. Some delays and setbacks do occur, but these are quickly identified, and efforts are then redoubled to get the work back on track.

Closing the Loop

Once the first assessment has been successfully completed, it is evident that this need not be a one-time event; it would be valuable to repeat the assessment at some point in the future:

- to verify that the initial improvement actions have been effective
- to learn from the implementation experience
- to develop a new improvement plan, building upon what has been accomplished.

So the leadership team discusses timing and agrees on an approximate date—perhaps in 12 months or so—to conduct the next assessment. This action also sends a powerful message to everyone involved in the improvement projects: there is no time to lose if this work is to be completed before the next assessment cycle.

● ● ● ● ●

These are typical steps in a fairly thorough and comprehensive assessment, using an internal team supported by an external process expert.

However, there is no "one right way" of doing this. Many variations are possible; in fact different approaches are *essential* to meet the needs of different situations. For example, you should use specific techniques that are helpful when:

- the organization is well advanced in the use of continuous improvement methods—or at the other extreme, has no experience at all
- the organization is small—or very large
- resources are particularly scarce
- the time frame must be compressed
- engaging the leadership team presents a challenge.

One of the most valuable benefits that you will glean from the following chapters is an understanding of how to design the process to fit your situation. For example, how to streamline the process by making it quick and painless as possible for an organization just getting started on continuous improvement—or how to make it sufficiently deep and searching to reveal valuable opportunities in a world-class organization.

What we described was a completely successful assessment, one that was well planned and executed and consequently led to effective action. However, like any powerful tool, this process has the potential to be misused. If an assessment is badly designed or poorly executed, through lack of knowledge or experience, this can result in:

- rejection of the process by the leaders at the outset, because of some misconception or groundless concern
- difficulty in securing an assessment team with suitable players, an adequate mandate, or sufficient time to do the job properly
- difficulty in obtaining the right information from managers and employees, or in making sense of it afterwards
- rejection of the findings during the feedback session. When poorly planned or badly handled, this meeting can become an unpleasant and traumatic experience for everyone involved
- failure to take effective action based on the findings.

However, there is no need for *any* of these things to happen. It's not a matter of luck; it's a matter of knowing what you're doing. The purpose of this book is to help you to pull off your next assessment like a seasoned professional, even if it is your first.

The following chapters will lead you through all of the phases of an assessment, setting out the steps in more detail, pointing out the pitfalls to avoid, and describing the tools and techniques that the experts use.

Whatever your role—leader, team member, or consultant— with this tried and tested roadmap in your hands you will always know what do next and what to expect.

GROUND RULES FOR SUCCESS

The assessment process is very flexible and can be implemented in many different forms, as we will see in the next chapter. However, regardless of what style of assessment is chosen, the following ground rules for success *always* apply.

Establish a Clear Purpose

This book focuses on how to use the assessment mainly as a planning process; to help create focused improvement plans. But you may have other aims. Whatever your main purpose in using the assessment process, you need to make this clear from the start, and design the approach accordingly. A clear purpose will help guide decisions such as who to involve, what mandate to give the participants, and what to communicate to employees.

This clarity of purpose is especially important to avoid mixed messages and unwanted behaviors. For example, if people believe that the primary aim is to win some kind of award or to achieve scores that will result in a bonus, then the process may be derailed by window dressing. If people believe that this process is in part a review of their personal performance, the data gathering may be impeded in a different way: by fear and defensiveness.

Fit the Process to the Situation

It is a mistake to think that there is "one right way" of conducting an assessment—the process has to be fitted to the situation. You don't give teenagers their first driving lessons in a 300 horsepower muscle car, and even the best driver cannot win a Formula One race in a Volkswagen Beetle. In the same way, an organization that is just learning about quality management is best served by a style of assessment designed for beginners—one that is quick and easy to execute, but will correctly identify the vital few priorities and create enough momentum to tackle these successfully.

One the other hand, an organization that is achieving world-class levels of performance requires a comprehensive and thorough assessment, using the most seasoned and experienced assessors. Anything less is likely to disappoint, by failing to identify valuable opportunities for improvement.

Sign Up the Leaders and Other Key Players

There is no way of pulling this exercise off successfully without gaining the informed support of the leadership team up front. Remember that success is not just struggling through the assessment phase and having the findings accepted.

Key Point
Success is not just completing the assessment, or even translating the findings into sound improvement plans. Success is implementing the improvement plans properly, in order to improve performance.

The leaders have to be clear up front that this is what they are committing themselves to.

Sometimes it is not easy to win this level of support, and you may be tempted to go ahead with merely passive approval or with an uninformed commitment. For example, you may hope that this process will provide a wake-up call for a leadership team that has become complacent and is expecting a glowing assessment report. Perhaps the leaders will be galvanized into action by a report that instead reveals major gaps between their perceptions and the current reality.

Don't try this—it hardly ever works! The most likely outcome is that the report will be trashed and the authors discredited. A report full of unexpected and uninvited bad news is not effective as a wake-up call. It is more likely to be treated as an insult or an irritation—easily ignored after the perpetrators have been dealt with. The leaders are much more likely to face up to the painful truths presented in the assessment report if they go into this process with their eyes open.

One other point—obtaining a consensus to proceed doesn't require unanimity, and the senior leader usually has the last say regardless of what everyone else feels. Sometimes management is under so much day-to-day pressure that the only way to get this process started is by a firm commitment on the part of the leader. TELUS Mobility (profiled later in this book as a case study) is a good example of this.

Give the Participants Ownership of the Process

The people who are involved in an assessment (at every level) will behave differently if they have the opportunity to make this process their own, rather than being herded through someone else's process. If they feel part of it, they will support and protect it as their own creation. They will also improvise and find ways to make it work when they run into obstacles.

For the leadership team, ownership means making the main decisions that will shape the process, taking personal responsibility for supporting the data gathering within their own departments, and committing to take action based on the findings. For the assessment team, ownership means devising their own game plan for how to proceed within the mandate provided by the leaders.

This ownership cannot happen in a vacuum. All of the participants need to be given sufficient information to understand the options available to them, the pros and cons and the pitfalls. They need knowledge about the assessment process *before* making important decisions on how to proceed.

Create a Sense of Urgency

There are several reasons why it is good practice to conduct the assessment process in an expeditious manner:

- It sends a message that reflects the attitude of senior management. "The results of this process are important, so let's have them soon so that we can get into action!"

- It encourages intelligent use of resources. There is less likelihood of "over-engineering" the process, or wasting effort in other ways, if the time frame is tight.
- It is easier to get high-caliber people onto the assessment team if the process is clearly a high-priority, fast-track operation.
- It demonstrates responsiveness to employee input. Often employees have been interviewed and surveyed before, but feel that "nothing happened" as a result. By completing the assessment process quickly, it is possible to get back to employees within weeks rather than months with action plans that clearly respond to some of the issues that they raised in the interviews. For them, this is very impressive and signals a significant change.

Creating a sense of urgency doesn't mean pressing ahead in such haste that the job cannot be done properly. It does mean communicating that this task is a priority, ensuring that commitments are honored, and holding to the agreed timetable.

Focus on Learning, Not Keeping Score

Although your main objective is to develop an improvement plan, this plan won't be as effective as it should be unless the participants accomplish some significant learning along the way. In fact the entire process of identifying the vital few correctly—and devising appropriate solutions—depends upon some new learning. If management already understood fully what was going on, they would have already solved these problems. So it is important to embrace learning as one of the key objectives.

The assessment process provides wonderful learning opportunities for the participants, and especially for those who serve as assessors. In one major petroleum company, even senior officers started to volunteer for this role,[6] because they heard their own managers raving about how much they gained from the experience. Not only did these managers learn about the criteria and about management systems, they grasped the "approach plus deployment equals results" concept in a way that changed how they managed.

The scores produced during an assessment are valuable to help differentiate between strong and weak areas of the management system, and to measure progress over time. However, the learning experience can be seriously undermined if too much significance is attached to scores. People can become preoccupied with the scores for a variety of reasons:

- They are striving for high marks in order to achieve some form of recognition or reward.
- They believe that simply measuring levels of performance will somehow cause improvement to happen.
- They have excessive faith in the significance and the precision of the numbers.

Key Point
When you're watching the scoreboard, you cannot see what is happening on the field.

In a well-conducted assessment, scores are developed and shared, but they are kept in perspective so that people can concentrate on understanding and learning.

Aim for Business Results, Not Recognition

Recognition is a powerful motivating tool that can and should be fully used to support improvement efforts. As the quality director of a large telephone company said: "I used to feel that I was pushing on a string, offering something that no one wanted. However, since we established our internal awards program, management are coming to me, asking for information and enthusiastic about participating. I feel now as if I own a giant, powerful magnet!"

All experienced examiners understand the motivational power of awards. However, problems begin to arise when stray fields from this "magnet" begin to deflect people's attention from the main purpose. It is ironic that the organizations that emerge as top performers in national awards programs are *not* those who adopted continuous improvement in order to win an award. They are organizations that are striving primarily for excellence and improved business results.

Key Point
Awards are like ice cream parlors that you pause at briefly during a long, dusty trek in the hot sun—refreshing and re-energizing, but not the purpose of the journey.

Make the Entire Process a Positive, Engaging Experience

So many management processes are no fun at all, and what's more, they are clearly not intended to be! But why should this be so? Let's take the planning process. Is there any good reason why planning for the future of the organization should be a painful, negative experience? It is hard to feel excited about a plan that was created through a process that is divisive, fear-inducing, or overly bureaucratic. A process like this often results in poorly conceived, fragmented plans that few people have really bought into.

Once you decide that there are real benefits in making the assessment process a more positive and engaging experience, it is not hard to accomplish. In fact it's easy, because there is so much opportunity for learning, for effective teamwork, and for having a positive impact on the organization. This strategy turns out to be a great advantage in getting the assessment done well, and it is completely consistent with the aim of creating sound, well-thought-out improvement plans that will get results.

Prepare for Tenacious Follow-Through

One of the most common failure modes for any kind of study, review, or audit is *failure to follow through*. All too often, good investigative work is done, and sound proposals are developed and agreed upon, but these are never fully implemented. Unexpected crises intervene, new priorities surface, key people change jobs, and so on. But the desired gains cannot be won unless the plans are executed.

Key Point

One of your design aims for an assessment should be to create a "fail-proof" process: one that will keep going and going in spite of the distractions, crises, and setbacks that are certain to occur.

You may think of this as your "Energizer Bunny" process—it keeps going like a toy with batteries that seem to last forever.

Fortunately, there are many things that we can do to help the organization be more persistent in its follow-through. Here are some of them:

- Integrate the improvement plans into the business plan, and build the improvement goals into the personal objectives of the leaders.
- Schedule regular, structured reviews of progress against the plans and the agreed-upon milestones.
- Create a measurement system that focuses attention on the performance indicators that we are trying to improve.

The secret of success is usually not luck or genius but persistence—and persistence is a *choice.*

• • • • •

You should now have a good idea of what the assessment process looks like and whether you could benefit from using it. In the next chapter we will show how to design an assessment process that is suitable for your organization.

• • • • •

ᵂᵂᵂ**Companion Website Materials:**

- The history of the awards
- The Baldrige and similar awards around the world
- The *Baldrige Index* and *Winners 600* studies
- Organizations using the assessment process

NOTES

1. The Baldrige Index is published by the Baldrige Office, National Institute of Standards and Technology, Washington DC.

2. "Award Winning Companies Improve Bottom Line" by Dr. Vinod Singhal of Georgia Institute of Technology and Dr. Kevin Hendricks of the College of William and Mary.

3. The list of principles given is typical of the principles listed in the documentation for various national award criteria. It is not taken from any one program.

4. This diagram is adapted from "Insights to Performance Excellence 1999" by Mark L. Blazey.

5. Chapter 7 describes the Affinity Diagram technique.

6. In many large organizations, "external" assessors are drawn from other divisions, so even the president of a division can participate in the assessment of another.

Chapter 2

Assessment Process Design

"Always design a thing by considering it in its next larger context—a chair in a room, a room in a house, a house in an environment, an environment in a city plan."
Eliel Saarinen, Time, 2 July 1956

Once the basic concepts are clear, the next step is to understand how to design an assessment, and the broad range of options available. The design phase involves selecting from these options and making adjustments in order to arrive at a process that is just right for the organization.

CHAPTER CONTENTS

- What makes for a great assessment
- Choosing the components of an assessment
- Selecting suitable criteria
- Selecting the best assessment process
- Basic types of assessment
- The pros and cons of different approaches
- Other design options
- Tailoring the process to your situation

• • • • •

WHAT MAKES FOR A GREAT ASSESSMENT

An assessment has three major components, as illustrated in Exhibit 2.1: the *criteria*, the *people* who perform the work, and the

Exhibit 2.1.   *The components of an assessment.*

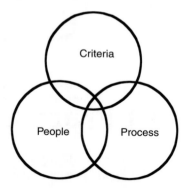

process that they use. In order to conduct a great assessment, you need to make good decisions about each of these.

People often believe that once they've decided to conduct a "Baldrige assessment" or a "CAE[1] assessment," they have pretty much defined what's to be done. They feel that there's little else to decide. Nothing could be further from the truth. When you conduct an assessment within your own organization, you will often choose to use criteria that are borrowed from an awards program, but the other aspects of your approach may look significantly different from the awards process—and for good reasons.

There is also a widely held belief that doing everything *"exactly the way that the award examiners do it"* is in some way desirable (to ensure rigor) or virtuous (to keep the process "pure"). This belief is understandable—but it is a misconception. In fact it is *not* a good idea to blindly emulate all the methods used by awards programs without considering carefully whether these will serve your needs.

You therefore have the freedom—indeed the obligation—to consider the range of possibilities that exist and to devise an assessment process that is suited to the needs of your organization. However, you need to know what you are about in order to do this successfully. This chapter aims to give you this knowledge.

Let's start by considering a few of the ways in which an awards examination may differ from an assessment that is conducted purely for planning purposes. Exhibit 2.2 sets out some of the typical contrasts. We have used a national-level award—the most stringent type—as the reference point.

Exhibit 2.2. *Contrasts between awards and assessment best practices.*

Typical Good Practice for a National-level Award Examination	Typical Good Practice for an Assessment
The process must scrupulously avoid becoming *prescriptive:* the examiners' report will set out in detail the areas for improvement, but it must not suggest courses of action. And the examination process cannot go further than providing a report. The award applicants themselves have to decide what to do with this information, if anything.	The assessment *has* to arrive at a prescription—that's the whole point! So the assessment process needs to include some kind of prioritization and planning steps that will lead to a sound, well thought-out improvement plan. And it is valuable to have the assessors provide some guidance and ideas, as input to the planning step.
The process goes to great lengths to avoid any bias or conflict of interest— real or perceived. This demands an arms length relationship between the examiners and applicants—for example there is little or no contact allowed before or after the site visit, and examiners are not allowed to become consultants for companies that they have site-visited.	In order to maximize the learning opportunities for people within the organization, it is desirable to have lots of contact between the outside experts and internal people— perhaps to develop a long-term working relationship. This need not compromise the objectivity of the assessors if conflicts of interest are avoided.
In order to be thorough and transparent, the examination process typically relies upon a very detailed and comprehensive "application report" which takes considerable effort to produce. The examiners use this document in two ways: to prepare for site visits, and to screen out lower-performing applicants— thus avoiding many expensive and perhaps pointless site visits.	If your aim is to plan for improvement, the application report can often be greatly simplified or even eliminated, thus saving considerable time and effort. An application report is not necessary if the assessment team is made up mostly of internal people, or if the organization is in the early stages of its improvement journey.

These are just a few examples of how differences of purpose translate into significant differences of approach.

It is worth noting that lower-level awards programs typically fall somewhere between the two extremes in Exhibit 2.2. In order to make the process less daunting and more helpful to the applicants, they often use simplified applications, and they devise ways of coaching and guiding applicants; to help them apply for an award, and then to help them understand the examiners' report and develop improvement plans.

Key Point
An award examination and an assessment have significantly different purposes, so they may require significantly different processes.

The assessment methodology relies upon valuable tools and techniques created by the award programs. We should be grateful for these—but feel free to adapt them and use them in ways that fit our goals.

• • • • •

CHOOSING THE COMPONENTS OF AN ASSESSMENT

As Exhibit 2.3 illustrates, you need to make decisions in three areas: the criteria, the people and the process. Your selection of which criteria to use is important—but this is usually your easiest, lowest-

Exhibit 2.3. *Designing an assessment.*

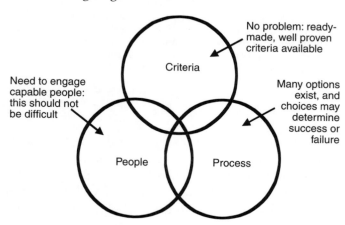

risk decision. It is your decisions related to the people and the process that will have the greatest impact on your success.

SELECTING SUITABLE CRITERIA

There is no need to agonize over this decision—it is usually quite straightforward. There are usually a few alternatives to choose from, and none of these is a "bad" choice.

In most parts of the world your natural choice will be the criteria for the relevant national quality award: Baldrige in the USA, EFQM[2] in Europe, CAE in Canada, and so on. However, this choice need not be automatic. It may be useful to consider other possibilities, such as criteria developed for specific sectors, or the criteria for a regional award (in your state or province, for example). The main factors that will determine your decision are:

- *Language.* Are the criteria materials available in the preferred language(s) of the participants?
- *Sector.* You need to choose criteria that will not seem alien to your colleagues—especially the leaders and the assessment team. Although the concepts are universal, many criteria use business-oriented language. This can be an irritation and a distraction for organizations that are not businesses—for example, parts of government, education, and health care. Fortunately, several sector-specific criteria do exist that use terms familiar to people in these sectors.
- *Complexity.* Many state or provincial awards have developed greatly simplified criteria, in order to provide "baby steps" for organizations just getting started. This is a great idea. However, if you choose criteria that have been simplified in this way, you need to be aware that these are intended only for beginners—they are not intended to support a truly comprehensive, in-depth assessment.

Many organizations are already familiar with some type of quality-related standards, such as ISO 9000 in industry, or the standards used for licensing health care and educational organizations. These standards are generally *not* suitable for the type of assessment we are describing: they are typically much narrower in scope and designed for compliance audit purposes.

Other Factors

There are some other factors that you may also consider, although these are usually secondary:

- *Widespread acceptance.* There are advantages in choosing criteria that many others are using. This makes it easier to share information and experience and to make valid comparisons.
- *Availability of support materials.* Some awards programs publish only the criteria and perhaps an interpretation guide. Others are supported by a wide array of useful materials—mini-assessment guides, case studies and other training aids, and detailed information from past winners about their practices.
- *Availability of expertise.* You will usually require some degree of expert support, either from outsiders or from a corporate function. Are there people available to you who are knowledgeable in the criteria that you are considering? Experienced examiners, trained by a national or state/provincial body, are among the most reliable sources of this type of expertise.

    On the other hand, most quality awards have strong similarities, and experienced assessors can easily make the transition from one to another. A good driver is equally competent behind the wheel of a Ford or a Toyota.
- *Awards eligibility.* Another factor that you *may* decide to consider is future eligibility for an award. Most national and state/provincial awards programs do not accept applications from organizations outside their geographic boundaries. If you intend to apply for one of these awards at some time in the future, you may decide to use these same criteria from the start.

SELECTING THE BEST ASSESSMENT PROCESS

One of the first important decisions you need to make is what type of assessment process to use—one of these will be better than the others for your situation. Fortunately, there is a fairly straightforward logic to this, which we will describe here.

The Key Design Decision: DEPTH

The main consideration is: how thorough do you need the assessment to be—how deep does it need to go? This depends upon how long your organization has been working on improving its management system.

As Dr. Jack Evans[3] observes, "if the organization is at a comparatively early stage of a quality improvement effort, it just isn't logical to bring up all of the heavy artillery of a full-scale assessment." This would be expensive, unnecessary overkill—and probably overwhelming and demoralizing for the participants.

In this situation, a fairly basic assessment is quite sufficient. This will quickly identify the most significant opportunities for improvement and enable these to be prioritized.

On the other hand, an organization that has been progressing steadily on the improvement journey for years absolutely requires an in-depth assessment—otherwise the findings will be just a litany of strengths. For an organization at this level it is frustrating to receive an assessment report that simply lists minor discrepancies but does not reveal valuable opportunities to improve. These insights can only come from a rigorous, in-depth assessment, using knowledgeable and experienced assessors.

Exhibit 2.4 illustrates the need to stay in the "just right" zone, where the depth of the assessment is matched to the maturity of the organization's improvement efforts.

Exhibit 2.4. *Matching depth to maturity.[4]*

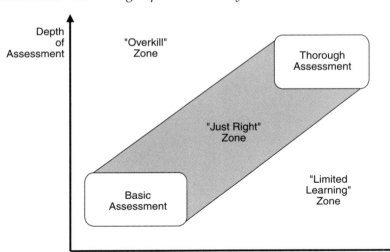

Maturity in the sense that we use it here does not necessarily correlate with size, market share, reputation, the longevity of the organization, or even current financial performance. Some large and well-known organizations have quite immature management systems, while some small and little-known organizations have been working on continuous improvement for years and have very mature systems.

If you have received training in the criteria you will be able to judge the maturity of your organization quite easily. If not, you will learn enough about the evaluation and scoring process (in Chapter 7) to make a rough estimate.

There is a continuous spectrum of assessment processes—like countless relatives, all within the same extended family. However, we will start by describing just four easily distinguished members of this family. These cover the full range of thoroughness required for organizations at all levels of maturity. Exhibit 2.5 illustrates how these can be chosen to stay within the "just right" zone.

Exhibit 2.5.   *Different types of assessment.*

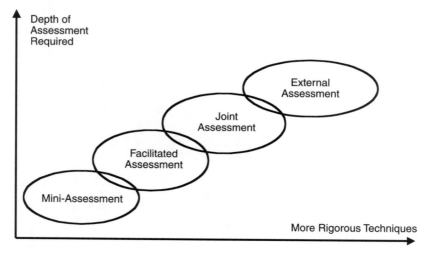

BASIC TYPES OF ASSESSMENT

These four types of assessment all use essentially the same criteria and evaluation system, but they are designed for different situations. They range from the quick and simple mini-assessment to the advanced and powerful external assessment. Each of these has strengths and drawbacks, and there are consequences to choosing one rather than another. Exhibit 2.6 summarizes the key differences in approach, while Exhibit 2.7 summarizes the steps in each.

The Mini-Assessment

The mini-assessment is simply a workshop in which the participants are guided through an evaluation of the organization using the criteria and the information that they have in their heads. There

Exhibit 2.6. *Types of assessment.*

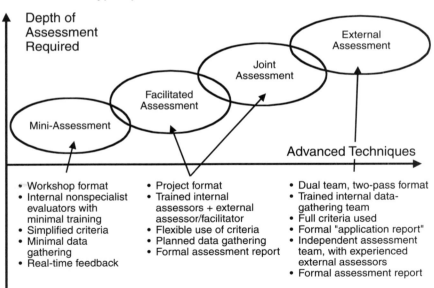

Exhibit 2.7. *Assessment process steps.*

Mini	Facilitated or Joint	External
Self-Assessment Workshop	Leadership Briefing Workshop	Leadership Briefing Workshop
Planning Workshop	Team Preparation, Data Gathering, Assessment Report	Team Preparation, Data Gathering, Application Report
	Report Presentation	External Validation, Assessment Report
	Planning Workshop	Report Presentation
		Planning Workshop

is no separate assessment team, no interviews, and no formal report—the findings are typically just captured on flipcharts. If the aim is to identify improvement actions, then a planning step is required. This can be a continuation of the self-assessment workshop or a separate workshop.

The Facilitated Assessment

The facilitated assessment is carried out by a team of internal people who are trained, guided, and supported by an external facilitator. This team gathers data by interviewing a cross section of the organization and reviewing key documents, creates a report summarizing the key findings, and presents this to the leaders. A planning workshop follows, to translate the findings into an action plan.

The facilitated assessment is a reliable and reasonably thorough, fact-based process that will get the job done at a modest cost. Its main limitation is a lack of perspective and objectivity, since it is essentially a *self*-assessment.

The Joint Assessment

The joint assessment is virtually identical to the facilitated assessment, but with the outside expert(s) playing a larger role. The external process expert works alongside the internal people as a full member of the assessment team. Rather than just guiding the team through the process, this individual contributes to the content of the report and shares responsibility for presenting and justifying the findings to the leaders.

The External Assessment

The external assessment is the most thorough approach, and it is significantly different from the others: it is an objective, independent assessment, conducted by outside experts.

The internal team does not try to evaluate the management system, but instead creates a detailed factual description of how it works and what results have been achieved. This document follows the structure of the criteria and resembles an application for an award, so it is usually called an *application report*.

The external assessors use the application report to understand what management is trying to accomplish and to prepare for their external "validation" step. During this validation, the assessors interview a cross section of the organization, obtain key documents and records, document their findings, and present their conclusions to the leaders. (See Exhibit 2.8.)

Exhibit 2.8. *Comparisons between types of assessment.*

Type	Assessor Capability	Independence of Evaluation		Extent of Data Gathering	Extent of Intermediate Documentation	Use of Criteria (Depth)
Mini	Internal people with minimal training	Self-evaluation only, with facilitator guiding the process but not contributing to the content		Little or none—perhaps some prework prior to workshop	A bullet-point evaluation report produced in real time	Minimal depth: high-level criteria headings only
Facilitated	Internal people with basic training and some external support	Evaluation by internal team with external guidance on the process and the evaluation logic		Planned interview process conducted by assessment team	A formal feedback report, developed in two steps: drafted during initial team training, then finalized after data gathering is complete	Flexible depth: the full criteria are used, "drilling down" more in those areas where there is more substance
Joint	Internal team members with basic training, plus one or more experienced external assessors		Evaluation by complete team, capturing internal and external perspectives			
External	Experienced external assessors with some internal support	External assessment team separate from internal data-gathering team		Two-pass process: first pass by internal team to create "application report," second pass by external team	A detailed formal "application report" created by the internal team / A formal feedback report created by the external assessment team	Full depth: the full criteria are used, including all elements

THE PROS AND CONS OF DIFFERENT APPROACHES
Mini-Assessment

The mini-assessment is an excellent tool for education and awareness-raising among the leaders. Its main advantages are speed, low cost, and minimal effort. It can also be used as a planning process, though in its basic form it is less effective than a more thorough assessment, for a number of reasons:

- The participants may not obtain such a clear picture of what is really going on because there is no data gathering phase—their view may be clouded by limited information and personal bias.
- The process has less perspective and objectivity because there is little external input—the participants may unwittingly collude to perpetuate existing false assumptions.
- There may not be such a strong and focused consensus regarding the priorities for improvement, because the picture obtained of the current state is less clear and fact based.
- It is less effective as a means of building a broad-based commitment to change because of the limited number of people involved.

In spite of these limitations, the mini-assessment is often the ideal first step for an organization in the early stages of continuous improvement. Sometimes it is the *only* feasible way forward when time and resources are particularly scarce.

Facilitated Assessment

The facilitated assessment is the value-for-money model, which uses a simple, efficient process to achieve a lot with modest effort and minimal external support. It provides good involvement and learning opportunities for internal people, and it can be made reasonably thorough up to a point. It is a safe approach because of the involvement of the process expert at key points as a guide and facilitator.

Its limitations are that: it is not as thorough and objective as a joint or external assessment; and it does not provide the type of insights and external comparisons that outsiders can bring.

Joint Assessment

The joint assessment in many ways achieves the best of both worlds: it retains the simplicity and efficiency of the facilitated assessment but gains the benefits of using outside expertise more effectively.

Strengthening the team by having an external assessor achieves much greater objectivity and perspective. An experienced outsider can bring valuable insights, as well as comparisons with "world class" organizations and their best practices.

This approach also provides a great opportunity for learning by internal people, since by definition they work alongside experienced assessors throughout the process. This type of assessment can also be done rather quickly: with an experienced assessor taking part, planning can be tighter with less allowance for contingencies; and there is no additional validation step.

External Assessment

Compared to a joint assessment, the main benefit of an external assessment is greater objectivity, and hence increased credibility of the report. This approach is also the most thorough, since the application report gives external assessors a big head start and enables them to dig down deeper during their data gathering. Other things being equal, the external assessment requires more elapsed time because there are extra steps involved: writing an application report and conducting a site visit.

One risk of the external assessment is that the organization may not have as much sense of ownership of the findings, resulting in less buy-in. However, this is offset by the greater credibility of the report, and it need not become a problem if the assessment is done properly. It is even more important with an external assessment to

Exhibit 2.9. *The pros and cons of different approaches.*

Type	Pros	Cons
Mini	• quick and inexpensive • simple, accessible • provides good experiential learning • can be a starter for more	• limited depth • limited use of data • limited involvement • no external perspective • risk of superficiality, lack of impact
Facilitated	• more depth • more use of data • less risk • modest cost	• more effort required • limited objectivity, external perspective • limited comparisons or insight into best practices used elsewhere
Joint	• greater objectivity and credibility of the report • external comparisons and insights into best practices used elsewhere • greatest learning experience for insiders • flexibility regarding depth	• more effort required • additional time/cost for external assessor(s)
External	• greatest objectivity, perspective • external comparisons and insights into best practices used elsewhere • learning experience for insiders, mainly in creating application report • most in-depth • reliable, comparable scores • credibility of an external report	• greatest internal effort required • more steps, more documentation • more elapsed time required • cost of external assessors • potential loss of ownership and buy-in

engage the leaders effectively at the beginning, to give them an excellent understanding of the findings at the end, and to follow up with a planning process that gives them full ownership of the priorities chosen and the action plans. (See Exhibit 2.9.)

• • • • •

The four types of assessment described so far are sound, tried and tested approaches, but they are certainly not the only ones. You can modify any one of these in many ways—boldly or subtly—to create your own more tailored process.

OTHER DESIGN OPTIONS

In most situations you can simply select one of these four types and use it as is. However, once you understand the options available and the design logic, you can fine-tune one of these designs or even develop a different approach tailored more precisely to your situation.

Some of the other options available to you are to:

- compress the time frame
- use a questionnaire survey
- simplify the criteria
- simplify the documentation requirements
- tailor the education and training.

Compress the Time Frame

An assessment can be designed to unfold in a rather deliberate fashion that consumes small amounts of people's time over a few weeks or months, or it can be designed more like a "blitz," in which the participants devote their full time and attention to the process and complete the assessment very quickly.

For example, it is often feasible to compress several steps—data gathering, report writing, and presentation of the report—into one working week (Monday through Friday). This can be achieved with any organization that isn't very large, complex, or geographically dispersed.

The benefits of this approach are that it makes very efficient use of the participants' time and it can increase the impact of the assessment. When people from several locations are involved—external consultants, or peers from other divisions—this approach can also significantly reduce travel-related time and costs by getting the bulk of the job done in one round trip. And by getting the assessment completed quickly, the organization can develop the improvement plans and get into action without delay.

Compressing the time frame in this way requires experience and excellent advance planning to pull it off successfully. It also requires advance preparations that may occur some weeks or months beforehand, such as training of the internal assessors and preparation of some type of application report, typically during a preliminary workshop with the leaders. And of course, the assessment has to be followed by a planning step and then implementation and follow-through. So this isn't really a five-day process, but it feels like one to most of the participants.

Use a Questionnaire Survey

A specially designed questionnaire survey (focusing on questions related to the criteria) may be valuable in certain situations, for example:

- if there is no employee survey data to draw upon
- as a means of strengthening a mini-assessment: A survey conducted beforehand can provide some data to counterbalance opinions and assumptions, and it can help overcome any denial within the leadership team about the concerns of middle management and frontline people.

Simplify the Criteria

Since the criteria were designed for examining world-class organizations, some of the content is irrelevant for an organization that has an immature management system. In this situation, simplifying the criteria can speed the process and avoid the risk of overwhelming or intimidating the participants the first time around. Later, as the organization makes progress, you can introduce people to the subtleties and the detail of the criteria.

Here are some ways of simplifying the criteria without compromising the integrity of a basic assessment:

- *Skip elements that deal with more advanced issues.*
  You can tailor the criteria to the level of maturity of the organization by simply skipping or removing many of the elements that deal with issues that they have not yet begun to think about and cannot deal with now. This is a kind of selective pruning—you trim off the parts that are far too advanced for the moment.

  For example, in the planning category, basic elements may call for some kind of improvement plan and a process for developing this, while more advanced elements may deal with monitoring the implementation of this plan and analyzing the results. You can safely remove the more advanced elements if you know beforehand that the basics do not exist.

  One caution: This type of pruning is not a job for novices—you should get expert help with this, or you may inadvertently lop off something that's needed to reveal one of the "vital few." Another point to bear in mind: changes designed to simplify the criteria may also distort the scores.

- *Skip the lower-level detail.*
  Many criteria have several levels of detail, such as seven or so categories, a number of elements within each category, and further explanations or expansions of each of these. For a basic assessment, you can work with only the higher levels, if the process expert explains the intent and provides examples. A one-page overview of the criteria (showing the categories and listing the elements of each) may be all that's needed to guide the process.

A Potential Pitfall   One idea that is often suggested is to simplify the assessment by focusing only on one or two *categories* of the criteria at a time. This may work, but it is usually not a good idea, because of the need to maintain a *system* view.

There is so much interdependence between the categories that focusing on just one or two may blindside you. For example, you might choose to focus on the process management category because the organization has made little progress here in the past.

But the *causes* of this lack of progress in process management may be rooted in other categories, such as leadership, planning, or the information system.

We are all well aware of the shortcomings of managing departments and functions independently as separate "silos." Let's avoid unintentionally creating new types of silos.

Key Point

To obtain a system view of the organization we need to overcome compartmentalization into silos—not just departmental silos, but process silos or category silos. These are all recipes for suboptimization.

Simplify the Documentation Requirements

There are two intermediate documents that may be produced during an assessment prior to the improvement plan: an *application report* (which describes the management system) and an *assessment report* (which identifies strengths and opportunities for improvement). Both of these can be simplified.

The assessment report will tend to reflect the thoroughness of the entire process, so a simple and basic assessment will tend to produce a simple and brief feedback report—perhaps just a list of bullet point findings. There is even more opportunity to simplify—or eliminate—the application report.

The application report is so called because it resembles the report that an award applicant is required to submit. For a mature organization, this report can take up dozens of pages of type, tables, and graphs and require a significant investment of time to create.

If you need the additional rigor and objectivity of a separate validation step using external assessors, then you need to create some type of an application report to enable the assessors to prepare for their task. For a mature organization, the benefits of preparing this document are significant.

However, it is not always necessary to create a full-blown application report, and trying to do so for an immature organization is a waste of time and effort. In this situation, a better approach is to create a simple, bullet-point application report rather than a comprehensive one. Or the application report can be eliminated entirely by using the knowledge of the assessment team as a substitute. This method, which we describe here for a facilitated or joint assessment, saves a great deal of time, and it is sufficiently thorough for a moderately mature organization.

Tailor, Personalize and Streamline the Training

The process used to train the examiners for a national awards program typically requires two to three days of classroom training on the interpretation of the criteria, how to evaluate submissions, and how to conduct site visits. For these examiners, this type of training is essential to achieve consistency within the examination process. However, there is no good reason to apply this format to every situation, other than the instructor's convenience, or the mistaken idea that such inflexibility is "maintaining the integrity" of the process. In some situations this "one size fits all" approach becomes an uncomfortable force-fit, like porridge before every meal. There are other equally legitimate training methods, and good reasons for sometimes turning to these instead. For example:

- It is often feasible to train assessors by having them evaluate their own company rather than a non-existent case study. The Cargill "CQA Week" is an excellent example of this approach.[5] As one of the designers of the Cargill system says: "We spend less time on the driving range and more out on the fairways. This is a playing lesson where the intensity helps the learning process."

  Similarly, in a facilitated assessment, the facilitator can coach the team members on the criteria as they work through a preliminary evaluation. After two days they understand the criteria quite well *and* they have completed their first cut of the assessment report.
- In many organizations the management system is so embryonic that a relatively simple, high-level assessment is all

that's required to identify the vital few areas for improvement. Providing training in the full glorious detail of the criteria may be beneficial for a few people, but for many it is just costly overkill that goes far beyond the needs of the task at hand.

Here are some general observations about education and training:

- The less mature the organization, the greater the risk of overkill. The critical need is for basic, essential knowledge, delivered in a fashion that avoids overwhelming people at the outset.
- In an immature organization there is a greater need for basic education in *quality management* (that is, the principles), and less need for extensive education in the *criteria.* In a mature organization it's the other way around.
- People playing different roles have somewhat different learning needs. For example, the leaders, people involved only in data gathering, and assessors who must critically evaluate and interpret the data, all have very different needs.
- The more advanced the organization, the greater the need (and the desire) for in-depth learning. However, there is much more to this than providing advanced training in the criteria for a few. The entire assessment process can and should be a learning experience for all participants.

For example, the leaders can learn more about the criteria and about their own management system by getting involved in creating the application report. The experience of serving as an assessor is a wonderful learning opportunity, and partnering with more experienced external assessors further accelerates this learning. In large organizations, leaders can also get this type of experience by helping to assess other divisions.

TAILORING THE PROCESS TO YOUR SITUATION

Here are some other situations that may call for additional tailoring of your approach (see Exhibit 2.10):

Exhibit 2.10.   *Tailoring the approach to your situation.*

Situation	Possible Approaches
The organization is very small.	• Consider including a sample of people from all levels of the organization in a workshop-style mini-assessment—or even include all employees.
The initial goal is education and awareness-raising only, or the leadership team wants to keep its options open about how to proceed.	• Conduct a mini-assessment without scheduling the planning session. When this is complete, the leaders can decide: (a) to do nothing more (b) to create improvement plans based only on the mini-assessment findings, or (c) to proceed with a more in-depth assessment.
Winning the support of the leadership team presents a challenge.	• Take the time to build support up front, before starting the formal process. • Explain that the demands on the leaders' personal time should not be excessive with *any* of the common approaches. • Lean toward a more streamlined and less in-depth assessment, but don't render the process ineffective through efforts to compensate for a lack of leadership motivation. • Use external resources at key points, to facilitate and to build the credibility of the process.
There is a climate of fear or mistrust.	• Use only external assessors for data gathering. • Use the leadership briefing not only to put across the key messages that should put the leaders more at ease, but also to gauge whether the process can accomplish anything for this group. • Consider carefully whether the current climate is likely to derail the assessment or to transform it into a negative exercise. If this seems likely, consider calling off any assessment for the moment. • Initiate a different, more limited process to address the climate issues only.

The Facilitated Process as a Demonstrator Model

This chapter has described four common assessment processes. It doesn't make any sense to describe the implementation details for *all* of these. So the later chapters that deal with implementation will focus on just *one* type: the facilitated assessment. By following the implementation of a facilitated assessment in these chapters you will learn how to execute the process, what pitfalls to avoid, and the tools and techniques to use. All of this information is equally applicable to other types of assessment.

And this does *not* imply that the facilitated assessment is in some way the *recommended* or *preferred* model. On the contrary, as you have learned in this chapter, you must choose a process that is right for your situation.

• • • • •

You should now have some idea of how to design a process that is geared to the needs of your organization. The next chapter shows how to develop a game plan that you can propose to the senior leadership team.

• • • • •

---

^{www}**Companion Website Materials:**

- Awards and criteria available around the world
- Contrasts between assessment criteria and compliance-oriented standards (such as ISO 9000 and regulatory standards)

NOTES

1. The *Canada Awards for Excellence* program (CAE) is the Canadian equivalent of Baldrige.
2. The European Foundation for Quality Management.
3. Dr. Jack Evans is a professor at Kenan-Flagler Business School, UNC-Chapel Hill, who has served as a Baldrige judge, and has conducted research into the assessment process.
4. This diagram is adapted from material by Dr. Jack Evans.
5. The Cargill case study at the back of this book describes an approach to training assessors using their own organization as the subject matter.

Chapter 3

Setting the Stage

*In preparing for battle I have always found that
plans are useless, but planning is indispensable.*
Dwight D. Eisenhower, U.S. general,
Republican politician, President

In order to set the stage for an assessment, the assessment process
sponsor explores the various options and puts together a plan to
propose to the leadership team. This phase starts when the sponsor
feels ready to develop a game plan for the assessment. It is complete when the sponsor decides to take the first substantive step—
to arrange a briefing workshop for the key decision-makers.

CHAPTER CONTENTS
- The leadership decision-making process
- The key issues
- Purpose
- Scope
- Timing
- Roles and responsibilities
- Budget, resources, and duration
- Using external resources effectively
- Finding competent help
- Winning support for your proposals
- Recognizing when this is not the right thing to do
- Check points

• • • • •

THE LEADERSHIP DECISION-MAKING PROCESS

Picture yourself as the assessment process sponsor. In setting the stage for an assessment, you will typically work through the following steps:

- First, you will identify some reliable sources of information and set out to learn as much as you can about the process. This book is a good start, and the companion website is a good next step. In most situations you will also need to identify a process expert—someone with knowledge and experience of this process that you can draw on.
- As you learn more, you will find that you can visualize how the various options might work in your organization. Soon you will have a game plan that you feel is workable, and you will want to discuss your ideas with the senior leader, and perhaps some of your colleagues.
- At some point you will feel ready to put forward a proposal to the leadership team and to seek their support for this approach—or you may decide that this approach is not right for your organization at this point in time.

THE KEY ISSUES

Before you put forward any proposal, you will need to think through a number of issues and form your own view of what would be best for the organization. Then you will be in a better position to share your views and seek the leadership team's agreement. Here are the main issues that you need to consider:

- Purpose—why should we do this, and what should we aim to accomplish?
- Scope—what should be the boundaries of an assessment?
- Timing—when should it be completed, and when would be the best time to start?
- Criteria—what criteria should we use?
- Process—what type of assessment process should be used?

- Participation—who should be involved, and in what roles?
- Budget, resources, and duration—what will it cost (including both direct and indirect costs), and how long will it take?
- Communication—when and how should we tell our employees, and what are the key messages for them?
- External support—what type of help will we need from outsiders?
- Approval—how can I gain the support of the leadership team for this proposal?

In this chapter we will examine each of these issues and show how to arrive at a decision.

PURPOSE

A clear purpose is essential, as this will influence many other decisions about the assessment process. You need to be able to answer questions like:

- Why are we doing this?
- What specifically will we get out of it?

It may help you to think about how the assessment process supports the organization's vision and strategic goals, and to develop a vision of where you want to go with the assessment process. There are many possible reasons for conducting an assessment, such as to:

- Develop a high-leverage improvement plan.
- Build a "critical mass" of support for implementation of the plan.
- Establish a yardstick for measuring the progress of continuous improvement efforts over time.
- Strengthen the leadership team's understanding of and commitment to quality-oriented improvement strategy.
- Enable the leaders to participate in improvement efforts.
- Obtain a formal analysis of what the organization is doing well and what it is not doing well.
- Build an improvement component into the normal business planning cycle.

- Document the management system for such purposes as education and reference.
- Build an inventory of current improvement initiatives and past achievements.
- Compare your methods with what other leading organizations are doing.
- Determine whether the organization is ready to apply for an award.

These are all valid aims. Your organization's needs will determine which are the most important in your situation. However, there is one common pitfall to avoid: viewing the assessment process as just a measurement tool. Measurement is important and valuable, but this process offers a wealth of other possibilities for learning, for clarifying priorities, and for building the case for change. Using an assessment for measurement purposes *only* is a serious lost opportunity.

Key Point

Using assessments just for measurement purposes is like buying a Ferrari for grocery shopping.

SCOPE

The scope of an assessment is usually the complete entity that the leadership team is responsible for. However, sometimes a different scope may be worth considering. For example:

- If the organization is large and/or complex, conducting some "pilot" assessments may be a prudent first step, even though the ultimate aim is to engage the entire organization in the process. However, it is important to differentiate between pilots used as vehicles for learning and pilots used as experiments or even as delaying tactics.
- If enthusiasm for the assessment process is evident in a few divisions of a large organization, but is not shared by most of the leadership team, then these proponents may have to demonstrate the value of their ideas by using the process

themselves first. This can pave the way for greater leadership buy-in later.

It is also feasible to apply this process to one department, to a specific business function, or to a headquarters group. However, the process works best when the unit being assessed has *all* of the following characteristics:

- It has some degree of autonomy (so that its own management team can act on the findings without having to seek approval).
- It serves a clearly defined set of customers (even if these are internal to the larger organization).
- It owns or controls the key processes used to serve these customers (so that it can work on improving these processes without running into external roadblocks).

TIMING

In most organizations, people are constantly under pressure, and from this perspective there is no "good" time to conduct an assessment. However, some times may be much better than others.

It is helpful to time the assessment to avoid clashes with other high-priority activities that also demand resources and management attention. You may have little room to maneuver—often you simply have to press on and get the assessment completed, regardless of competing priorities and unexpected distractions. But it would clearly be unwise to conduct an assessment of a toy store chain during the pre-Christmas shopping rush, or a marketing firm right in the middle of a high-profile product launch.

A second timing-related issue has to do with getting the resources that will be required to implement the improvement plans.

Key Point
Conducting an assessment without some strategy for acting on the findings is like setting off on a long safari with the gas gauge on Empty and no provisions.

Ideally, the "back end" of the assessment—the planning workshop—should occur at a time that makes it easy to integrate with the normal planning and budgeting process. In this way the improvement plans can become part of the regular business plan, with priorities assigned and resources allocated in the budget. If this is not feasible, then the leaders must understand at the outset that the improvement plan will require additional resources and budget.

A third factor that can sometimes affect timing is the need to distance the assessment from negative or threatening events—such as a major restructuring or layoffs. If an activity like this is going on at the same time, it will be difficult to get people's attention—or to establish sufficient trust for them to share information freely. It may also be difficult to convince people that these activities are not linked in some way. For example, if a layoff is under way, they may see the assessment simply as a devious way of identifying whom to let go. In this type of situation, it may be best to delay the assessment.

Nevertheless, many organizations operate in such a reactive and unpredictable fashion that there is no point in trying to fine-tune the timing. If you obtain support to proceed, you may just need to get on with it, hoping to complete the first cycle quickly and demonstrate the benefits before the process is derailed by unforeseen events.

ROLES AND RESPONSIBILITIES

The following descriptions cover roles and responsibilities throughout the assessment process, up to the point where the improvement plans have been developed. At this stage, most participants will take on different roles related to the implementation of improvement plans.

The Assessment Process Sponsor

The leadership team typically will not spontaneously decide to conduct an assessment. Someone has to come up with the idea, do the necessary research, and put forward a proposal. We will call this person the *assessment process sponsor.* This is typically someone who has a passion to improve the organization and is therefore acting as a change agent, either at the request of the senior leader or on their own initiative.

This individual will typically:

- research the assessment process, the options available, and the support resources required
- develop a proposal for the leadership team, setting out alternatives, decisions required, and the pros and cons
- set up a workshop for the leaders to launch the process.

Later, once the assessment is launched, this person will typically take on formal responsibility for the assessment process. This typically involves:

- ensuring that a suitable assessment team is assigned, adequately trained, and supported as required
- monitoring progress during the assessment
- engaging other leaders where necessary (for example, to remove roadblocks).

This person may also play a strategic role, working to ensure the assessment process is integrated into the regular planning cycle, and evolving the process over time as the organization's needs change.

One key point about this role—this person must provide the necessary leadership *without taking ownership and accountability away from the rest of the leadership team.* He or she may provide guidance and support, but the entire leadership team must own the resulting improvement plan.

The Process Expert

When embarking on an exercise like this, it is a great help to have someone available who already knows the ropes. We will call this individual the *assessment process expert*—someone with solid experience who knows how to make the process work in a variety of situations and how to deal with the typical problems that are likely to arise.

This person's responsibilities will vary according to the situation and the type of assessment, but they will typically include:

- helping the assessment process sponsor to develop a sound plan for the assessment
- providing training and support for the assessment team
- helping to design and facilitate the key working sessions: the executive briefing workshop, the report-writing, the executive feedback session, and the planning workshop.

If a joint assessment is selected, the process expert will also act as an assessor. For an external assessment, the process expert will lead the external assessment team.

Like the sponsor, the process expert must provide guidance and support, and lead parts of the process, without taking ownership away from the internal participants.

The Senior Leader

It is best to ensure the support of the senior leader at an early stage, and certainly before arranging the executive briefing workshop. In order to ensure the success of the process, the senior leader needs to:

- visibly lend his or her support, and thus help build a shared commitment within the leadership team
- ensure that there is adequate communication to employees about the purpose and nature of the exercise and its importance
- maintain a sense of urgency once the improvement plans are developed, and ensure that there is follow-through.

Other Roles and Responsibilities

Once the decision has been made to proceed, the leadership team collectively takes on certain responsibilities, and an internal team must be formed, with a team leader and perhaps some administrative support.

Role	Responsibilities
Leadership Team	• Help create a climate for open communication by taking part in communications about the process. • Support the data gathering within their own functional areas, removing barriers if necessary. • Participate in planning for improvement. • Collectively own the improvement plans, and take on individual responsibilities for sponsoring specific initiatives.
Assessment Team	• Take part in training to acquire the knowledge and skills required for the task. • Conduct the data gathering and document their findings. • Participate in presenting the assessment report. • Participate in planning for improvement.
Assessment Team Leader	• Act as the link between the team and the assessment process sponsor (and the process expert), and call for guidance or help when necessary. • Coordinate planning and logistics. • Act as the focal point for pulling together the internal team's report.
Administrative Assistant	• Provide logistics support, for example in setting up interviews and organizing working sessions. • Provide word-processing assistance during report writing.

BUDGET, RESOURCES, AND DURATION

Before you propose anything to the leadership team, you will want to have a fair idea of the likely costs and duration. They are certainly going to ask: how much of *my time* will this require; how much of *my people's* time; *how long* will the process take; and what is the *price tag*?

You will need to develop your own estimates for your own situation, but the following material provides some pointers. To arrive at an estimate you will work through the following steps, with input from your process expert:

1. Decide what depth of assessment is required, and hence what type of process you will use.
2. Map out a rough plan for the data gathering in order to estimate the total number of interviews required and the number of locations to be visited.

Exhibit 3.1. *How resource requirements vary for different approaches.*

		Typical Effort (Person Days)			
	Duration	Leader	Team member	Total internal	Process expert(s)
Mini	1 week	½	n/a	30	3
Facilitated	10 weeks	2	14	140	12
Joint	8-9 weeks	2	10	90	14
External	12 weeks	2	12	130	19

3. Estimate the size of the assessment team required, and consider which locations should be represented on the team.
4. Map out the steps, and estimate the effort required for each.
5. Estimate travel and accommodation costs.
6. Determine the costs of whatever outside help is required.

Notes:

- These estimates are for an organization with one line of business and about 500 to 1000 employees, all based in the same city.
- The actual numbers may look quite different for a different organization, but the differences between approaches will usually be similar.
- Since the mini-assessment involves only the leaders (and perhaps a handful of others), it does not vary with the size of the organization. The duration shown for the mini-assessment does not include any prework or survey.
- Other things being equal, the joint assessment is slightly quicker than a facilitated assessment because a team that includes experienced external assessors can work faster and requires less contingency time.
- The joint assessment assumes only one external assessor. The external assessment assumes two.
- The external assessment takes longest because of the need to prepare a detailed application report, and because of the additional external validation step.

The Schedule

Exhibit 3.2 shows the logic of calculating the timetable for a typical *facilitated* assessment. A large, complex, and geographically spread organization would probably require more elapsed time to complete the interviews.

Expediting the Process

Completing an assessment very quickly can heighten the impact and enable the organization to get into action quicker. This can be achieved by assigning assessment team members full time and by conducting most of the process as a nonstop "blitz," as described in Chapter 2. Using this approach, the training, data gathering,

Exhibit 3.2. *The logic of developing a timetable.*

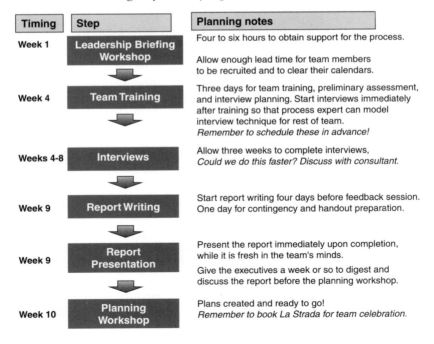

Timing	Step	Planning notes
Week 1	Leadership Briefing Workshop	Four to six hours to obtain support for the process. Allow enough lead time for team members to be recruited and to clear their calendars.
Week 4	Team Training	Three days for team training, preliminary assessment, and interview planning. Start interviews immediately after training so that process expert can model interview technique for rest of team. *Remember to schedule these in advance!*
Weeks 4-8	Interviews	Allow three weeks to complete interviews, *Could we do this faster? Discuss with consultant.*
Week 9	Report Writing	Start report writing four days before feedback session. One day for contingency and handout preparation.
Week 9	Report Presentation	Present the report immediately upon completion, while it is fresh in the team's minds. Give the executives a week or so to digest and discuss the report before the planning workshop.
Week 10	Planning Workshop	Plans created and ready to go! *Remember to book La Strada for team celebration.*

report-writing, and feedback phases can usually be compressed into just two weeks (ten working days), even for a fairly substantial organization. If the assessors are already trained and can do adequate preparation beforehand, the data gathering, report-writing, and feedback phases can often be compressed into just one week (five working days).

This approach includes little contingency, and there is no room for error. So the planning and logistics have to be superb, and the assessment team must contain a solid core of thoroughly experienced assessors.

Factors That Affect Effort and Cost

For any given size and shape of organization, the three factors that affect the effort required and the cost are:

- the type of assessment process selected
- the nature of the organization
- the size of the assessment team.

There is surprisingly little difference between the different types of assessment in terms of overall effort required (with the exception of the mini-workshop). However, there are *major* differences in who does what, and therefore significant differences in *visible cost*. For example, a facilitated assessment may actually require more effort than a validated assessment, but most of the work is done by internal people. In an external assessment the external assessors take on a much larger share of the work, so the external costs are higher.

The second factor, which you have no control over, is the nature of the organization. The number of interviews required increases with:

- size—the number of employees and layers of management between the senior leaders and the frontline people
- complexity—the number and diversity of divisions, each with different products and services, different types of operations, and perhaps distinct sets of customers
- geographical spread—number of locations in different parts of the country, and/or international divisions.

The third factor that drives cost is the size of the assessment team, since the entire team must take part in each of the key steps in the process. Chapter 4 (page 101) provides guidance on team size and the attributes to look for in selecting team members.

USING EXTERNAL RESOURCES EFFECTIVELY

All of the assessments described in this book assume that outside help is being used in a way that's appropriate for that particular approach. An assessment is a very knowledge-intensive process, which requires the involvement of someone who has the necessary training and experience. For this reason most organizations will need help at least the first time around, either from a corporate staff group or from an external consultant. However, the timing and the nature of this can vary considerably.

Here are some rules of thumb:

- An organization conducting its first assessment has a critical need for help during the *early* stages of the process: while planning the assessment, briefing the leaders, and educating the assessors. This support will be used mainly to gain an understanding of the *criteria* and to help establish the assessment *process.*
- An organization that is more advanced on this journey needs the experience and perspective of external assessors in order to obtain a sufficiently thorough, probing, and objective assessment. In this situation the outsiders' contribution is most valuable in the *later* stages of the assessment, and is focused mainly on the *content* (of the assessment report). (See Exhibit 3.3.)

It's helpful at any stage to have some external input to the process, however small, to provide a kind of sanity check. Insiders, no matter how capable, often cannot see certain things that are immediately obvious to an outsider. Insiders who have never been exposed to a world-class organization are likely to be over-optimistic about how well their own organization is doing. And the

Exhibit 3.3.   *Using external resources for different types of assessment.*

	Basic Assessment	**Advanced Assessment**
Planning phase	**Critical**	Helpful
Briefing the leaders	**Critical**	Helpful
Training the internal team	**Critical**	Advisable
Data gathering and report writing	Helpful	**Critical**
Feedback to the leaders	Helpful	**Critical**
Planning for improvement	Helpful	Helpful

additional credibility granted to an outsider helps to ensure that leaders will believe and accept the findings.

Giving Insiders an Outsider's Perspective

Smart organizations set out from day one to build internal expertise so that they will not always be dependent upon outsiders, and so they can become knowledgeable enough to make their own decisions about the process. This is an excellent strategy; it creates self-sufficiency but does not prevent them from using outsiders *when this will add value.*

For example, several of the organizations featured in the case studies have some of their own people involved as examiners in state and national awards programs. This has many benefits for these people:

- They acquire considerable expertise through the training, the assessment work itself, and the interaction with other experienced assessors.

- They obtain a broader perspective by seeing what other high-performing organizations are doing.
- They acquire a type of credential—the status of an examiner—that grants credibility.

And these are all benefits to the organization. With employees of this caliber and experience, they have much less reliance on external consultants: they have given some of their insiders an outsider's view of the world.

FINDING COMPETENT HELP

If you choose to employ an external consultant, you need to make certain that you are getting someone who can do the job well. *This is a critical success factor,* and it's the process sponsor's responsibility. If you don't do your homework here and the assessment fails because of incompetence or poor guidance from your helper, you cannot attribute this to bad luck or an act of God—it is negligence on your part.

But how can you verify the capabilities of an expert in an area where you are not an expert yourself? Take heart—it can be done. It involves some work, but it really isn't very difficult. In this section we will describe how to go about this, so that you can make a good choice with reasonable confidence and certainty.

Clarifying Your Requirements

Depending upon your situation, you may have quite different priorities regarding external support. For example, if your main challenge is winning the support of the leadership team, then you may need someone who can be a guide and mentor for this group—someone that they will respect and pay attention to, and who can challenge their views from the perspective of a peer.

On the other hand, you may be confident about working with the leaders, but simply require training for some people in the criteria. Or perhaps your people are already familiar with the criteria but need guidance on how to conduct the assessment process—for example, how to plan and organize the data gathering, and how to conduct the interviews.

Exhibit 3.4 sets out the attributes for someone who could play any or all of these roles. Depending on your situation and the role that you want your process expert to play, some of these attributes may be vital, and others may be less important. You must decide.

One important caution: If you do engage someone to work directly with the leaders and exert a personal influence, you *must* make certain that this person is also technically competent as a subject matter expert, or you may set up the worst possible scenario— bad advice accepted without question!

Don't be shy about asking your chosen expert to refer to this book, no matter how well qualified he or she may be. In our experience, true experts *never* feel they know it all, and they are *always* looking for additional information. Also, by referring to the same

Exhibit 3.4. *Desirable attributes of a process expert.*

Attributes	Comment
Integrity, trustworthiness	If you cannot rely on advisors to tell you the truth—such as when there is a clash between their own short-term interests and the needs of your organization—then you cannot trust their advice, however well qualified they may be.
Ability to relate to senior executives and to be perceived as credible	When dealing with issues that affect them directly, experienced executives (rightly) won't pay much attention to someone who doesn't understand their role and their challenges. The best qualifications are experience in dealing with executives and personal maturity.
Experience of successfully implementing continuous improvement initiatives and orchestrating organizational change	The assessment process is a powerful vehicle for change and continuous improvement—but only if you go about it in the right way. Understanding the concepts is relatively simple; it is the doing that is difficult. So it is invaluable for the process expert to have some hands on experience of a significant organizational change process, preferably one based upon quality principles.

(continued)

Exhibit 3.4. *(Continued)*

Attributes	Comment
Experience of conducting *this* type of assessment process successfully	This book makes a strong case for differentiating this process from others, such as compliance audits. Traditional audit experience can be an asset, but only if such individuals can adapt their style. Assessors who come across as critics or faultfinders do not create the kind of atmosphere in which people will share information readily and become engaged in the process.

A sound understanding of the criteria	Past experience as an examiner for a national awards program is a reliable qualification.
	    A good assessor can explain the essence of the criteria in simple terms and has a clear mental image of what a world-class organization's management system looks like.
	    Having total recall of criteria paragraphs and subparagraphs doesn't prove a thing.

Facilitation, interviewing, listening, report-writing and presentation skills	These are fundamental skills that a consultant in any discipline should possess, but some people are much more skilled in these areas than others.
Education/training skills	Subject matter knowledge is necessary but not sufficient: process experts should also be able to deliver education effectively and communicate their knowledge to others.

source material, you will be able to align your thinking and your strategy more precisely.

How to Find and Qualify Your Process Expert

When you are ready to start looking for your process expert, there are a few golden rules that you should *always* follow:

1. Clarify your needs before you start. For example, you could prioritize the key attributes required for your situation by reviewing Exhibit 3.4.

2. Focus on the capabilities of the person who will do the job, not the so-called "capabilities" of a consulting group. Consulting firms usually list in their proposals similar assignments undertaken for other clients. But you need to know what *the consultant you are being offered* has done—it is this individual's capability that matters to you, not what other consultants in the firm have done.

3. *Always* follow up on references unless you already know the person's abilities *relative to this specific process*. The person you employ should have already performed this type of task successfully before—preferably many times. Why would you pay for a novice to practice on your company at your risk? So ask for the names of a few recent clients for similar work, call them up, and get the full story. Make sure that the project is complete, and ask them how they know that it was successful. Ask what kind of contribution your prospective consultant made, what he did well and what he could have done better.

4. Look for a "fit" in terms of values and style. You are paying mainly for a core technical competency, and you must not compromise on this. But you can make better use of this person's knowledge if you can develop mutual trust and a good working relationship. It may be hard to accomplish this, for example, if the consultant seems more concerned about selling her services than helping your organization, or seems to consider himself about a million times smarter than you.

Timing

If you decide to use an external process expert, it is best to identify and engage this person at an early stage, well before your plans are set in concrete.

Even the brief preliminary discussions that you will have with your process expert, prior to requesting a proposal, will usually cover enough ground to ensure that you are at least heading in the right direction. From the consultant's point of view, it is most frustrating to be called in partway through an assessment, only to discover that it's too late—the process is already in trouble because of mistakes that could easily have been avoided.

Key Point
One of the most valuable—and least expensive—services that you can obtain from a process expert is sound guidance in the early stages of planning your assessment approach.

Early involvement will also help you to qualify your chosen expert and confirm that you have made a good choice—before it's too late to change.

Potential Conflict of Interest and Bias

There is potentially a serious conflict of interest for external consultants involved in an assessment if they hope to be involved in implementing the improvement plans. There is an equally serious risk of bias if an external assessor's expertise is narrowly focused within a certain part of the criteria—for example, in process management, or in human resource practices—and she lacks expertise in the other categories.

In both of these situations the assessment report may be biased toward the areas where the assessors can offer services, or toward the areas that they know best. Imagine that you engage a team of "construction industry experts" to inspect your home thoroughly, from basement to shingles. If this expert team comprises mostly plumbers, how many problems do you think they will spot in the foundations, the plastering, the wiring, or the roofing? It would not be a big surprise if most of the problems found are . . . in your plumbing. Especially if these same people expect to be employed to fix the problems!

Even if no real conflict or bias exists, there is a perception problem when the same consultants who performed the assessment reappear to implement the recommendations. It is natural to wonder: just how objective was that assessment? Did we just pay for a sales pitch? And of course you will need to find different assessors to conduct the next assessment—you cannot have the same people conducting an assessment of their own work.

What is the answer? One clean and simple way of avoiding this type of problem is to build a "wall" between assessment and implementation. You can make it clear from the start that any out-side consultant (or firm) that is involved in the assessment will not take part in implementing the improvement plan, and vice versa. This can help avoid financially motivated conflicts of interest.

You need to use your own best judgment in this area. There is also value in having continuity of support throughout the process, and conflict of interest may not be an issue if:

- the process expert is an employee (such as a member of the corporate staff)
- the process expert acts only as a facilitator (that is, guides the process but does not influence the content of the findings or recommendations).

"Functional" bias—the tendency to see problems only in one's own area of expertise—can be minimized by ensuring that the team members as a group are reasonably well rounded in their experience.

A Final Word—about Gurus

There is a mysterious phenomenon that occurs quite often when companies employ a highly respected external consultant: a complete suspension of critical judgment on the part of the client. This behavior is apparently caused by a belief that the consultant:

- is never wrong
- has supernatural powers
- knows God
- might possibly be God.

In other words, the consultant is given the mantle of a 'guru'.

Now the consultant in question may have a lot to offer. But ironically, uncritical acceptance of everything that the consultant says will often result in failure of the consultant's methodology. Here's why.

When this phenomenon occurs, people begin to act as if under a powerful spell. When they encounter problems in using the methodology, they simply persist—often beyond all reason. But they cannot bring themselves to make even simple, practical changes that might solve the problems, if these changes appear to contradict the guru's teachings. They have surrendered their ability to think critically and to learn from experience.

This is tragic. Quality management is not about blind faith in mysterious rules, or following procedures without understanding why. It is about the scientific method of inquiry applied to the task of management.

It is essential to use external consultants (and their methodologies) simply as resources: to understand their limitations, and to challenge information or advice that doesn't seem to make sense. Above all, people within the organization must take final responsibility for figuring out "what will work here" and for making informed decisions about how to proceed.

WINNING SUPPORT FOR YOUR PROPOSALS

Before you can hope to convince others, you must first satisfy yourself that this is the right thing to do. Then you need to interest your colleagues sufficiently for them to invest some of their time in learning about the process and about your proposals.

Although an assessment is not an unduly expensive process, it is not the type of exercise that can be neatly cost-justified using a simple formula, like a program for reducing accounts receivable or cutting inventories. What value can you place on a strategy for achieving world-class levels of performance? There is strong evidence that a quality-oriented strategy pays off handsomely in long-term bottom-line results. It may also be helpful to provide information about other leading organizations that are using this process. Exhibit 3.5 provides some ideas for arousing your colleagues' interest.

You will know you are on the right track in making your case when some people begin to say "We should find out more about this process—can you organize a presentation or a workshop for us?"

Once you have generated some interest, it's time to give the leadership team some direct exposure to the process, and to your proposals. The next logical step is a workshop that enables them to experience how the assessment process actually works. This is usually an engaging and enlightening experience. The next chapter describes some of the key elements of this.

Perhaps you can see the benefits yourself, but you are at a loss as to how to sell this process to the leaders. In this case, perhaps you are not the best person to take on this task. If you don't currently have sufficient rank or status to influence the leadership team, your best plan is to seek out and lobby a suitable leader. Perhaps he or she may see the potential and decide to become the sponsor.

Exhibit 3.5.   *Some ideas for generating interest in an assessment.*

- Clarify what the other leaders' major goals and concerns are (if you don't already know this) and identify specific ways in which this approach can help address these.
- Discuss with leaders their ideas about what makes a great company, and compare these ideas with the quality management principles that underpin the criteria.
- Discuss with the other leaders methods of planning for breakthroughs in performance. It may be clear that a more reliable approach is required—especially if the results have begun to plateau, if the competition is catching up, or if there is a history of ineffective, ad hoc initiatives. You may be given a mandate to investigate and recommend a suitable method.
- Use case study material from past award winners to illustrate specific best practices that are particularly relevant to your situation.
- Provide information about the Baldrige Index, a hypothetical portfolio of stock in Baldrige winners, and the Award Winners 600, a study of 600 recipients of quality awards, showing that they outperform others.
- Arrange contact with peers in other leading organizations that are using the assessment process. The companion web site lists some of these organizations.
- Ask your process expert(s) for references—other clients who will attest to the effectiveness of the assessment process.

RECOGNIZING WHEN THIS IS NOT THE RIGHT THING TO DO

There is no tool or methodology that cannot be misused in a way that causes harm. For this reason, when you are considering any methodology, it is a great idea to ask the proponents: "When would this **not** be the right thing to do?" If they do not have a thoughtful answer to this question, then you may suspect that their judgment has been overtaken by their enthusiasm.

You should be asking yourself this question about the assessment process. Here are some answers—situations where conducting an assessment might not be the best thing to do, or at least not the first thing.

- *The only item on management's agenda is short-term survival.* If your organization is in the midst of some crisis, it may not be sensible—or feasible—to conduct an assessment. It may be impossible to gain the leaders' attention or to spring free the necessary resources. And if the crisis is truly severe, it may be irresponsible to do anything that diverts attention from fixing it.

On the other hand, some organizations seem to operate in a mode of perpetual self-inflicted crisis. If the company's survival is not actually hanging in the balance, an assessment right now might help the leaders to understand what they are doing wrong.

- *The leadership team seems to lack what it takes to pull this off.* Exercising effective leadership is a great challenge, and it's easy to be critical—there are leadership issues in every organization. In most cases the assessment process will help the leaders to identify and deal with these issues, and to do some good for the organization. However, there are some situations in which the assessment is doomed to fail because the leadership team does not have "what it takes." What does it take? Here's my list: 1) a willingness to face reality, even if this is painful; 2) a willingness to put the good of the organization ahead of narrow self-interest and ambition; and 3) the ability to make some decisions and see them through to completion.

- *There are some more fundamental issues that need to be dealt with first.*

  For example, if the leadership team is not clear about what business they are in or where the organization is headed, or if there is no business strategy at all, then these issues need to be tackled first, and management shouldn't need an assessment to realize this. There isn't much value in trying to make the ship more efficient if there is no agreement about the cargo or the destination.

- *There are major organizational changes under way.*

  If the organization is undergoing major structural changes, or the membership of the leadership team is being altered radically, or some kind of merger, acquisition or divestment is under way, then an assessment may not be feasible (or useful) at this time.

  However, once the overall direction has been set and some stability of staffing has been achieved, an assessment may be both feasible and valuable. An assessment can shed light on how the transition is working, and it can facilitate integration, for example by bringing together people from different sides of a merger to provide a "nonpartisan" view of the situation. It can also be used to help clarify what management practices the new organization intends to adopt, rather than have these decisions be made unconsciously or by default.

- *An improvement plan has just been completed and people are eager to get on with implementation.*
  Unless the current improvement plan is fatally flawed, you will achieve better results by taking advantage of the momentum and enthusiasm that already exist and pressing on with implementation. However, the leaders should monitor closely how this plan is working, so that any weaknesses can be identified quickly and corrected before people lose heart. And it *does* make sense to plan for an assessment at some time in the not-too-distant future, to verify what is working and what isn't.

- *The organization already has an effective method of developing improvement plans.*
  If your organization already has an effective, reliable way of planning for improvement, you would be foolish to replace it or to tinker with it casually. Instead, you might study how it works and figure out what makes it effective. Then you can reinforce the best features and find ways to improve it further. Perhaps some of the techniques in this book will help. Most planning methodologies include some type of assessment, but this is usually far from comprehensive, and it often examines everything *except* the organization's management methods.

  If your organization has adopted an advanced planning methodology—for example, one based on Hoshin Planning—the assessment process can complement this by helping people to understand better where the levers are to achieve higher performance.

CHECK POINTS

Here is a list of things to consider before you begin to engage the leaders in a formal way—for example, by arranging a briefing session. This list will help you determine whether you are set up for success or failure:

Success	Failure
I understand pretty much how to go about conducting the assessment—I can visualize how it will work in this organization.	I expect that it will work exactly as described in the book.
I can picture how my colleagues are likely to react to my proposals—the benefits that will strike a chord and the likely objections.	The approach seems so sensible that I cannot imagine why anyone would object to it.
I can anticipate the main questions that will probably be asked, and I know how to respond to these.	I expect my colleagues just to trust my judgment and accept my recommendations.
I am clear about the nature and the extent of the external support that we will need, and I have already identified and involved suitable expert resources (if any).	It seems quite simple—I don't see why we would benefit from external support. OR We plan to find a guru and put ourselves completely in their hands.
I am confident that we can pull this off and that this process will help move us forward.	There's no harm in trying this approach anyway: if it doesn't work we will just try something else.

Once you feel that you are set up for success, it's time to go for it!

• • • • •

ᵂᵂᵂCompanion Website Materials:

- Using the assessment process in large organizations
- How to calculate assessment resource requirements
- Organizations using the assessment process
- Past winners of quality awards
- How to obtain case studies
- Hoshin Planning and the assessment process

Chapter 4

Engaging the Leaders

The real voyage of discovery consists not in seeking new landscape but in having new eyes.
Proust

Once their interest has been aroused, it is important to engage the leaders and make them active participants in the assessment process. An interactive workshop enables the leaders to gain an insight into the assessment process, to discuss the proposed plan for an assessment, and to make an informed commitment to proceed.

CHAPTER CONTENTS

- Workshop objectives and design
- Introducing the assessment process
- Introducing the assessment criteria
- Using the criteria: a test drive
- Agreeing on the assessment plan
- Confirming the next steps
- Check points

• • • • •

WORKSHOP OBJECTIVES AND DESIGN

The leadership briefing workshop is a critical step because:

- It sets up the leaders' expectations for the entire assessment process—and especially for the all-important feedback session when the assessment team will present its report.
- Some important commitments must be secured—not just to support the assessment process, but to act on the findings.

A key aim of the workshop is to enable the leaders to become active participants in the process. In doing so now they will have greater ownership of the report to be presented later—and they will be more committed to act on the findings.

Key Point
For the assessment to be successful, you need to do more than just obtain permission to proceed; you also need to sign up the leadership team as full participants in the process.

The specific objectives of the workshop are to give the leaders a good grasp of the assessment process, to set out a proposed plan for an assessment, and to involve them in making the final decisions about how to proceed.

This chapter describes how to accomplish these objectives using a workshop with the following steps:

- *introducing the assessment process,* including the purpose, the benefits, who is using this approach, the basic flow, key success factors
- *introducing the assessment criteria,* including the management principles, the concept of a management system, the framework of the criteria, and the approach-deployment-results evaluation logic
- *using the criteria* to perform some self-assessment—typically focusing on a category close to the hearts of the leaders
- *presenting the assessment plan,* focusing on the key decisions—such as timing—that the leadership team needs to understand and perhaps discuss

- *confirming the next steps,* especially those that involve the leaders: choosing assessment team members and blocking their calendars for the feedback session and planning workshop.

The following sections describe each of the key steps in the workshop.

INTRODUCING THE ASSESSMENT PROCESS

After the normal welcomes and context-setting, the first step is to establish the credentials of the assessment process and to outline briefly how it works. This calls for a brief but compelling presentation, setting out:

- how the assessment process works as a way of planning for improvement
- the case for assessment—for example, evidence regarding the performance of award-winning organizations
- other organizations using this methodology
- the potential benefits of this approach
- key success factors.

Properly delivered, this presentation whets the leaders' appetite for more information.

INTRODUCING THE ASSESSMENT CRITERIA

Previous chapters explained the management principles and the idea of a management system. These are very important, fundamental concepts that everyone involved in the assessment must grasp. The challenge is to accomplish this quickly and effectively for a group of leaders who are typically more interested in results than in management theories, and who have many pressing demands on their time. You can lose them very quickly!

The Management Principles Exercise

The most effective method that we know for achieving this understanding is a process of organized self-discovery, leading from the management principles to the idea of a management system. This consists of the following steps:

1. *A brief presentation and discussion about the management principles*
   The aim is to ensure that everyone understands the core concept behind each principle—perhaps by associating it with a catch phrase.
2. *Individual work assignments on the management principles*
   For the exercise, each participant is assigned responsibility for making one of the principles operational within the organization. Their task is to provide some answers to the following two questions:
   - What would success look like? What would be happening, what would people be doing, to indicate that this principle is being adhered to?
   - What supporting mechanisms would be required to sustain this way of working and make it the norm?
3. *Paired discussion and group debriefing*
   After some discussion with a partner, the entire group is debriefed and the participants share their answers for each of the management principles chosen.
4. *Review of a handout with model answers*
   This handout provides good examples of supporting mechanisms, which are the most difficult answers for people to devise, and the most valuable. These examples reinforce the participant's own ideas and help bring them back on track if they have gone off on a tangent.
5. *Discussion of a series of questions that elicit the key learnings*
   If suitable questions are now put to the group in the right sequence, the participants will volunteer most of the key learnings from this exercise. (See Exhibit 4.1.)

   The final step in the exercise is to explain the connection to the assessment criteria. The criteria provide an excellent, purpose-built tool for testing and designing an *effective* management system—

Exhibit 4.1. *Learnings from the management principles exercise.*

Question	Learning
Is this a good set of principles on which to base a management approach?	Yup, it's a pretty good list.
Would we be more successful if we could consistently operate according to these principles?	We certainly would!
What linkages can we see between the principles? What would be the effect of ignoring one of them, like customer focus, or management by fact, or leadership?	The principles are all intertwined. Neglect any one of them and the others begin to unravel, too.
Do most organizations work like this? Why not?	This approach is *not* common practice—even though people would much prefer to work in such an environment.
So why isn't this way of working common practice?	Facilitator's proposal: One key reason is that most organizations lack many of the supporting mechanisms required to support this way of working. They lack an effective management system.

one that is based on the management principles and designed to obtain results.

This exercise is powerful because it enables the participants to identify for themselves many of the components of a management system. They have really been devising parts of the management system during the exercise. So when they see the structure of criteria, this immediately makes perfect sense, without lengthy explanations. They have grasped the essence already, even though they don't yet know much about the details.

After some final discussion, this exercise is complete. In well under one hour the leaders have internalized the principles and grasped the basic idea of a management system. Magic!

This may be a good time for a short break.

• • • • •

USING THE CRITERIA: A TEST DRIVE

Once the leaders have learned about the management principles and grasped the concept of a management system, they are ready to try their hand at examining their own organization—to take the criteria out for a test drive. This is perhaps the most important part of the workshop, because it gives them first-hand experience of how the assessment process works. This experience of *doing* some assessment is worth a thousand explanations.

This exercise typically involves:

1. ***Explaining a portion of the criteria***
   The exercise will normally focus on a small part of the criteria—typically a portion of the leadership category. This part of the criteria needs to be explained clearly.
2. ***Setting up the evaluation exercise***
   The participants need to be shown how to identify strengths and opportunities for improvement.
3. ***Small group work by the participants***
   The leaders may work in small groups, discussing how the organization works and coming up with their own findings.
4. ***Sharing and discussion of the findings***
5. ***Demonstrating the scoring system***

Some of these steps are straightforward, others are not. It's worth taking a closer look at each of them.

The term *evaluation* is used a lot here. Evaluation means identifying strengths and opportunities for improvement—and scores too, if required.

Explaining a Portion of the Criteria

To conserve time, the exercise will normally focus on a small portion of the criteria—perhaps one item of the leadership category. This item needs to be explained clearly. A useful technique is to "paint a picture" of the methods used by a world-class organization, perhaps a company that they already know about.

Setting Up the Evaluation Exercise

This evaluation exercise—identifying strengths and opportunities for improvement—builds on the technique that is taught to the examiners for any quality award. There is little value in trying to make the leaders experts in this technique, and there is not enough time to do so. However, it is essential to help them focus their discussion on the organization's methods and use the evaluation logic properly.

The following techniques can help greatly:

- describing the evaluation logic (approach times deployment equals results) in a way that they won't forget
- modeling how the process works by following a simple step-by-step procedure, and providing written instructions for this procedure.

Describing the Evaluation Logic   This is pretty dry stuff, so it is important to describe the evaluation logic in a memorable fashion. Perhaps something like this:

"You can always tell when someone has been trained as an assessor, because they often "talk funny." For example, an assessor might ask: "Is this an *approach* issue or a *deployment* issue?"—What?

Here is a true story that may help shed light on this strange way of thinking:

While conducting an assessment of a financial services company, the assessors discovered within hours of starting the site visit that this organization had developed management by fear into an art form. At the headquarters, people lived in constant fear of being dismissed for the most minor infractions. The assessors were shocked by what they saw, but speculated that probably the branch offices wouldn't be so bad. They expected that, like most field operations, the branches would not always follow headquarters' directions to the letter—especially if these directions didn't seem sensible. Right? The assessors soon found out that they were wrong! The company's system of management by fear extended consistently in full force right out to the frontline people in every branch office.

What is the point of this story? This was an example of *a bad approach, fully deployed.* The company was actually very good at implementation: everyone was aligned and using the same approach. But the approach was deeply flawed. You don't get points for this in an assessment! Good results (and good scores) require a combination of effective approaches and good deployment of these. Thus the evaluation logic can be expressed as: approach × deployment = results.

• • • • •

Demonstrating the Evaluation Process The next step is to model the evaluation process. Exhibit 4.2 shows a simple procedure that can be used to demonstrate the process with the whole group, step by step, before they use it on their own. This should be done "for real"—that is, by evaluating their own organization, using an item of the criteria.

Some readers will immediately see an apparent flaw in this procedure. "Not all of the policies and practices will be strengths!" we hear the plaintive cry. This is true, but it doesn't matter at this stage. Here is how the discussion might begin, led by the facilitator:

"OK, so you have a written policy of flogging anyone who arrives late for work. Thanks for sharing that. Let's write up the strength:– *you do have some defined HR practices. Now we can critique these practices. Does anyone see how this particular policy may not align with good management principles? Perhaps we can also write up an opportunity for*

Exhibit 4.2. *A robust evaluation procedure for novices.*

Evaluation Procedure

1. Make sure that you are clear about the scope of the criteria item.
2. List as **strengths** any policies, practices, or routines used in the organization that seem relevant to this part of the criteria.
3. Critique these to identify **opportunities for improvement:**
   - What's missing—that is, what do the criteria call for that isn't addressed?
   - Are these practices fully implemented?
   - Do they appear to be effective?
   - Are they consistent with the management principles: for example, customer focus, valuing employees, management by fact, etc.
   - Are there any evaluation and improvement cycles?

improvement here . . . Now is this an approach *issue or a* deployment *issue?"*

"*It's a deployment issue—we never have the guts to carry out our policy.*"

The main purpose of this procedure is to keep the group focused on methods, not symptoms. If they are not given this type of guidance, many of the findings will be about symptoms (for example, "we don't have an agreed strategy") rather than methods (for example, "we do not have an effective process for developing strategy"). If they proceed in this way, churning out only symptoms, they may produce lots of strengths and opportunities for improvement—but they will learn nothing about how to "see" their management *system.*

This evaluation logic is a key component of an assessor's "X-ray glasses," and the leaders should develop this skill, too. With practice, this way of thinking and observing becomes second nature.

● ● ● ● ●

The evaluation procedure just described is a valuable learning tool, although trained assessors don't work in *quite* this way. Experienced assessors don't need to be guided by such a restrictive procedure, and they have to consider a broader range of factors, as illustrated in Exhibit 4.3. The award criteria typically describe such factors in some detail.

Small Group Work by the Participants The leaders are now ready to break into small groups and begin their own evaluation work. Depending on the numbers, and the time and space available, they may spread out and work round flipcharts in different corners of the room or just huddle in twos or threes where they sit. The time required will depend on how large a portion of the criteria they are asked to cover. They should also be asked to write up their findings for sharing with the group.

Sharing and Discussion of the Findings When most of the groups seem to be about done, it's time to share the findings, have some discussion of these, and then reinforce some of the key learnings.

Exhibit 4.3.   *Factors to consider when examining approach, deployment, and results.*

When Examining . . .	Ask Yourself . . .
Approach	• Does the approach use methods that are effective and appropriate to the task? • Is it systematic? • Is it integrated into the management system (as opposed to being an isolated add-on)? • Does it employ reliable information and data? • Is it "closed loop"—that is, does it embody some form of evaluation and improvement cycle? • Is it aligned with the organization's needs (for example, does it address what's important for this organization)? • Is there evidence of innovation?
Deployment	• Is the approach used whenever and wherever it could be used effectively, such as in different parts of the organization and in different situations?
Results	• Are there favorable performance *trends* and/or sustained *levels* of good performance? • Are there *comparisons* available to demonstrate how performance levels stack up against the outside world—competitors, industry leaders, "benchmarks" for specific processes? • How broad, deep, and important are the performance improvements? • Are the results improving in areas that are key to the achievement of the strategic plan?

What the Findings Look Like   What will the results of this evaluation exercise look like? Exhibit 4.4 shows a typical set of findings that might be produced by experienced assessors. The initial outputs from this type of learning exercise will be much less polished and less precise. But these findings should still shed some light on how the management system currently works, and they should reinforce the need for a more systematic approach.

Exhibit 4.4. *The format of findings.*

Strengths	Opportunities for Improvement
+ There is a systematic process for gathering information from the leaders to help determine the strategic direction. + There is a sound method of processing various inputs, using appropriate tools, to determine the strategic direction. + The strategic direction is communicated thoroughly to all managers by means of the all-manager briefings and follow-up sessions.	− Input from other stakeholders, and from other levels in the organization, is gathered in an ad hoc fashion, or not at all. − Communication of the strategic direction to nonmanagement employees is patchy—there is not a consistent, defined way of doing this. − There is not a reliable method of obtaining feedback on whether the strategic direction is adequately understood at various levels in the organization.

Symptoms or Methods: A Pitfall in the Evaluation Process As already noted, when people are learning the evaluation process for the first time, a common pitfall is to focus on symptoms and to fail to examine methods. When this happens, the people involved may seem to have done a good job: they have identified many strengths and opportunities, which are accepted as accurate. But on closer scrutiny, these findings do not properly cover the ground called for in the criteria, and they do not shed much light on what practices are working well or badly. Exhibit 4.5 illustrates the difference between findings that are focused on symptoms rather than methods.

There is no reason to completely avoid describing symptoms in the findings—in fact, this type of information is often needed to provide a complete and convincing picture of what is going on. But findings that don't address methods at all are like a hamburger without the patty—there's lots of tasty sauce and relish, but nothing nourishing or substantial to get your teeth into. They don't give any indication of what process needs to be fixed.

• • • • •

That's how the body of evaluation exercise works. In wrapping up this exercise, the message to the leaders is: "You've done a good job, and now you understand how the evaluation process works. The assessment team will receive a lot more training and spend a lot

Exhibit 4.5.   *Symptoms or methods: Examples.*

Symptoms	Methods
Employees in some departments are still unaware of the company's direction following the merger and are therefore very concerned about job security.	The process for internal communications is not systematic, and consequently many employees do not receive important messages intended for all staff.
Many technical employees lack basic knowledge about new technologies.	The professional development program does not address the needs of technical staff.
New product launches over the past year have been consistently behind schedule, and post-launch problems have seriously affected sales and margins.	The new product introduction process is not well defined and seems to be frequently ignored in practice. Also, by focusing on narrowly defined functional responsibilities it hinders rather than facilitates cooperation between the various groups involved in the process.

of time gathering data. You can expect their findings to be more detailed, more precise—and to contain some real surprises."

Now they need to understand the scoring system.

Demonstrating the Scoring System

The scores will form a valuable part of the assessment report. The scores for individual items complement the text; they confirm which aspects of the management system are the strongest and which are the weakest. These scores also provide a baseline for measuring improvement in future assessments. And the overall score provides a useful indicator of the maturity of the whole management system on a scale that reaches from "not started yet" to "world class."

There are two reasons why is it important to demonstrate the scoring system during this workshop:

1. to reinforce (again) the evaluation logic—approach times deployment equals results—since this logic is also built into the scoring system
2. to set the leaders' expectations for their own organization's scores.

First, the scoring system needs to be explained briefly. (This is described in the next chapter.) Then the leaders are asked to score individually one item of the criteria based on the findings that they have just produced. Polling the group reveals the distribution of their scores, and this can lead into a brief discussion of why some people scored high and others low. The bottom line is: At this stage no one knows the "correct" score—it is unknowable, because the facts are not yet clear. After the data gathering has been completed, trained assessors can arrive at reliable scores.

The leaders also need to understand that this scoring system uses a scale very different from the familiar school grades. The Baldrige scoring system—like most of its counterparts—is designed to give most organizations low scores (below 30 percent) and to stretch out the high performers over the upper part of the scale (above 50 percent). This makes it easier to identify potential award winners.

Exhibit 4.6 provides a "guesstimate" of the distribution of scores in industry, based on assessments of many organizations. Note that this can only be a guess: it is impossible to measure this distribution because most organizations either haven't conducted

Exhibit 4.6. *Estimated distribution of scores in industry.*

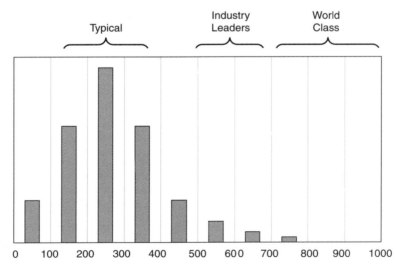

an assessment (and therefore don't know what their score is) or do not wish to publicize their scores.

Do not on any account omit the scoring part of the workshop. If the message about scoring is not internalized, the leaders will be shocked by the scores in the final report. This reaction can quickly translate into disbelief ("this is nonsense") anger ("the assessment team blew it"), and even rejection of the entire process. Don't take the risk of this happening!

This explanation of the scoring system shouldn't make the leaders feel proud of a score of 250, but they shouldn't feel astonished or humiliated, either.

Survival Tip

It is vital to explain and demonstrate the scoring system during the executive briefing, and to set expectations accordingly.

What Leaders Need to Know about the Scoring System

- The scoring system was designed to relegate most organizations to the 10 percent to 30 percent range, in order to differentiate high performers.
- Fifty percent is a *very* good score, indicating that an organization is on track to become world class–all it has to do is persist, and keep turning those improvement cycles.
- A score in the 10 percent to 30 percent band doesn't mean that this is a badly managed organization. It usually means that although lots of good work is done, many tasks are done in a way that is dependent upon who is around at the time. Many good practices may exist, but these have not been made systematic in a way that allows them to be managed, sustained over time, and fine-tuned.
- Having a low score doesn't mean that the organization cannot be successful–but it will need a lot more of those lucky breaks to sustain success in the long run.

Everyone *knows* that his or her own baby is beautiful. So even when the leaders have been shown what typical scores look like, they may still expect *their* organization's scores to be much higher. That's why it is important to stress the unusual nature of this scoring system and to emphasize that the scores are not the most important output. It is important to keep the focus on the main substance of the assessment: the strengths and opportunities for improvement.

The Dynamics of the Process

It is always interesting to watch how this part of the workshop unfolds, as the leaders work with the criteria for the first time. All leadership teams have some blinds spots, especially when viewing their own performance, and occasionally a group will seem quite out of touch with reality at this stage. However, many are surprisingly tough on their own leadership approach and come up with insightful findings. Most groups even assign quite realistic scores, once the scoring system is explained to them. And they almost always find the process worthwhile, not just a silly exercise. Why does this process work so well?

It would be easy for a discussion of leadership among the leaders to degenerate into an acrimonious debate with the subtext "I'm doing a great job of running my department—if only you guys could get your act together." However, the evaluation process avoids this tendency, because it focuses attention on methods, not individual competence. Since the leaders collectively own the management system, they can discuss this freely and honestly without anyone feeling threatened.

The leaders usually enjoy this process—they often haven't had the opportunity before for this *type* of discussion. Rather than receiving a boring, academic presentation about the criteria, they have used the criteria to learn more about how their own organization actually functions. Sometimes they find this discussion so engaging that they are reluctant to stop, and the workshop leader has to intervene to get the group back onto the agenda.

Handy Tip
Hold onto the flipcharts and acetates with the leaders'
findings—these will prove useful later in the process.

Misconceptions about the Criteria

This workshop is just a brief introduction to a rather large topic. So you cannot expect all the leaders to understand everything perfectly

Exhibit 4.7.   *Common misconceptions about the criteria.*

Misconception	Correction
The criteria are checklists of things that must be done to achieve some *arbitrary definition of excellence.*	The criteria set out the major *components of a management system.*
The criteria are *standards* that can be used to measure *compliance.*	The criteria provide a tool for examining and measuring the *effectiveness* of a management system.
The management system is a set of *documentation* setting out "how things are *supposed to be done* around here."	The management system is a set of practices: "how we *actually do* things around here."

right away. Exhibit 4.7 presents a few common misconceptions about the criteria, which may come out at some stage and may be worth correcting tactfully. These probably won't be stated explicitly—you need to listen for the false assumptions that lie behind some of the discussion.

Wrapping Up the Evaluation Exercise

Once the evaluation exercise is complete, one of the questions that should be put to the group is, "How valid are these findings?" The answer should be obvious: "We cannot be the only judges of how we're doing as leaders." Clearly the leaders' views are just one perspective, and a very biased one at that. To arrive at valid conclusions, the perspective of other employees is required, as well as any data available from surveys. It's obvious that a data gathering step is essential. The leaders now want to know how this will be done.

AGREEING ON THE ASSESSMENT PLAN

The next step is to present your proposed plan to the leadership team.

Chapter 3 discussed the main decisions that shape the assessment process, such as purpose, scope and timing. By the time you arrange for an executive briefing, you will have made these decisions and developed your own plan for an assessment.

There is no need to revisit and explain all of these decisions now—your colleagues are relying on you to make use your judgment on their behalf, especially regarding the technical issues.

But it is essential to give the leaders due ownership of the process by sharing the decisions that will affect them most, and those where they may feel entitled to have a say. Usually this means discussing the following topics, as a minimum:

- the main tasks and the schedule
- assessment team selection
- communications to the employees
- other questions: anything else about the process that they want to know about or discuss.

The Main Tasks and the Schedule

You can simply set out the main steps in the assessment—showing the process that you have selected—and this largely determines the schedule. It is wise to have some other options also worked out in advance so that alternatives can be examined easily. For example, you may have prepared two schedules: one with the assessors assigned part-time, the other with them full-time.

Assessment Team Selection

One of the most important decisions that the leaders have to make is how to staff the assessment team: how many team members to assign, and what types of people to select.

A team of five or six people is economical, efficient, and easily managed. You may need a larger team—for example, to handle a large number of interviews or to allow for adequate representation of a complex organization. However, a team of more than ten people is unwieldy and should be avoided if possible.

Exhibit 4.8. *Guidelines for choosing the assessment team.*

The team members should be:

- knowledgeable about the organization
- able to access information
- able to communicate with people at all levels
- trusted and credible (to leaders, peers, front line people)
- role models for the desired behaviors (dependable, team players . . .)

The team as a whole should be a cross section of the organization (to avoid the perception of bias).

It usually isn't feasible (or desirable) to select the team members during the workshop, but it is essential to agree on what types of knowledge and skills you are looking for, and to agree on which leaders are going to provide team members. Exhibit 4.8 provides some guidelines for use in choosing the team. This is a starting point for discussion; the leaders may also want to consider other factors.

Clearly, the assessors should not be people who are easy to spare! It is worth explaining the benefits of putting forward some of the most capable people to take part in this team. For example:

- The assessment process is a unique development opportunity for up-and-coming people—giving them a broad understanding of how the organization works.
- A strong team will provide a more powerful resource to support the implementation of the recommendations.

Team members should, if possible, be willing participants, not reluctant draftees. This means that the leaders may need to explain to their preferred candidates the importance of the assessment, and to convince them that this is valuable work. Being selected as a team member should be viewed as recognition, not as a punishment. For people who are already heavily loaded—perhaps already sacrificing their personal time to get their jobs done—it's wise to provide relief from some of their other duties.

Most of the leaders—and especially the more influential ones— should provide someone for the assessment team whom they trust to represent their own department or function. If any of the leaders do not feel represented on the team in this way, then they will have less ownership of the report.

Setting up an assessment team is in many ways just like setting up any other cross-functional project team. If your organization often establishes cross-functional task teams, and generally does a good job of this, then the process will come naturally and the participants will readily understand their roles and responsibilities. If your organization rarely sets up such teams, or typically does this badly, then a lot more care and effort will be required to get the team started on a sound footing.

Communications to the Employees

If employees aren't told in a timely fashion what's going on, they will speculate, and the resulting rumors can spread like wildfire—especially if they confirm people's pet theories or worst fears. For example, stories may circulate that the purpose of the assessment is to identify who should be let go in an upcoming layoff. Messages like this do not encourage open sharing of information!

So once the decision has been made to proceed, it is important to get the message out to people in a timely fashion.

The main purpose of these initial communications is to establish a suitable climate, in which people will speak openly and honestly during interviews. Here are the key messages that will help accomplish this:

- Many people will be involved in the process, by taking part in interviews. Of course these interviews will not cover everyone, but they will touch on a cross section of the organization.
- The assessment is an examination of methods, not of individuals' competence or performance. So no one should feel that they are personally under the microscope. The underlying assumption is that everyone is doing the best they can with the knowledge, skills, information, and tools that they have. The assessment is designed to identify the barriers that get in their way.
- There are no right or wrong answers. Everyone's perception of the situation is accurate in the sense that it reflects their personal experience—it is the view from where they sit.

- The purpose is to find opportunities to improve, not to check up on people or to find fault. So interviewees should be frank and open with the assessors. The organization cannot improve unless it knows where it is falling short.
- The interviews will be confidential. The feedback report will not pull any punches about what was discovered, but the assessors will not identify individuals or reveal "who said what."

This is the type of message that should go out at the start of the process through whatever channels are chosen. It may also be important in these communications to differentiate the assessment from an audit.

The leaders also communicate by their actions, which can have even more impact than written communications, however carefully crafted. So it is important that these points are also covered properly during the leaders briefing. The assessment team will receive the same messages during their training.

Differentiating the Assessment from a Compliance Audit If your organization is already familiar with some form of compliance audit, it is natural for people at all levels to assume that this process is similar, and to go about it in a similar fashion—after all, you've had experience of doing things successfully this way in the past. This is a trap.

For an assessment to be most effective, an environment must be created in which people feel free to discuss opportunities for improvement. Most people don't open up like this in an audit setting, because doing so often has negative consequences of some sort—for the organization and for themselves. (See Exhibit 4.9.)

Other Common Questions

Here are some other common questions that may arise during the executive briefing.

Do We Really Need an Internal Team? Some of the leaders may be thinking about the assessment team, "This seems like an awful lot of effort to produce a report—isn't there an easier way?"

Exhibit 4.9. *Audit vs. assessment—warning signals.*

Here are some of the warning signals that will tell you when people are still thinking of the assessment as a compliance audit:

- People refer to the criteria as a "standard" and talk about "compliance" or "conformance."
- The scores seem unduly important to people, and the idea keeps recurring that there is a "pass mark."
- People feel their own performance is being scrutinized, rather than the system within which they work—for example, they may show concern that any "problems" identified will be seen as being their fault.
- People become concerned about the number of opportunities for improvement being identified, perhaps saying things like, "how are we going to deal with all of these?" In a compliance situation, usually *every* significant shortcoming must be corrected, while in assessment the aim is to find many opportunities in order to identify a *few* that have the greatest leverage.
- There is a recurring tendency to talk up the strengths, and to downplay, minimize, or even conceal problems—perhaps because of the above concerns.
- The process is perceived as being "owned" by a third party—and the "auditors," not the organization, determine how the assessment is conducted.
- People seem to be concerned that there will be few choices available at the end regarding what action to take—the report will indicate what must be done, rather than providing a framework for deciding what issues to address.

If you see many of these warning signals, then you have more work to do in getting the message across.

The short answer is that an internal team is not essential—the data gathering and report writing can all be done by outside consultants. However, there are some compelling reasons for involving internal people in the process, rather than relying on outsiders in this way.

Picture the following scene: The assessment has been completed by the consultants and the report presented. Based on their new understanding of what is going on, the leadership team members all agree on three key improvement priorities, and they are strongly committed to act on these.

However, no one else has this information or understands the reasons for selecting these particular priorities. The leaders have to start from scratch in winning the commitment of others to their plan.

Wouldn't it be better to have some of their best people already on board, fired up and ready to go?

This is exactly what having an internal data gathering team accomplishes. The team members inevitably become strongly committed to seeing their findings acted upon. These people can help develop the improvement plans, act as ambassadors for the initiatives being undertaken, and serve as consciences to ensure that the leaders follow through. Some may also take part directly in the improvement projects.

Key Point

One of the most important reasons for establishing an internal team is to provide a "power plant" to help drive implementation of the improvement plans.

Should We Plan to Share the Assessment Report with Employees? Sometimes the leaders are nervous about being completely open with the findings. This is a pitfall. If there is any secrecy about the report, employees are likely to become skeptical about management's sincerity and to view the entire exercise with scorn.

On the other hand, the leaders' credibility will be greatly enhanced if they acknowledge the shortcomings that have been identified, as well as the strengths, and demonstrate commitment by taking effective action.

In any case, the findings usually contain few surprises for the employees—and it's the follow-up action that they really want to see. So there should be a plan for communicating with all employees after completion of the assessment, to share the key findings and to set out the actions that are planned. To avoid any aura of secrecy around the findings, it is good practice to ensure that all employees have access to the full assessment report, even though few of them will want this level of detail.

CONFIRMING THE NEXT STEPS

Before calling a close to the workshop, you need to review the decisions made and the next steps, and ask the group if there are any loose ends from their point of view. When these have been dealt with, the workshop is complete.

CHECK POINTS

As the leaders head off after the workshop, already focused on their next tasks, you will probably huddle with the process expert and reflect on how it went. Here's what you should ideally have accomplished—and avoided:

Success	Failure
The leaders view the assessment process as their own (collective) project.	The leaders view the assessment as your project and your responsibility.
The leaders feel accountable for the success of the assessment and are clear about their roles in supporting the process.	Having given their approval, the leaders expect you to run the project on their behalf.
The leaders feel that the workshop was a planning and decision-making session, as well as a learning opportunity.	The leaders feel that the workshop was just a presentation or a tutorial.
The leaders feel that they discussed "how we run our organization."	The leaders feel that they were just "taught Baldrige."
The leaders feel that they have explored the key issues and have arrived at the best decisions for the business (with guidance from the sponsor).	The leaders feel that they have been shepherded or manipulated toward predetermined decisions made by the sponsor.
The leaders plan to free up some of their best people to assign to the assessment team.	The leaders plan to nominate people whom they can easily spare for the assessment team.
The leaders realize that they *must* take action based on the findings and are eager to receive the report.	The leaders plan to wait and see if they like the look of the report before deciding whether any action is really necessary.
The leaders understand that the scores are likely to be numerically quite low and are not overly concerned about this.	The leaders believe that although most organizations get low scores, *their* scores should reflect the excellent job that they are doing.

Success	Failure
The leaders expect the report to reveal lots of opportunities for improvement, some of them potentially very significant and valuable.	The leaders expect the report to highlight a few problems that in an ideal world ought to be fixed.
The leaders leave with the dates of the report presentation and the planning workshop blocked in their calendars, and with some personal tasks noted down (e.g., recruitment of a suitable assessment team member).	The leaders leave expecting to be informed later about the next steps (e.g., via the minutes), and to be reminded if they need to do anything.

If you seem to have achieved most of the desirable outcomes and avoided most of the pitfalls, then you can celebrate a job well done. For those that you missed—well, at least you know where some of the rocks lie that you will have to steer around later.

However, there's no time to waste. Your colleagues are now committed and so are you—you have an assessment to run and a schedule to meet. Now you can look forward to some real action.

Postscript: If the Decision Was Not to Proceed

What if the leaders decide that they are just not interested in an assessment? How should you feel about this? Have you failed?

If the workshop was badly run, then you already know the answer. But if the workshop was conducted properly, so that the leaders' decision was a well-informed one, then this outcome may be a blessing in disguise. Even though it is disappointing, it would be *far* more damaging for the organization (and for everyone involved) to start the process in a half-hearted fashion and then fail to follow through.

If you have a passion to help your organization improve, and you have run into a roadblock like this, then for your own safety and sanity you *must* master the number one survival skill of change agents: understanding how to size up the situation and gauge your chances of success.[1]

Most organizations go through periods when they lack the basic ingredients needed to create positive change. For example, if management is weak or has become complacent, some kind of crisis may be required before any progress can be made. So in some situations, even the most committed and talented change agent can have little or no lasting impact. Don't squander your precious time and energy trying to build a lake in the desert.

● ● ● ● ●

---

www**Companion Website Materials:**

- Sample communication to employees
- Managing change

NOTE

1. *The Change Agents Handbook,* by David W. Hutton. Chapter 2: [Sizing Up] The Situation.

Chapter 5

Preparing the Assessment Team

Well begun is half done.
Unknown

Once the leaders have given the go-ahead for an assessment, the next step is to select and assemble an assessment team and prepare this group for its task. This includes training the team in the assessment process and the criteria, conducting a preliminary evaluation, making detailed plans for the data gathering stage, and learning interview technique.

The process described here is part of a facilitated assessment. However, this phase is very similar for most types of assessment.

CHAPTER CONTENTS

- Assembling the team
- The training process
- Initial team training
- The preliminary evaluation
- Planning the data gathering process
- Other team preparation issues
- Check points

• • • • •

ASSEMBLING THE TEAM

In this chapter you may picture yourself in the role of assessment team leader. Now that the leaders have given their blessing and support to the process, there is no time to be lost in bringing together the members of your team and getting them started on their task.

Team Composition and Availability

Armed with suitable guidance from the assessment process sponsor, the leaders should have made the following key decisions during the leadership briefing session: what type of people are to be assigned to the team, which leaders are to provide team members from their own departments, and when these individuals must be available to start work.

The team typically comprises five to seven people drawn from the major functions or departments, with one person assigned as team leader. Once it has completed its training, the team's mandate is to conduct the data gathering process, evaluate the data and develop an assessment report, and present the report to the leadership team.

What if the Assessment Team Members Are Not All Available?

In spite of the commitments made by the leadership team, sometimes there may be problems and delays in getting the full team together. This is the first test of whether the leaders are truly committed to the process—and whether the senior leader and the process sponsor will provide adequate support. This is not a time to accept compromises that may hurt the process and cause problems later. The team cannot be assembled and trained properly until it is complete.

The assessment team generally has a stronger mandate when it "mirrors" the leadership team—that is, each of the *key* leaders feels represented by someone in whom they have confidence. Later, when this team presents its report, these leaders will feel more ownership of the process and hence the findings. On the other hand, if a leader does *not* provide a team member as promised, then this individual may have little sense of ownership, and he or she is more likely to start "taking shots" at the team and its findings.

So it usually makes sense to hold out for the promised complement of team members, especially if the delinquents are influential members of the leadership team. This helps to ensure that the team represents the organization, and it is also like taking hostages for defense purposes: having the right people on the team provides some protection against irresponsible attacks on the team's findings.

Key Point
An understaffed team has an incomplete mandate, which may prevent it from delivering its message effectively.

This does not mean that *every* member of the leadership team must have a representative on the assessment team—just that the commitments made to provide team members should be honored.

THE TRAINING PROCESS
Training Strategy

The most important learnings during an assessment come not from seeing new things, but from seeing things differently. The quality principles and the criteria provide the lens that enables assessors to do this. However, new assessors need training and practice to learn this new way of looking at an organization. So it is important to give the team a proper grounding in the criteria at the outset, and then coaching and guidance during the assessment. This education should provide a good grasp of the fundamental concepts and thought processes, not just a literal interpretation of the clauses in the criteria, like a checklist.

A team that is well prepared and supported in this way will produce far better findings—not just a litany of symptoms that many people are already aware of, but new insights into causes and possible solutions.

Steps in the Training Process

This section describes a training and preparation process for the team that typically requires about three days of intense work.

1. *Initial team training*
   Like the leadership team, the assessment team learns about the criteria and the assessment process—but in greater depth.

2. *The preliminary evaluation*
   The team conducts a preliminary assessment based upon what they currently know about the organization. This process helps the team in several ways: they learn about the criteria in more depth, they hone their evaluation skills, and they identify parts of the criteria where they need to obtain more information.

3. *Planning the data gathering process*
   The next step is to prepare a data gathering plan. The team decides on the questions to be asked, select a suitable sample of interviewees, and assigns team members to specific interviews.

4. *Interview technique*
   During this training the team also learns about the interview technique that is most effective for an assessment. This technique is described in Chapter 6.

A key feature of this training is that, as far as possible, it is learning on the job. For example, the team members have a fairly quick introduction to the criteria, similar to the executive briefing process. Then, as they work through the preliminary assessment, they are coached by the process expert in each category and item of the criteria. The process expert provides examples of what world-class organizations do, and tutorials on subjects such as process management where they may have no prior knowledge. This approach is quick, relatively painless, and highly effective.

Interview technique is handled in a somewhat similar fashion: the team members are taught a simple process, and then they practice it during the early phases of data gathering—during interviews led by the process expert.

INITIAL TEAM TRAINING

The very first two to three hours of team training cover the same ground as the leadership briefing, and they can be conducted in much the same manner. In fact, it is valuable to use the same material, so that the assessment team members can see what their leaders have been told—including the criteria for selecting assessment team members, and the emphasis on follow-through after the assessment.

This is also a good time to share the results of the leadership team's evaluation exercise. This material can help the assessment team members in several ways:

- It provides the leadership perspective of some key issues.
- It will enable them to make better use of their time during interviews with the leaders, since they already have some of the leaders' input.
- It is reassuring for them to see that the leaders don't think everything is perfect!

THE PRELIMINARY EVALUATION

Once the team has grasped the fundamental concepts, it is ready to conduct a preliminary evaluation. Guided by the process expert, the team simply reviews and evaluates what it already knows about the organization's methods, following the structure of the criteria. This takes the form of a list of strengths and opportunities for improvement, like the example in Exhibit 5.1.

At the same time, the team identifies areas of uncertainty and tags these with codes like *??* or *DOC*. These codes indicate where the team needs to ask questions during the interviews and/or obtain documents.

Once this preliminary evaluation is done, it is a simple matter to extract the lines that have been tagged; and move these into a separate document. This will be reviewed and formatted into a *master list* of issues for the data gathering process (Exhibit 5.2). These are the areas where the team needs to ask questions during interviews or obtain key documents.

Exhibit 5.1.   *Sample of a preliminary evaluation.*

Strategic Planning

+ There is a systematic, fact-based process for developing the strategic goals.

− There is little use made of external comparisons (e.g., benchmarking of key processes or comparisons with competitors) during strategic planning.

?? How do we consider the capabilities of key suppliers during strategic planning?

?? Communication of the strategic direction. (Do people below manager level understand the strategic direction? Do the leaders and managers understand it?)

DOC: Review strategic plan for supplier and benchmarking information.

DOC: What is our track record in achieving the goals set out in past strategic plans? Need comparison of past strategic plans with actual results.

?? Improvement of the process. Have there been any reviews of the strategic planning process?

Legend:

+ = strength

− = opportunity for improvement

?? = question to be asked

DOC = document to be reviewed

This master list will be invaluable throughout the data gathering process for planning each interview, for staying on track during the interviews, and for jogging memories afterwards regarding what topics were covered. It is extremely helpful to summarize this information onto *one* sheet of paper so that the entire sweep of the data gathering topics can be seen in a glance. In this way it serves as a kind of instrument panel during the interviews—a quick reminder of "which way is up" when things get confused or bumpy.

PLANNING THE DATA GATHERING PROCESS

Now your team knows exactly what information it has to gather. The next task is to develop a data gathering plan. This involves:

1. selecting the interview sample
2. assigning team members to specific interviews and to other data gathering tasks, such as obtaining key documents and results data
3. scheduling the interviews

Here is how you will go about these tasks.

Exhibit 5.2.   *Typical master list of interview topics.*

XYZ Alphabet Soup Company—1999 Assessment	
Leadership	**Planning and Information**
• Is the company direction clear?	• Design of the new annual
• Personal involvement with	planning process (how are
improvement teams	customer priorities and supplier
• Senior management	capabilities considered?)
decision-making process	• Cascading of the company
• Format of review process	goals (is there any mechanism
(linkage to strategy, preventive	for alignment between
actions vs. firefighting,	departments?)
information package)	• What process performance/
	capability measurements have
	been established?
Customer	**People**
• Customer survey methodology	• How does new performance
(segmentation, analysis	management system work (does
of findings)	it encourage teams, is it fully
• Method for determining customer	deployed)?
priority for specific requirements	• Retention: why are so many
• Complaints management system	new people leaving (what
(nontechnical as well as technical	analysis, what conclusions,
complaints)	what actions)?
	• Employee development (how is
	this supported—budget, linkage
	to performance management)
Process	**Other**
• Senior management role in process	• Experience of three improvement
ownership	teams: brightway bandits,
• Inventory of "key" company	accounting aces, market ears
processes (cross-functional or	• Acquisition: done in a fashion
within departments only)	consistent with principles;
• Reasons for using three different	monitoring/feedback
process improvement	mechanisms
methodologies	

Selecting the Interview Sample

The interviews will be conducted as a top-down sweep, starting with the leadership team, and ending with frontline employees.

The interview "sample" is the list of individuals and groups that the team will talk to in order to reach a representative cross section of the organization (see Exhibits 5.3 and 5.4). It typically includes:

- individual interviews with *all* members of the leadership team
- individual or group interviews with other levels of management
- group interviews with some frontline employees.

If the organization has begun to use improvement teams, then some of these teams should also be interviewed.

The interview sample should also be designed to include:

- a cross section of each facility
- the owners of key processes

Exhibit 5.3.   *The interview sample.*

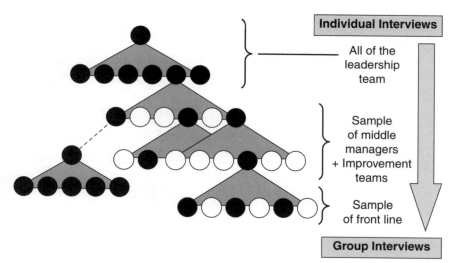

Exhibit 5.4. *The interview sample.*

Target Population	Include	Type of Interview
The leadership team	• All	• Individual interviews
Other levels of management	• Any specialists required • Owners of key processes • Interface people • A sample of the rest	• Mostly individual interviews • Group interviews if there are groups of managers performing essentially similar jobs
Improvement teams (if any exist)	• A few of the most successful teams	• One group interview for each team
Frontline employees	• A sample	• Group interviews

- specialists on any key topics, such as the strategic planning process or human resource practices
- "interface" people, such as individuals who work with customers and suppliers

The interview sample must be adequate from two different perspectives:

1. It *must* be adequate from the point of view of your *assessment team*—to answer the questions that have been identified, and to provide a good understanding of how the organization operates today.
2. It must also be credible to the *leadership team*—that is, not biased in any way, covering the key functions, and reaching sufficient people.

Once you have designed a sample that the assessment team is satisfied with, you should ask yourselves what the leadership team may think of it.

Group interviews are a valuable way of reaching many people quickly in order to find out how the management system actually works, as opposed to how it is supposed to work. Other things being equal, it is best to structure the groups so that the participants have a common experience—for example, they are from the same department and/or perform somewhat similar jobs.

If your organization has many locations, geography will play a big role in the selection of the interview sample. For example, it will be desirable to include a sample of locations that is somehow representative—the new West Coast branch office because that represents the future direction of the organization, the Central region branch because that is typical of most branches today . . . and so on.

If the organization is using teams—for example, to solve problems or improve cross-functional processes—then these are an important part of the management system, and should be studied. The most effective way of doing this is to pick a few of the most successful projects and conduct a group interview with each team, to allow them to tell their story. This type of interview is described in detail later. Why choose the most successful teams? This is explained later in this chapter.

When planning group interviews, you need to be very careful about mixing people at different levels.

Key Point

Interviews should almost never include people who report to each other, since this will inhibit open communications about certain topics, such as management's actions and how these are perceived.

The only exception to this rule is during an interview of an improvement team, where the team leader may also be the supervisor of some team members. Although this may inhibit discussion somewhat, it is usually more effective to interview the whole team as a unit. However, it would not be wise to include someone who is very senior or was not an active member of the team—such as the team's sponsor—since this might completely change the dynamics of the interview.

Assigning the Interviews

Once the assessment team has a complete list of the interviews to be conducted, the next step is to assign the interviews.

Typically, each interview is conducted by two assessors, who work as partners and share the tasks of leading the discussion with the interviewee(s), keeping the interview on track, and making notes.

It is good practice to have the same assessors interview people at different levels within the same department. This enables the assessors to compare answers for consistency and build up a more accurate picture of what is going on. One way of achieving this is to split the assessment team into smaller *interview teams* of two to three people, each of which will cover a certain department.

When choosing the interviewers for a specific department, it is helpful to have an insider who understands the work of that department and also someone from outside the department who can be more objective. However, just as we avoid setting up group interviews with people who report to each other, it is also very important to avoid the situation where assessors interview their own managers or people who report to them (directly or indirectly). This awkward situation can easily be avoided by switching interview assignments where necessary.

As you are deciding on these assignments, you begin to see how many interviews each team will be involved in, and some trading may be required in order to balance the workload. Once the interview sample has been selected, you know the total number of interviews that will be conducted. For interest, you can also estimate the total number of people who will be interviewed (by guessing the number in each group interview).

Scheduling the Interviews

The next step is to establish a timetable for the data gathering phase. The following key dates need to be agreed upon:

- a deadline for the completion of all *leadership* interviews
- a deadline for the completion of *all* interviews
- the dates of regular team debriefing meetings.

The team should review what it learned from the leadership interviews before proceeding much further. There may be a need at this stage to fine-tune the master list of interview topics, to eliminate issues that have already been dealt with, and to add new issues that have emerged. All of the interviews should be completed before the final report-writing session begins.

Once the training is complete, the assessment team members will schedule their own assigned interviews within this timetable, choosing dates that suit their interview partners as well as the interviewee(s). Each assessment team member will also keep the team leader or administrative support person informed of interview dates and status.

Planning the Documentation Review

Interviews are not the only source of information to draw on during data gathering. Certain key documents, records, and reports will also be required in order to:

- Provide formal descriptions of the management system and how it works. These documents may include the organization's strategy and plans; roles, responsibilities, and individual and departmental objectives; policies, procedures and methodologies.
- Provide data on a range of results areas, such as customer satisfaction and loyalty, market share, employee morale and involvement, product and service quality indicators, indicators of the performance of key business processes (transaction costs, error rates, cycle times . . .), and of course overall financial results and trends.

An effective way of planning this work is to:

- Identify required documents or data during the preliminary assessment, as already explained.
- Assign each document to a member of the team, to review it. This should not be a "trawl"—the review should be planned to identify specific information, generally as required by the criteria.

- Assign other data gathering tasks to team members in a similar fashion. For example, the financial results need to be reviewed to determine past trends and current levels of performance. Similar information is also needed for customer and employee satisfaction, product and service quality, process performance and operational efficiency, and supplier performance.

The most effective way to obtain all this information is to work with the individuals who own the documents or the data required. By reviewing documents or reports with a knowledgeable person, an assessor can quickly gain an insight into the overall picture and extract the required information without countless hours of reading and sifting.

An assessor may want a copy of a key document to share with the team, or for reference but some documents may be highly confidential. If there is a problem in sharing a document, look for solutions such as restricting disclosure to one member of the team, disclosure of only certain parts of the document, or disclosure of the nature of the content, but not the actual content.

For example, the team may learn that confidential exit interviews are documented and analyzed to determine why people leave. An assessor can verify how this process works by seeing the interview format and a report summarizing the findings over a period. There is no need to see the confidential records of specific interviews.

Exhibit 5.5 lists some documents that are often useful, especially to outsiders or people who have not experienced first-hand how certain things are done in the organization. For example, none of the assessment team members may have taken part in the annual senior leadership retreat, where the first planning session takes place. Documents from this event may clarify what process was used and how this worked.

Note that Exhibit 5.5 is not a comprehensive list!

In most organizations the team can very quickly assemble enough documentation to sink a ship. It is important to be selective and focus on what is really needed—or risk wasting a lot of time for little result.

Exhibit 5.5. *Typical useful documents.*

Document	Purpose
Strategic plan, operational plan, and departmental plans	Examine flow-down of long-term goals into strategies and tactical plans.
Personal objectives of senior leadership team	Examine alignment of objectives— cross functionally and with the strategic plan.
Agenda, minutes, presentation materials from regular leadership team meetings	Gain some insight into how the senior leaders operate as a group: the topics discussed and what information is provided (e.g., how often are customer and employee issues considered); how decisions are made, communicated, and monitored; how much is strategic vs. tactical vs. operational; how much is proactive vs. reactive.
Employee surveys, analysis and action plans	Understand what the survey covers and how the organization seeks to understand the survey information and to take effective action. Also use survey results to determine some of the interview questions: for example, "what action is being taken regarding [survey topic]?"
Customer surveys, analysis and action plans	Same rationale as for employee surveys.
Reports containing results data, including levels and trends over several years	Obtain data for evaluating all the results category topics: financial, market, people, customers, and processes.

Learning Interview Technique

The final portion of the team's training involves learning about interview technique for an assessment, as described in the following chapter. Usually a brief presentation and discussion of the technique will be sufficient. However, sometimes the team includes people who are quite nervous about the interviews—with justification, because their jobs do not involve doing anything like this. In this case some role-playing should be sufficient to build their skill and confidence in the technique.

However, confident or not, all of the internal team members need to learn the process properly before they lead any interviews. A very effective way of doing this is to have the process expert lead the first round of interviews with members of the assessment team taking part. By participating in a few of these interviews, each assessment team member can see the interview technique in action, practice in a safe environment, and get immediate feedback and coaching from the process expert.

This approach works best if the first interviews start immediately after the training workshop.

● ● ● ● ●

This completes the team's three days of intensive preparation—a combination of training and learning on the job. The team members are now well equipped for their task.

The time spent preparing the team is time well spent, which will pay off in spades as the process unfolds. By performing a preliminary evaluation, the team has already laid some of the foundations of its final report, and the preparations and planning will ensure a highly focused, efficient, and professional interview process.

OTHER TEAM PREPARATION ISSUES

Here are some of the questions that new assessment teams often ask.

Should We Work out the Exact Wording of the Interview Questions? Assessment teams sometimes spend large amounts of time and effort perfecting the wording of the interview questions. This may seem like a good idea at the time, and novice assessors may feel strongly that they *need* to do something like this in order to be well prepared. But this time-consuming effort usually leaves the interviewers still poorly equipped for their task. After being asked one of these carefully crafted questions, the interviewee may respond "I don't understand—what do you mean?" and the interviewer is stuck!

Good preparation *is* essential, but trying to word-smith the questions isn't the best method. An approach such as the one described here (developing a list of well-defined topics and learning a conversational style of questioning) is a simpler and more effective approach.

Should We Ask Everyone a Standard List of Questions? A common technique is to use a standard—sometimes proprietary—list of questions that touch on the various parts of the criteria, and then put these questions to everyone. This method will work, but it has some serious drawbacks:

- Very few interviewees will have knowledge about a broad spectrum of standard questions.
- A lot of time may be spent asking people questions for which the assessment team already knows the answers—or questions that they already know people in this organization cannot answer.
- The interviews will take much longer. Two hours may be barely sufficient, when a more focused set of questions would require only one hour.
- The assessors may not be focusing on what is important to this organization, as they would by developing a customized list of questions.

An approach such as described earlier in this chapter (using a preliminary evaluation to identify the interview topics) will be more effective in most situations.

Should We Visit the Best Units or the Less Successful Ones? A common discussion point is whether to include certain locations or groups that are known to be atypical—for example, because they have been particularly successful or because they are known to be in difficulty. Here are some thoughts on this subject:

- The more successful units within the organization usually face the same problems with the management system as the other units, but they have been more successful at dealing with them. So the assessors can identify the systemic weaknesses of the management system just as readily in successful units. They will also find more examples of best practices that are worth emulating elsewhere.
- The leaders of the most successful units tend to have more credibility, so the feedback report will carry more force if the interview sample is seen to include these rising stars.
- By looking at the most successful examples of an approach—for example, the use of teams to improve cross-functional processes—the assessors can often see more clearly the limitations of the organization's approach. Improvement teams that fail are often the victims of poor deployment, pure and simple. Teams that succeeded can help the assessors evaluate the approach. They can explain where the methodology and the management system helped and where these got in the way.
- Sometimes it may make sense to include an area that is in trouble—if, for example, their problem is typical of some recurrent problem in the organization, or if this area is key to the success of the organization. However, the assessment must stay focused on the management system as a whole, and it must not be seen as a substitute for proper investigation of a local situation.

• • • • •

The team is now ready for its task. However, before everyone rushes off, it's a great idea to have a final wrap up, to go around the table one last time and find out how everyone feels about the task ahead.

CHECK POINTS

As the team preparation draws to a close, you will know that you are on track if the situation is beginning to look like the "success" column below:

Success	Failure
The *"why and how"* of the data gathering process are understood—the team is now focused on *"who, when, and where."*	The team members are still unclear about the basics: the reasons for conducting an assessment; and some of the steps in the process.
The team members are clear about where they still need or want some additional preparation—perhaps some extra interview practice for certain people—and suitable arrangements have been made.	Some team members feel they are not adequately equipped for their task, but their concerns have not been acknowledged or dealt with.
The team has developed an atmosphere of mutual trust and support, recognizing each others' strengths and weaknesses, and perhaps coaching and helping each other when required.	The team has not "gelled"—the team members are operating independently from each other, and some seem to be pursuing personal agendas.
The team members seem to trust the process they have been taught; they don't know exactly how everything is going to unfold, and some of them lack experience, but they feel that if they use the methods they have learned, they will look professional and obtain the information that they need.	The team members are not sure that the process is going to work: they have begun to propose changes which may be unnecessary or even damaging.
The task ahead looks much less daunting. The team members are looking forward to getting into action, and they can see that this could be a lot of fun!	The team members are neither excited nor confident about the task ahead.

It's time for the team to go back into the real world and put their game plan into action. It's going to be fascinating to find out what really goes on around here.

● ● ● ● ●

---

^{www}**Companion Website Materials:**

- Training workshop sample agenda
- Data gathering plan spreadsheet

Chapter 6

Data Gathering

It is a capital mistake to theorize before one has data.
Sherlock Holmes,
in *The Adventures of Sherlock Holmes,*
by Sir Arthur Conan Doyle

Once it has been trained, the assessment team begins the process of gathering data. This data gathering phase starts when the assessment team has completed its preparations, and it ends when the team has obtained all the information it needs to create the assessment report.

The process described here is part of a facilitated assessment. However, this phase is very similar for any assessment in which a team is used to gather data.

CHAPTER CONTENTS

- The data gathering process
- Data gathering strategy
- Interviews and documentation review
- Frequently asked questions about data gathering
- Other data gathering issues
- Check points

• • • • •

THE DATA GATHERING PROCESS

With the training complete, the assessment team is now ready for action. The assessors, working in pairs, will conduct a set of *structured interviews* of a cross section of employees at all levels, starting with the leaders. These interviews normally last for about one hour and include group interviews of front-line employees, as well as improvement teams, if these exist. The team will also obtain and review *key documents,* to complement the information obtained from interviews.

Data gathering is a vital step in developing a fact-based understanding of what is going on. However, it is also important because of its immediate effect on the organization. It is the most visible part of an assessment—the team will interview many people at all levels within the organization—and the interviews affect people's opinions about the value of the exercise. Well-conducted interviews reinforce the credibility of the assessment and build support for it by:

- providing an opportunity for people at every level to have their say—and to know that they have been heard
- demonstrating that the assessment team is well organized and knows what it is about
- inspiring confidence that action will be taken on the key findings, while avoiding unrealistic expectations that every problem is going to be fixed overnight.

The interviews also stimulate the learning process. Interviewees, especially management, usually find the questions thought-provoking and realize that they could do their jobs better if they had more of the answers.

DATA GATHERING STRATEGY

The data gathering phase is the most expensive part of an assessment, because of the time and effort required to interview a representative sample of people. So it's important to conduct this phase efficiently. The following strategies make for rapid, effective, and credible data gathering:

- Creating an open atmosphere, so that people will share information freely
- Focusing the interviews by concentrating on areas where the team needs information
- Using group interviews and sampling to achieve adequate coverage with the least disruption to the organization.

Creating an Open Atmosphere

In many ways, the success of the data gathering process is in the hands of the interviewees. If they feel safe, confident in the assessors, and motivated to cooperate, they can provide a great deal of valuable information in a short time. On the other hand, if they feel threatened for any reason, or don't feel that this is a useful exercise, then getting at the facts can be like pulling teeth—and a lot of information will never be shared.

Key Point
The secret of effective data gathering is to create a situation where the interviewees **want to tell you everything.**

If the assessors succeed in doing this, they will be "fire-hosed" with information rather than having to pry it out of people who are fearful or reluctant to cooperate.

People can be put at their ease by suitable advance communications before the interviews begin, and by setting up the interviews correctly as described in this chapter.

Focusing the Interview Process

Some organizations conduct an assessment by asking everybody interviewed about everything in the criteria. This is very wasteful of time. Most internal assessment teams know a great deal about the organization before they even conduct a single interview. By sharing this knowledge effectively among themselves at the start, the team can clarify what they already know and what additional information they need to gather. This enables them to prepare for a much more focused and productive interview process. It's also unnecessary and wasteful to put the same questions to everyone. By planning the interviews according to the data that the team needs and who is being interviewed, the assessors can focus on topics for which the interviewees can provide useful input.

Using Group Interviews and Sampling

It is a common mistake to undertake far more interviews than is really necessary. This is costly for the organization, and it is also frustrating for the assessors, especially when they realize only part-way through the process that they already have all the information they need. After this point the interviews stop being interesting and surprising and start to feel like watching the same movie over and over and over. . . . Soon, even the interviewees begin to suspect that the assessors are bored out of their minds. This is not a good situation!

This pitfall can be avoided by selecting an appropriate sample of people to interview, and by using group interviews to achieve more coverage with fewer interview sessions.

• • • • •

These are the main strategies that the team will employ to ensure effective data gathering.

INTERVIEWS AND DOCUMENTATION REVIEW

When the overall planning work has been done, the assessors should all be clear about what information is required, who is being interviewed, and who is doing what. It's time to start scheduling and conducting interviews.

Exhibit 6.1 shows the overall flow of the interview process. This includes:

- scheduling the interview in advance
- preparing just beforehand
- the interview itself
- debriefing immediately afterward

The following section covers each of these phases.

Interview Strategy and Style

As already emphasized, one of the keys to successful data gathering is to create an open atmosphere in which people freely share information and perceptions. The key points should have been already made in the initial communications after the executive briefing workshop, and these should be reiterated at the start of each interview.

Exhibit 6.1. *The anatomy of an interview.*

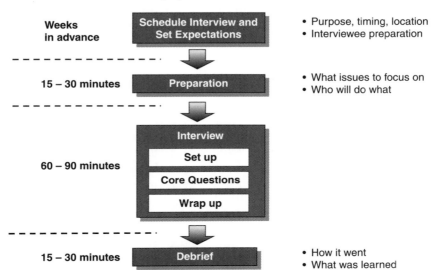

Everyone develops their own interview style, but it is essential that assessors do not come across like mean-spirited inquisitors seeking to find fault. They should be perceived more like sympathetic listeners who are keen to learn more about the interviewees' work, their achievements, and the problems that sometimes get in their way.

To create the desired open atmosphere, the tone of the interviews should be relaxed, good-humored, and not too formal. Some assessors may be concerned that a very formal approach is required to appear "professional" to the interviewees—especially to senior management. You need to match your approach to the style of the organization, but it is usually a mistake to conform to a stereotype that does not fit your purpose. The competency of the team will come across in other ways, such as:

- a professional approach—setting expectations clearly in advance, turning up on time, working as a team during the interview
- clarity regarding the areas of inquiry—you should be clear about what you want to find out, and you should not accept evasive or superficial answers at face value

- the nature of the questions—these often probe into areas that people have not thought about much before, although they are clearly important
- active listening and replaying of key points to demonstrate understanding—interviewees really appreciate having their views properly understood
- courtesy and consideration.

Key Point
*Don't confuse **seriousness** with **solemnity**. Assessors can be deadly serious about conducting a thorough and accurate assessment, but still go about it in a good-humored fashion and have fun too.*

In fact, you will probably get the best results if you can make the process enjoyable—for yourself and for others.

Taking Charge of the Interview

When you are the interviewer, *you are responsible for managing the interview.* The interviewee—regardless of his or her position—has temporarily put you "in the driver's seat" by agreeing to the interview. This means that *you* must take responsibility for keeping the discussion on-topic and using the time well. You must be polite and courteous, but you must not be intimidated by rank and thus be too timid to take a grip on the proceedings. You are in charge! Well, for an hour anyway.

Interview Logistics

When you contact interviewees to schedule the interviews, you need to set clear expectations regarding the purpose, the duration, and any preparations required.

Individual interviews should generally take place in people's own offices, where they will feel more at ease and have their documents and records readily available. An exception might be when the person has an open office that offers no privacy. In this situation, be alert for signs that the person wants privacy, such as low-ering the voice or looking around apprehensively. You may ask at the start whether they would rather conduct the interview here or in a nearby closed meeting room. Group interviews need to be con-ducted wherever there is space available, but you should try to avoid surroundings that may intimidate the interviewees. Think twice about summoning frontline people to an opulent penthouse boardroom.

Normally the interviewees do not need to do any preparation, since the interview questions are simply about how they do their jobs and other topics that they already know well. Occasionally you may ask them to have a certain document available for discus-sion or to take away for review.

Planning an Interview

Most of the planning of interview content has already been done when the team drew up its master list of interview topics. How-ever, you should also have a game plan for each specific interview. By referring to the master list, you can quickly identify the main issues that you need to explore, based upon who is being inter-viewed and what has already been learned in previous interviews.

All that's needed is a quick review of the master list with your interview partner to decide the key issues to be explored, who will take the lead on each, and any specific requests to make, such as for documents or data.

The Phases of an Interview

An interview may feel quite informal to the interviewees, but to be effective it needs to follow a definite flow, and there are several steps that must not be overlooked or forgotten. The complete process consists of three phases: *setup,* the *body,* and *wrap-up.*

Phase 1: The Interview Setup   Your aims during the opening moments of the interview are to put interviewees at ease, to set their expectations, and to set the tone for the rest of the interview.

The setup should cover:

- *Purpose and duration.* It may help to remind interviewees about the communication that went out about the assessment and to explain the purpose again. Check that the scheduled duration of the interview (typically one hour) does not present a problem.
- *The nature and scope of the exercise.* This is partly a reminder of the key points in the earlier communication to staff, and partly new information. Interviewees need to understand that the aim is not to evaluate their individual performances or to find fault. It is about examining management methods to find out what's working and what isn't. There are no right or wrong answers. Many people are being interviewed, at all levels in the organization, and the aim is to examine how the organization is managed.

  The interviewee might describe the criteria in a nutshell, rather like this, "We are using a framework that looks at how the organization is led, how we figure out what our customers need and organize ourselves to meet these needs, how we plan our work, how we use information and measurements to understand what's going on, and how we manage the flow of work so that it's easy for everyone to do their jobs well. And of course we look at the results to see whether what we are doing is working."
- *Confidentiality.* Interviewees need to feel secure that they can speak freely and that what they say will not be used against them. So you should promise that the report will pull no punches, but that you will not reveal who said what. In a group interview you cannot vouch for all the other participants, but you can ask them to respect the same rules that you are following.

  When you give this reassurance, some interviewees will brush it off with a remark like, "Don't worry—anything that I tell you now I would repeat in front of anyone." However, twenty minutes later, this same person may pause in the middle of particularly candid statement and say something like, "You did say that these interviews are confidential, right?" You can smile at this point, but don't laugh out loud. The point is that this reassurance is helpful.

Confidentiality is clearly important to frontline employees, who are the most vulnerable to intimidation or retaliation. However, it is also important at other levels in the hierarchy. For example, when there is a climate of fear within the organization, this usually affects the leadership team, too. Even senior people may be nervous about giving information that could be interpreted as hostile to the "party line" or to the senior leader. In this situation, confidentiality is important to the leaders, too. You should *always* promise confidentiality, even to senior leaders who may not seem to need it.

Key Point
Leaders need to feel safe, too, even though they might be embarrassed to admit this to you—or to themselves.

- *Note-taking.* Mention that you need to take notes to assist your memory, since you are doing so many interviews. These notes are just personal memory-joggers—they are not part of the formal record of the assessment.
- *Other questions.* It is courteous to ask interviewees if they have any questions about the process before you go further. This will also help flush out any issues that might be bothering them or could cause them to hold back.

Dealing with Skepticism Sometimes, especially in frontline group interviews, people feel that they have already been questioned many times but nothing has happened as a result—why will this exercise be any different? The implied question is "why should we bother to tell you what we think?" and the underlying issue is management credibility. This question provides an opportunity for you to explain why *you* have confidence that the leaders will take action this time. Explaining the timetable may help by showing the interviewees when they can expect to see an outcome. However, you probably shouldn't go overboard on this or you may destroy your own credibility. Everyone knows that you cannot *guarantee* that management will take action: the proof of the pudding will be in the eating.

The Importance of the Interview Setup Occasionally an interview may not go well. You may find that you are talking at cross-purposes, or that the other person is becoming defensive or angry or uncooperative. These problems most often occur because the setup part of the interview was inadequate in some way.

This can happen easily if you are not alert. For example, you go to interview Joe, supposedly the expert in the strategic planning process, but soon find out that the real expert is Ann down the corridor. Before you know it, you are conducting an interview with Ann, perhaps without having set it up properly. Or due to schedule changes you have to conduct an interview at very short notice and you skip some of the setup.

Key Point

To avoid problems later, always remember to go through a proper setup at the start, even when you have drifted or been suddenly thrown into an interview.

This chapter reviews later some typical difficulties that may arise and shows how to deal with these. However, simply being diligent about the setup will prevent many interview problems.

Phase 2: The Body of the Interview Now you can plunge into the body of the interview—the questions that you came to get answers to. For the next forty-five minutes or so, you and your partner work together as a team to gather the information that you want.

It is good practice for one person to take notes while the other leads the interview, maintaining eye contact and showing interest in the answers, and clarifying key points. The assessors may take turns leading the interview, and either assessor may jump in with subsidiary questions—for example, when an answer is unclear to them or when they spot a new line of inquiry.

Questioning Technique The following is the step-by-step process that you will use for introducing a topic and exploring it with the interviewee. This is an easy and natural process to use, because it resembles the way that people elicit information during normal conversation. Most people can learn this technique in minutes and be reasonably confident and proficient after using it in one or two interviews.

When the assessors have mastered this approach, they no longer need "scripted" questions. All they need is a list of interview topics that are well defined and understood. These topics don't even need to be written down in question form. And using this technique they conduct better, more intelligent interviews. Magic!

Of course, this approach in itself cannot guarantee a good interview. Success still depends upon the interviewer's skills, and these improve with practice and experience.

Exhibit 6.2 illustrates the questioning technique and Exhibit 6.3 provides an example of this method in action.

A Search for Understanding The interview should not be a "checklist" exercise, in which the interviewers simply check off items—"We do this . . . We don't do that." Rather, it should be a search for a clear understanding of how the management system works. For example, suppose you find out that there is a defined strategic planning process. That's great, but how does it actually work? Who is involved, what is the timetable of events, what information sources are used, what are the interviewee's observations about how well the process works . . .? You need to find out enough about the process to evaluate it.

Key Point
Once started on a topic, you should keep asking questions until you feel that you understand how the process works—or you conclude that the interviewee cannot (or will not) help you further.

Following Threads Another technique that will help you to see the management system as a whole is to follow the threads that hold the whole structure together. For example, there is a thread of *purpose* that starts with the mission and strategic direction of the organization, and then works its way down through more detailed levels of planning and into people's personal objectives. You can follow this thread, for example, by asking people at different levels about whether they understand the direction of the organization and how their personal objectives are linked to the organization's goals. Alongside this purpose thread is a "how are we doing" thread that runs in the opposite

Exhibit 6.2. *Questioning technique.*

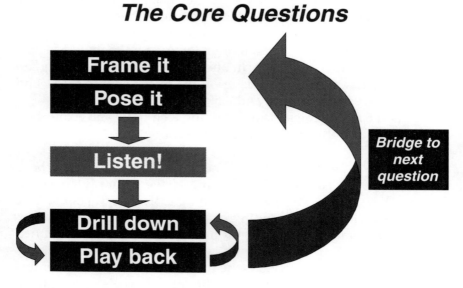

Exhibit 6.3. *Questioning technique in action.*

Interview Step	**Example of Dialogue**
Frame the issue	"We're interested in strategic planning—especially the way that customer information is used during this process."
Pose a question inviting the interviewee to speak	"How does this work in your experience?"
Listen	Interviewee shows interest and pays attention.
Play back (for confirmation) and *Drill down* (for more detail) until satisfied	Play back: "So what you're saying is that market share data is used formally during strategic planning, but data on customer satisfaction is not." Drill down: "Can you tell us more about how the market share information is used?" "Who is considered the owner of the strategic planning process?" "Is there a document that describes all of this?"
Bridge to the next issue	"Thanks, I understand this a lot better now. You mentioned the customer satisfaction data—we're interested in . . ." next topic

direction. This is the monitoring of progress against objectives. This thread should go from the individual right back up to the strategic plan, with the question being asked at each level, "how are we doing?" and measurements in place to provide answers.

Another set of threads has to do with customer focus. The "customer requirements" thread starts with the identification of customer groups and their needs and works its way back into product specifications and service standards, and then into the processes and procedures that deliver these products and services. The matching "how are we doing" thread runs back out to the customer, starting with the monitoring of process compliance, the achievement of product specifications and service standards, and finally, monitoring of the customer's satisfaction with the end result.

When these threads are broken, the organization doesn't function well: people's efforts are not aligned with the strategy, and our business systems don't deliver what customers want. As you go from one interview to the next, remember that you are not examining a patchwork of separate pieces—you are examining strands in a fabric that should be seamless and tightly woven.

Key Point

Often the most valuable findings from an assessment have to do with "broken threads"—breakdowns in the linkages between different parts of the management system.

Listening for Methods, Not Outcomes   You have already heard a lot about this focus on methods. It applies equally to how you put questions during an interview—but especially how you *listen and probe*. It is another way of differentiating between opinions and facts.

Sometimes the data gathering process feels like watching a soap opera unfold, with lots of subplots and surprises. And it is natural for the interviewees to spend time on issues that they feel emotional about. However, regardless of how absorbing this may be, you cannot just sit back and take it all in like a movie. *This approach will not give you enough information to produce useful findings.* This show may look like a soap, but you need to treat it like a murder mystery. You need to climb out of your seat, get onto the set, and become the detective.

As a detective, when you are being presented with incidents and emotions, you need to acknowledge and understand these, and show empathy. But you must also listen and probe for systemic causes—the processes, practices, and behaviors that cause these outcomes.

People are upset about being kept in the dark? Ask about communications: How is information relayed to them? What have they been told? What haven't they been told? Ask them how things should be done to avoid this problem in the future.

You may never have the cachet of Sherlock Holmes, but you will often have the satisfaction of exposing the culprit behind some problem—typically a broken or nonexistent process—complete with conclusive evidence that everyone else had overlooked. Elementary, my Dear Watson!

Dealing with Interviewee Difficulties   With proper preparation, interviews usually go smoothly and without incident. However, occasionally a situation will arise where there may be a potential problem. Exhibit 6.4 lists a few to look out for, and suggested actions to take.

The Talkative Interviewee—A Case Study

The fact that an interviewee is very talkative doesn't *always* mean you have a problem. I once had a particularly memorable interview with a senior executive where I hardly spoke a word.

After the normal setup, I posed the first question, and he got started. He continued to talk, almost without drawing breath, for a full hour. I allowed him to continue because he was answering the questions on my list, as well as giving me some valuable additional information and insights. Only occasionally would I stop him to clarify a point. When our time was up and he had to rush off to his next appointment, he shook my hand and *congratulated me warmly on conducting an "excellent interview."*

As it happens, it *was* a good interview. I had obtained all the information that I wanted, and more, mainly by keeping quiet—because there was no need to do otherwise.

Note: This is *not* the recommended way of conducting an interview. The story is just to help you recognize when you *must* interrupt and when you don't really have to.

Exhibit 6.4. *Dealing with interviewee difficulties.*

Interviewee Behavior	Possible Interpretations	Possible Actions
• Avoids scheduling an interview	• Is too busy • Feels threatened • Is not supportive	• Remind of leadership commitment made. • Identify any concerns and clear up misconceptions. • Describe the aims of the interview (as in setup).
• Looks surprised when you arrive • Is not there • Has office full of people	• Is not ready for interview	• Allow the interviewee to choose: to reschedule now or to continue as planned.
• Hostile or unhelpful tone, body language • Gives single-word answers	• Feels threatened by the process • Feels offended in some way • Is having a bad day	• Ask whether there is a problem. • Probe feelings about the assessment. • Try to clear up any misconceptions.
• Won't stop talking	• Is proud of achievements • Is putting up a smokescreen • Has an ax to grind	• If the interviewee is telling you what you want to know, interrupt only to clarify or summarize. • If the interviewee is off track or providing too much information, regain control quickly. Jump in at the first pause for breath. Explain that you have a number of other questions and limited time. • Ask more specific, focused questions.
• Is distracted and keeps searching for a document or diagram to show you	• Feels unable to explain a point properly without the exhibit that cannot be found	• Ask interviewee to draw the diagram by hand or jot down the key points, and continue. They can send you the real document later.

(continued)

Exhibit 6.4. *(continued)*

Interviewee Behavior	Possible Interpretations	Possible Actions
• Won't talk much • Seems preoccupied or withdrawn	• May be preoccupied by a serious personal or business problem • May be just naturally quiet	• Explore whether the interviewee grasped the points made during the setup. • Get off the business agenda for a moment (e.g., ask for a coffee or nature break), and use a more personal approach to inquire whether this is a bad time for the interviewee.
• Breaches confidentiality or etiquette; e.g., starts to trash colleagues or to discuss personalities	• It doesn't matter why the interviewee is doing this	• Switch off. Do not acknowledge comments either by agreeing or disagreeing. Stop taking notes. • Interrupt as soon as possible and get back onto your questions about the management system. Perhaps remind the interviewee that the focus of this process is on methods, not individuals.
• Asks for feedback on findings	• Is just showing natural curiosity • Believes that the findings may highlight his or her department (favorably or unfavorably)	• Talk about how well the assessment is going, but don't get into content. If pressed, explain that you just don't know yet—you only have a part of the picture. Tell the interviewee when the final report will be available.

Interviewing a Group   Group interviews are a very efficient way of obtaining information from a lot of people quickly, especially when they are likely to have a lot in common—for example, they all perform similar work. All interviews of frontline people will be done in groups, and there may also be some group interviews of middle management or supervisors.

There are a few differences in the way that a group interview is conducted, compared with an individual interview. Your aim is to get input from everyone. So you may ask all the participants to introduce themselves at the beginning, take enough time during the setup to establish some rapport, and then try to draw everyone in.

Group interviews generally work somewhat differently from individual interviews:

- They are somewhat less structured and focused, even with good facilitation—that's just the nature of the beast.
- They take longer to cover each issue, since there may be several perspectives.

On the other hand, a group interview of frontline people usually does not cover as many issues, because the participants are not involved in *operating* the management system. They have limited information about how it works—they just experience the consequences.

Group interviews of frontline people generally feel quite different from any other type of interview. Typically they are great fun; there is less caution about what is said, no posturing and no politics. And there's often a strong sense of camaraderie within the group, with lots of leg-pulling going on between people. They can also be quite emotional events, for many different reasons. Sometimes it's because there are serious problems:

- You may find yourself becoming angry as you listen to people explaining patiently and sincerely the senseless barriers that they have to try to surmount in doing their work, and the extraordinary lengths that they go to in order to get the job done properly.
- You may be saddened by the rage and deep mistrust of management displayed by people who feel that they have been abused in some way.

Sometimes interviews are emotional because what you're seeing is so good: occasionally you will encounter a workplace so different that it's inspiring. People will share their great pride in the improvements they have made as they explain how their workplace has been transformed from the hell-hole that it once was. They may even discuss the team spirit that exists and how they now feel valued as human beings. They will also show you charts showing that they are saving the company a *bundle* of money. At this point even the accountants on the assessment team are getting emotional.

Interviewing an Improvement Team Interviews of improvement teams are important because these provide insight into the basic machinery that the organization uses for solving problems and improving processes. These efforts are the cutting edge of the improvement process, where actions are taken that *directly* improve quality and productivity and reduce costs and cycle times.

This type of interview is also quite different from a regular group interview; it follows a different pattern and has its own special agenda. How is this related to the criteria? This type of interview is

Exhibit 6.5.   *Questions for an improvement team.*

Phase	Typical Questions	Listen for
Formation	• Why was the team formed? • How was the team formed? • What did you do at your first meeting?	• A clear, measurable objective, linked to the organization's goals • An appropriate mandate for the team • Assignment of a high-level sponsor • Selection of people with the required capabilities • Allocation of sufficient time and resources • Establishment of a mechanism for regular monitoring and review of progress—to completion
Preparation	• Did you use any tools or methodology? • Did you have any type of training?	• Choice of suitable methodology and tools • Timely provision of training and guidance • Development by the team of a game plan
Execution	• What difficulties did you encounter? • Did anyone review your progress? • Would anyone have noticed if you gave up?	• Access to support resources • Effective application of methodology and tools • Regular communication, monitoring, and review of progress • Removal of barriers by the sponsor • Intervention by the sponsor to recover from setbacks
Completion	• Were you successful? • How do you know? • Did you receive any type of thanks? • Was it a good experience—would you do it again?	• Recognition of the team's efforts • Debriefing, to learn from the team's experience • Acknowledgement of the personal development gained

a way of probing deep into the process management category. If there isn't much process management work being done, there won't be any suitable team and you won't have such an interview.

The best technique for interviewing an improvement team is simply to have the participants tell the story of their improvement project, from A to Z. You need to:

- prompt the team to start at the very beginning
- ask questions to clarify what happened at each phase before moving on to the next phase
- ensure that all of the team members have a say, for example, by restraining any tendency for the team leader to dominate the discussion.

Exhibit 6.5 sets out the typical flow of questions and the issues that you will be listening for.

If there is any time left when this ground has been covered, you may change course and continue with questions from your master list, just like a normal interview.

The criteria do not specify *how* process management should be done, and you should remain open-minded about this. For example, you may discover that much process improvement is done without creating separate teams or projects. This template still provides a good way of finding out.

Phase 3: The Interview Wrap-Up   You always need to conduct a proper wrap-up, otherwise you may miss important additional information, and interviewees will also sense a lack of closure. So you must always leave enough time for this—say ten minutes— even if you have not covered all of the topics intended. You owe this to the interviewees.

Here is what the wrap-up should cover:

First, ask if there are any other issues that *they* feel you should be discussing, or anything else that they feel you should know. While they are thinking about this, you may remind them about the framework that you are using: leadership, customer focus, etc. . . . Very often, interviewees will simply confirm that the interview has covered the ground, but sometimes this question will reveal something unexpected and important.

Second, ask them what they would do if *they* were running the show—the one or two key things that they would focus on to improve the organization and to make it more successful. You can wave your "magic wand" and make them the senior leader for the moment. This is the "King for the Day" question.

The King for the Day Question   This is a great way to end an interview because:

- It goes back to what the entire process is about—identifying the best actions to improve the organization.
- It allows interviewees to let their imaginations loose on problems that they may feel stuck with.
- It reveals what they see as truly important.
- It puts responsibility back on their shoulders—at least for a moment—and if necessary jolts them out of the role of victim. For example, someone who has been sounding off about how messed up the organization is will often reflect for a moment and then say, "Gee, I'm not sure **what** I would do. You know, this situation isn't easy to fix, even for the president."

So although it may seem light-hearted or even frivolous, this is actually an important and revealing question.

You can ask everyone this question—except the senior leader, who already runs the show. For this person, you could ask what is the one problem he or she would fix if they owned a magic wand. In group interviews, you can set up this question by telling the interviewees that they have all just been appointed as the top management team, and each of them should now come up with their own view of what needs to be done.

This question will elicit slightly different types of responses at different levels in the organization. Members of the leadership team will often give fairly guarded answers—since *any* answer could be interpreted as a criticism of their boss's current strategy—but listen carefully, because often they *are* suggesting significant changes to the direction or the priorities. People at lower levels may be unable to imagine what they would do as head of the organization, but they are happy to suggest what they would do if put in charge of their own department or group. If anyone is completely stumped by the question, just move on—you should not cause embarrassment by pressing for an answer.

FrontLine People Provide Insights

Interviews of frontline people are extremely important and provide a perspective that you cannot obtain in any other way. These interviews are usually fun, and sometimes inspiring. Even experienced assessors are often humbled by the dedication and pride of workmanship demonstrated by people who perform unpleasant jobs, have little say in what goes on, and are shown little respect in all too many organizations.

Given their working environment, you might not expect frontline staff to come up with deeply considered answers about what they would do as the senior leader. But every so often someone in a low-paid job steps up to this particular ball and bats it right out of the park. Sometimes a clerk or a cleaner has his game plan for the company all worked out, starting from day one when he steps into the big corner office. And sometimes this person's ideas seem more sensible than what the company is actually doing.

No single group has a monopoly on the insights that may help you understand what is really going on and where the leverage points are.

• • • • •

The interview is almost done. Thank the interviewee(s) for their time and for their help, remind them briefly about the next steps, concentrating on what they will see next, and ask them if they have any final questions. Also review any actions that either of you has agreed to. For example, if the interviewee promised to provide a certain document later, confirm this commitment, including the time frame, and *write it down*. If you don't notice the interviewee writing this down, all the more reason for you to do so.

Most interviewees are quite happy for the interview to end now, but some want to know more about the process—what will happen next, what do other organizations do, and so on. Sometimes a group of particularly smart and interested people wants "equal time" now to put *their* questions to *you*. If your schedule allows it, you owe it to interviewees to answer their questions as best you can. This isn't just courtesy. By doing so you are being an ambassador for the process, and you are drawing more people into the circle of those who understand and support what management is trying to accomplish. In this way you are already having an impact on the organization.

Debriefing After the Interview

You should debrief with your partner immediately after the interview. This is simply a review of what you found out, especially any surprises or new information. Sometimes you may feel that the interviewee didn't answer a certain question, even though you asked it two or three times in different ways. Your partner can confirm or deny this. Sometimes you have each heard quite different answers to a question—different interpretations of what was said. You can usually resolve this difference of perceptions simply by replaying how each of you heard the conversation. If this doesn't work and it's an important issue, you can always double-check with the interviewee.

This debriefing process is important because it crystallizes what you found out and helps you to remember the key points. It is important to absorb the main findings from the interviews as you go along. The final report will come mainly from the team's recollection of these key findings, not by crawling through mountains of detailed interview notes. The notes are there only for reference when necessary to jog memories on specific points.

Documentation Review

During the training workshop, the team identified what documents it needs and assigned responsibilities among the team for obtaining these documents, reviewing them, and sharing the findings. Now the team members need to do their jobs.

A convenient way to obtain an important document and at the same time get some insight into the content is to review it briefly with the owner in the course of an interview. Or you may simply request it and study it off-line.

All team members need to study their assigned documents sufficiently to answer the team's questions about each document. There should be no reason for anyone else to have to study the document.

It is often possible to find out quickly what the team needs to know about a document just from the table of contents, the executive summary, and reference to a few key pages. What does the employee induction course cover? A few minutes with the training manual will tell you.

Other documents may require in-depth study. For example, if you want to examine the flow-down of objectives and operating plans from the strategic plan, you may need to assemble and read several documents—including many people's personal objectives—and do a lot of cross-checking. You can lighten this task somewhat by asking people during the interviews whether their own objectives align with the strategic objectives. Their answers might even make this part of the documentation review unnecessary.

How is the information from the document reviews shared? It is good practice during the team's debriefing sessions to summarize briefly what people have learned about each document studied. The information gleaned from the documentation reviews will also come out naturally during the report writing.

Team Debriefing

In addition to debriefing after each interview, the entire assessment team should meet several times during the data gathering process to share what they have learned, and to revise their game plan if necessary in the light of new information. Each successive debriefing session answers more of the team's questions, brings the findings into sharper focus, and enables the team to identify the questions to pursue in the next round of interviews.

For example, if top management feel that they themselves do not understand the strategic direction, there's little point in asking people at other levels if they understand the direction. That issue has been dealt with and can be crossed off the master list. Thus, during a top-down interview process, the team can usually form conclusions early on about many topics, and skip these topics during subsequent interviews. Of course, where the team is testing *perceptions,* they cannot make any assumptions; they have to ask.

As the data gathering proceeds, new issues may be revealed that need to be investigated. Thus, additional topics may be added to the master list. It is important to corroborate data rather than accept isolated incidents or anecdotes as being typical. All key findings must be corroborated by several sources. The team debriefing is the place to discuss any not-yet-proven theories about what may be going on and ask the other team members to try to confirm or disprove these in future interviews.

An Example of Effective Corroboration

During an assessment it was found that one corrective action team did not find the root cause of a problem and therefore arrived at an inadequate solution. Further examination revealed that several teams had the same problem. In developing this finding, the assessors determined that there was a serious flaw in the training provided to the teams. Without the additional pursuit, this significant finding would have been lost.

The team should also challenge itself to ensure that it is doing a good job. It can do this by reviewing the master list of topics and asking questions like:

- Are we determining whether there is real ownership of processes?
- Are we finding out whether there is full deployment?
- Are we looking for systematic improvement cycles?
- Are we looking for linkages from top to bottom (threads)?

FREQUENTLY ASKED QUESTIONS ABOUT DATA GATHERING

The following are questions about data gathering that often arise.

How Much Should We Say about Our Report Before It Is Done? Depending on the situation and the assessment approach, the data gathering process may be done within a few days—or it may take many weeks. If the data gathering is going to be a lengthy process, then communications during this period become important:

- What information should be shared with whom?
- What can the team say about what they are discovering and about what may be in the report?

The way that these communications are handled can have desirable or undesirable effects:

Desirable	Undesirable
• Maintaining an open atmosphere during the interviews • Keeping the leaders aware of the assessment process • Paving the way for good acceptance of the findings	• Giving the impression of a hidden agenda • Causing rumors to circulate that are distortions of the supposed "findings" • Having the leaders feel as if they are the last people to know what's in the report • Giving the impression that the confidentiality of the interviews has been breached • Causing rumors to circulate because it is a mystery what the assessment team is up to • Surprising the leaders when the assessment report is presented

Clearly, there are some potentially conflicting considerations here: inappropriate confidentiality is seen as secretiveness, and inappropriate openness becomes indiscretion.

A good general rule is "no secrets, but no leaks"—in other words, be open about what issues the team is investigating, how they are going about it, and (in general terms) what the data gathering is revealing. But do not preempt the report by a premature disclosure of the findings—that is, the specific conclusions drawn from the data. This is a "leak."

When interviewees ask, "How are we doing?" this is how to handle the question. And remember in this situation that the interviewees already have a lot of information about where the assessors are headed, from the specific questions asked and from the way that the assessors summarized the answers. You are really doing little more than confirming what they can infer from the interviews.

Sometimes there are interviewees who seem overly concerned to know what is going to be in the report—they *really* want to know the actual findings. This may be an indication that these people still see this as a pass-fail situation, or they fear that the report may reflect badly on them or their group. Some people won't believe that this process is any different from a compliance audit until it is complete. So it may help to discuss again the nature of the report. If pressed hard, you can explain that it's too early to form definite conclusions: each team member has only a piece of the picture, and until all of the team get together to develop the final report, you really don't know yet what the findings will be.

During a lengthy data gathering process, it is also good practice to brief the leaders periodically, so that they will not be caught completely off-guard by any of the major findings in the report. This keeps them aware of the assessment and helps pave the way for acceptance of the report.

Is It Good Practice to Write Up Interview Reports? There should not normally be any need to formalize interview notes and these should not be considered part of the formal record. Writing up a formal report on each interview is a lot of work. And if you begin to do this, interviewees may ask to review your report on their interviews, which is hard to refuse. If this happens, the next step is for them to start asking for modifications and fine-tuning, thus creating even more work! You can begin to see why this is usually a bad idea.

If interviewees seem concerned about the team's notes, to the extent of wanting to see them, this may be a sign that something is wrong. Perhaps these people feel threatened or feel that their own performance is under scrutiny. If the nature of the assessment process has been explained properly, they should not demonstrate this type of concern.

Should We Conduct a Questionnaire Survey? A commonly used technique is to conduct a kind of mini-survey of employees, using a questionnaire that relates to the categories of the criteria. This may be useful if there is a lack of other data—for example, if there is no recent employee survey, or if the employee survey does not shed much light on how people feel about the way that they are managed. This type of survey may provide some useful data to complement the interviews. It can also be used to strengthen a mini-assessment by providing the leadership team with some data on employee perceptions. However, a questionnaire survey is not a substitute for interviews, and it is not a rigorous examination of the management system, since it yields opinions but few facts.

Consider strategic planning, for example. A questionnaire may provide input from many people about how they feel about the planning process as it affects them. But this may be like asking people riding around in horse-drawn buggies how they feel about their transportation when none of them has even heard of automobiles or aircraft. It's unreasonable to assume that people within the organization know what a great planning system looks like, especially if most of them only have experience with the current system. A proper examination of the planning process requires an understanding of how the current process actually works, as well as expertise related to planning methods (including the methods used by world-class companies) *and* expertise in the criteria.

Finally, don't fall into the trap of thinking that conducting a survey is necessarily a quick and easy option. There is often significant effort involved: agreeing on a methodology and questionnaire design, communications to explain the purpose and encourage people to participate, the capture and analysis of the results, and the presentation and sharing of this information in formats that are useful. Confidentiality issues may also require the use of third-party administration of parts of the process.

OTHER DATA GATHERING ISSUES

The "Moose on the Table": Encounters of the Unexpected Kind   This may be an issue for an assessment team and especially for any outsiders involved.

During an assessment, it is normal for some issues to surface that are not directly related to the criteria. However, occasionally one turns up that has so much emotion attached that it has to be acknowledged and discussed in the interviews, even though it is not directly related to the mandate of the assessment. Sometimes the issue seems quite important—perhaps it is central to the success of the organization. And often there is some kind of fear or conspiracy of silence that is preventing the issue from being acknowledged and dealt with by management.

As an external assessor, you may feel like the guest at a party where there is a dead moose on the dinner table, but the other guests don't appear to notice. Or like the mechanic giving his customer's car a routine service—only to find a dead body in the trunk. What do you do? Pretend that you didn't notice anything amiss? Is it fair to your client to play dumb in this way?

Insiders usually cannot do much about such situations—and it is often too risky for them to try—but outsiders can do something and are morally obliged to do so. Here's the logic of how you might decide on a course of action.

1. How big is the problem? It has to be big to justify stepping outside the mandate of the current assignment, even as a side trip.
2. Are senior management already aware of it to the extent that they are discussing it and working on it? If you're not sure, you cannot risk leaving them in the dark.
3. Who needs to be informed, and what is the best way? Usually a confidential meeting with the senior leader is the most appropriate course of action. This may start out along the following lines: "I know that this is not part of our mandate, but during the assessment we could not help observing what we feel is a serious issue. This seems sufficiently important that we feel obliged to bring it to your attention. Of course, you may already be fully aware of this—we have no way of knowing."

Responsible consultants hate these situations, because they feel obliged to take action that may put the current assignment at risk, and may even damage their relationship with the client. But if you are the consultant, you have to make a judgment call about what's the right thing to do—and then act on your decision. Remember that the client is trusting you to act in their best interest, not to keep your head down and play safe while they dig themselves into even deeper trouble. Getting this issue out in the open may be a major contribution; it may even provide a breakthrough that enables the organization to reach for a new level of performance.

Example of a "Moose on the Table"

In one financial services company, a particular department was viewed with considerable fear verging on paranoia. Many people believed that this department spied on employees, acted as a kind of thought police, and exerted a Svengali-like influence over the senior leader. When no one from this department was present in an interview, this issue came up immediately and dominated the initial discussion. But when *anyone* from this department was present, no one would say a word about the subject.

The external assessors had to be alert to spot this unexpected issue at an early stage and to corroborate it while there was still time available. When the lead assessor brought this issue to the attention of the senior leader, this person was already aware of some concerns, but had no inkling of the strength of feeling among employees or the impact that this situation was having on senior management's credibility.

CHECK POINTS

As the data gathering proceeds, you will know that you are on track if the following descriptions of success are close to the mark:

Success	Failure
The interviews are generally taking place as scheduled.	There have been many postponements (caused either by team members or by interviewees).
The team members seem confident and comfortable with the interviews, and people who have been interviewed are generally positive about the process.	The team members are all over the map in terms of their interview technique and level of comfort with the process, and many interviewees have voiced concerns about how their interview was conducted.
The team is debriefing regularly, sharing new findings, and fine-tuning and aligning the remainder of the data gathering process.	The team members are working independently, perhaps coming to contradictory conclusions, and their lines of inquiry are diverging.
Key documents and results data are being obtained and reviewed in parallel with the interview process.	Non-interview-related tasks—such as assembling and reviewing key documents or obtaining results data—have not been assigned or are being overlooked.
There is growing team spirit as people work together and get to know each other better.	The team is split by conflicts, jealousies and personal agendas.
The team is having fun and is looking forward to the next steps.	Many of the team members are figuring out how to avoid being in the firing line at the feedback session, or how to avoid being associated with certain findings.

Sooner than you think the interviews will be complete. Then it will be time to capture and analyze what's been learned.

> ### ^{www}Companion Website Materials:
>
> - Using tools and technology during data gathering

Chapter 7

Developing the Assessment Report

A fact is like a sack—it won't stand up if it's empty. To make it stand up, first you have to put in it all the reasons and feelings that caused it in the first place.
Luigi Pirandello, Italian author, playwright

Once the data gathering is complete the team begins the process of analyzing the information acquired, developing the findings, and creating the assessment report. The team must know how to reinforce the credibility of the report, how to make the findings clear and easily understood, and how to sequence the information for presentation to the leadership team.

CHAPTER CONTENTS

- Steps in completing the assessment report
- Initial impressions
- Developing the findings
- Report-writing technique
- Scoring
- The results category
- The overall summary
- The assessment team's vital few
- Planning the presentation

- Final cleanup of the report
- Other report-writing issues
- Check points

● ● ● ● ●

STEPS IN COMPLETING THE ASSESSMENT REPORT

Finally, the last interview has been completed and the last document reviewed. It is now time to analyze what the team learned and to complete the assessment report.

Since this is a facilitated assessment, the team has already conducted a preliminary evaluation during its initial training and preparation. This document greatly simplifies the task of creating a final report, by providing a good starting point for developing the findings—the strengths and opportunities for improvement. The full assessment report also requires some additional pieces: some data to show the extent of work done by the team, scores, a summary of the key findings, and the assessment team's view of the "vital few" priorities for improvement. Then, once the report is complete, the team members need to prepare themselves well for a clear and convincing presentation.

In a facilitated assessment, the process expert plays an important (though low-key) role by guiding the team's consensus discussions, helping the team members to interpret what they have learned, and suggesting suitable language for the findings. With the benefit of greater experience and an outsider's perspective, this person will often challenge the team's initial conclusions and submit alternative points of view, to find out whether these are supported by the facts. The team members make the final decisions by consensus, since it is their report. The process expert's involvement also provides assurance that the scoring system is applied properly, so that scores will be in the right range.

Contents of the Assessment Report

Exhibit 7.1 sets out the typical contents of a complete assessment report. There are many components to this, but these fall into three main groups:

Exhibit 7.1. *Typical assessment report content.*

Topic	Typical Content	Comment
Assessment Process	• List of team members • Interview statistics: number of interviews and interviewees by level, by function, and by location • List of documents reviewed • Any comments on how the process went: e.g., good cooperation from interviewees, assessment team worked well together	Show that the team has followed the agreed-upon process and covered the ground.
Findings	• Strengths, opportunities for improvement (and perhaps scores) listed item-by-item, following the structure of the criteria • Category summaries if appropriate	This is the heart of the report, and the bulk of the material.
Overall Scores	• An overview of what the scores indicate: e.g., percentage scores by category; overall score	Confirm impressions about which categories are strong or weak.
Summary	• A bullet-point list of the key observations, positive and negative	Paint the "big picture." May be presented before or after the findings.
Assessment Team's Vital Few	• The top priorities for improvement identified by the assessment team	To be presented as an input to the final decision-making process.

- a summary of the work done by the team, to show that the team has followed the agreed-upon process and done its job thoroughly
- the main body of the assessment report, which includes the strengths and opportunities (organized according to the structure of the criteria) plus the scores and a summary
- the assessment team's view of what the priorities for improvement should be.

Steps in Completing the Report

The team's task now is to complete all of this material and prepare to present it. This chapter describes the entire process for doing this. It's not just a matter of starting at the beginning of the report and working through it; the sequence of preparation is important, and to make best use of the team's time, some tasks should be done off-line.

The main steps are as follows:

- A brief discussion of *initial impressions* from the entire data gathering process.
- Development of *findings for all categories of the criteria,* item by item. The preliminary evaluation is used as a starting point and is modified and rewritten as necessary in the light of the information obtained since by the team. *Each item is also scored as it is completed.*
- Creation of an *overall summary* (and perhaps category summaries).
- Development of the *assessment team's view of the vital few* priorities for improvement.
- *Preparations for the presentation:* deciding roles, logistics, evidence to be cited, handouts and supporting materials required.
- *Formatting and clean up* of the report off-line.

INITIAL IMPRESSIONS

Before starting to work through the criteria, category by category, it is good practice to brainstorm a list of initial impressions of the organization. This exercise helps to clarify the team members' thoughts by forcing them to summarize at a high level before plunging into the detail of the report. These initial impressions won't appear in the final report, but they will be valuable when the team is developing an overall summary for the report.

DEVELOPING THE FINDINGS

The main task of the team is to arrive at a consensus about strengths, opportunities for improvement, and the score, for each element of the criteria. This will take up most of the report preparation time. The process expert facilitates this process, keeping the team on track, explaining the criteria, and guiding the discussions on each element toward a consensus.

The Value of Consensus

People often believe that striving for consensus will lead to endless, rambling discussions, with no means of getting closure. This is not the case.

When team members don't agree about a finding, this is generally because they have different information. Seeking consensus ensures that this additional information is shared. Also, consensus does not mean unanimity. A good working definition of consensus is:

- Everyone believes that their point of view has been heard.
- Everyone respects the process used to arrive at a decision.
- Everyone can live with the final decision—even those who put forward a different point of view during the discussion.

Key Point
The value of seeking consensus is that this gets the facts out on the table and thus ensures alignment on the key issues.

If the team has been debriefing properly during the data gathering, it is easier to arrive at a consensus, since everyone already has the same information—just as if they had personally been present in every interview.

The Consensus Process

For each element of the criteria, the team goes through the following steps:

1. A brief review of that element of the criteria, to clarify the main focus and the scope. This answers the question, "what are we looking for here?"
2. A brief, unstructured discussion of what the team has learned. Most of the main points emerge spontaneously, but there is no attempt to capture these just yet.
3. A brief review of the preliminary assessment, to see whether this provides a useful starting point for capturing the findings. For some criteria, the preliminary assessment may be fairly accurate and may simply require some editing. For other criteria, the team may find its preliminary assessment lacking and decide to start afresh. Reviewing the preliminary assessment may also trigger some new thoughts.
4. Capturing the key findings (strengths and opportunities for improvement). After some discussion by the team, the process expert should usually be able to achieve a consensus by suggesting a suitable phase that captures the essence of the finding.
5. Scoring. Each item in the report needs to be assigned a score.

During its training, the assessment team had lots of practice developing strengths and opportunities for improvement as it conducted a preliminary assessment. And all of this was done under the guidance of the process expert. So by now the team is quite skilled in this technique. The team has also had lots of opportunity during its regular debriefing sessions to discuss the information emerging from the data gathering.

So the main challenge in writing the final report is not so much agreeing on the points—it is in expressing them with precision and clarity and in appropriate language. Here are some report-writing "rules" that will make this a lot easier.

REPORT-WRITING TECHNIQUE

The phrasing and sequence of the findings can make a huge difference to how the report is received when it is presented to the leadership team, so it is important to get the language right. This does *not* require meticulous fine-tuning of every word—in fact this is a pitfall you must avoid! You simply need to adhere consistently to certain writing practices.

By sticking to the following rules, you can avoid a lot of unnecessary misunderstandings, resistance, and even hostility. This will make the presentation of the report easier for everyone involved—and much more effective.

Focus on Methods, Not Individuals or Groups

One of the keys to maintaining an open atmosphere throughout the entire assessment process—and especially during the presentation of the report—is to keep the focus on methods, not individuals. This places the emphasis where it should be—on the management system. This approach also depersonalizes the shortcomings identified, and it is therefore less threatening to the leaders.

So the report should stick to descriptions of *what* is working and *what* is not, rather than *who* seems to be doing a good job and *who* is messing up. For the same reason, it should not focus attention on specific groups or departments.

It *is* important to point out when there are major *variations* between departments and functions in their approach, since these usually indicate a shortcoming in the management system. Typically, each department simply follows the preferences of the person in charge at the time. This will work—some of the time, in some departments—but it is not a management system! There is usually no need to single out the leaders or the laggards. The key finding in this situation is that there is not a consistent approach.

Sometimes one group has developed a best practice that the team wants to highlight because others could benefit from emulating it. Again, this should be done by focusing attention on the method, rather than on the group itself.

Absolutely Avoid Absolutes

Black-and-white statements tend to irritate your audience and just cry out to be challenged. Even if you believe that one of these statements is accurate, you could be proved wrong in some minor detail, and you are courting trouble if you lapse into using this style. Here are some examples of slightly softer statements that make your point without goading the audience into challenging you—or offending people who naturally feel proud of their departments.

Absolute Statement	Qualified Statement
There is *no* evidence of . . .	There is *little evidence* of . . .
No one understands . . .	*Few* people seemed to understand . . .
Managers *always* . . .	Managers *frequently* . . .
There is *no* system for . . .	There is not a *formal* system for . . .

Separate Strengths and Opportunities

Findings often come out initially as a mixture of positives and negatives. Here is an example: "The strategic planning is systematic and fact-based, but there is no formal mechanism for obtaining input from key suppliers and partners."

Combining strengths and opportunities in one sentence like this can be confusing to your audience. It is much better to split a statement like this into two statements, the strength and then the opportunity for improvement. Statements should also be labeled (for example, with plus or minus bullets) to indicate clearly which are strengths and which are opportunities.

Having split a finding into its positive and negative components, you must not space these too widely, since this may also confuse your audience. After the report has been written, you may need to experiment with the sequence and layout, to keep closely related points close together during the presentation.

Achieve a Balance of Strengths and Opportunities

Most sections of your report will include both strengths and opportunities. It is good practice to try *always* to identify *some* strengths, even if these are relatively soft, since these help to cushion the blow of the opportunities. And it is usually undesirable to have a section where there is no opportunity at all for improvement—unless the organization is doing a truly stellar job in this area. Insightful opportunities are the "gold nuggets" that the organization is looking for, even if it cannot act on all of them immediately.

The reader should be able to judge the overall strength of each section by looking at the balance of strengths and opportunities. If the organization is strong in a section, then there will usually be several significant strengths cited, and the opportunities will usually be fewer and/or less significant.

It is often helpful to highlight strengths and opportunities that are especially significant—for example, by using *double*-plus and *double*-minus bullets.

Don't Get Into Solutions

The findings section of your report should not contain prescriptions for action. You may sometimes find yourself writing descriptions of *how* to improve (for example, "the recognition system could be improved by training all managers in . . ."). You should avoid this style—it will obscure the very points you are trying to make.

It is much clearer to write your findings as straightforward observations of fact, describing what is in place and working and what is missing or not working. Of course, the team has lots of ideas about what could be done—many of these suggested by the people interviewed. Some of these ideas will be captured later in the report, to support and clarify the vital few. However, they don't belong in the findings.

Match the Report Structure to What You Have to Say

Although the structure provided by the criteria is essential to ensure thorough and comprehensive data gathering, sometimes this very structure can get in the way of expressing your findings clearly. Rather than let this happen, you should use your own discretion to change the structure of your report so that it fits what you have to say. Here are two examples:

- There may be some important observations about the organization as a whole that don't seem to fit well under any particular criteria heading. Assessors refer to these as "cross-cutting issues"—findings that are valid and directly related to the criteria, yet they don't fit properly into any single category. The best way to deal with these important points is to include them in an overall summary.
- Sometimes it may be difficult to write something about every item within a category, usually because the organization is weak in this area, so there isn't much to say, and these few findings apply equally to all of the items. You can often deal with this situation by writing one set of findings at the category level and ignoring the individual items (although you may still need to provide a score for each item).

Key Point

The criteria have a structure that helps you investigate *thoroughly what is going on. This structure should not be allowed to get in the way of* communicating *what you've found out. The criteria provide the basic format, but you should structure your report in a way that fits the message.*

SCORING
When to Score

The team needs to develop a consensus score for each item of the criteria. The best way to do this is to score each item immediately after completing the findings for that item, while the details are still fresh in people's minds.

An alternative is to wait until all of the findings are done and then go back to do the scoring later. *Don't do this!* This method invariably becomes an exercise in pure frustration, as the team members struggle to recall the discussions that they had a few hours earlier, when they were writing up the findings.

Following is an outline of how the scoring system works.

The Scoring System

The scoring system is an integral part of the criteria and is based upon the evaluation logic: approach × deployment = results. Most categories of the criteria deal with the approach and deployment of methods, and these are scored using a table like that shown in Exhibit 7.2. This method is more precise than the type of system where people simply pick a number between 0 (meaning poor) and 10 (meaning excellent). There are definite marker points within the table that narrow down the range of possible scores for any given situation.

For example, to score 50 percent or more, there must be some kind of mechanism for "closing of the loop" around the processes being examined, so that they can be refined over time. (The scoring system calls for a fact-based, systematic evaluation and improvement process to be in place.) To score 70 percent or more, this mechanism must have been used to fine-tune the process over time. (The scoring system calls for *clear evidence of refinement.*)

This table is used only for scoring approach and deployment. A different table is used to score results. The results scoring table is designed for evaluating graphs and other results data, and

Exhibit 7.2.   *Typical scoring guidelines (Baldrige Criteria).*

Score	Approach/Deployment
0%	• No systematic approach evident; anecdotal information
10% to 20%	• Beginning of a systematic approach to the basic purposes of the Item • Major gaps exist in deployment that would inhibit progress in achieving the basic purposes of the Item • Early stages of a transition from reacting to problems to a general improvement orientation
30% to 40%	• An effective, systematic approach, responsive to the basic purposes of the Item • Approach is deployed, although some areas or work units are in early stages of deployment • Beginning of a systematic approach to evaluation and improvement of basic Item processes
50% to 60%	• An effective, systematic approach, responsive to the overall purposes of the Item • Approach is well-deployed, although deployment may vary in some areas or work units • A fact-based, systematic evaluation and improvement process is in place for basic Item processes • Approach is aligned with basic organizational needs identified in the other Criteria Categories
70% to 80%	• An effective, systematic approach, responsive to the multiple requirements of the Item • Approach is well-deployed, with no significant gaps • A fact-based, systematic evaluation and improvement process and organizational learning/sharing are key management tools; clear evidence of refinement and improved integration as a result of organizational-level analysis and sharing • Approach is well-integrated with organizational needs identified in the other Criteria Categories
90% to 100%	• An effective, systematic approach, fully responsive to all the requirements of the Item • Approach is fully deployed without significant weaknesses or gaps in any areas or work units • A very strong, fact-based, systematic evaluation and improvement process and extensive organizational learning/sharing are key management tools; strong refinement and integration, backed by excellent organizational-level analysis and sharing • Approach is fully integrated with organizational needs identified in the other Criteria Categories

examines *levels* of performance, *trends* in performance, and *comparisons* (for example, with competitors, similar organizations, or similar processes).

Scoring Consensus Process

The process expert plays an essential role in achieving proper scoring by coaching the team on how to interpret the scoring guidelines and by providing a "sanity check," challenging any scores that seem inconsistent with the findings.

The following is an effective method for the process expert to guide the team to a consensus score:

1. Allow the team to peruse the findings.
2. Have each team member silently decide on a score.
3. Share these individual scores and chart the distribution.
4. Have the high-scoring and low-scoring team members explain what influenced their decisions.
5. Repeat the individual scoring and charting of the distribution. The distribution of individual scores will often look somewhat different after this discussion.
6. Propose a team score—usually near the mid-point of the distribution—and seek consensus by asking if "everyone can live with this."

Exhibit 7.3 provides an example of how to chart individual scores as the team works towards a consensus.

Exhibit 7.3. *Charting scores.*

1.1 Leadership											
	0	10	20	30	40	50	60	70	80	90	100
First round		x	xx	xxx	xx						
Second round			xxx	xxxx	x						
Consensus				**30**							

How to Set Out Scores

The way that the scores are set out in the report makes a difference to the thought process of the recipients, and this can affect how the report is received. If the findings have been well written and presented (and if the leaders' expectations have been set properly during the initial workshop), the scores will not come as a surprise, since they simply reflect the findings. You may elect to provide scores at the end of each category, or you may summarize all of the scores at the end. Either approach can work. But whichever approach you choose, there is one golden rule:

Key Point
To avoid causing unpleasant surprises when presenting the report, always use the sequence "findings first, scores second."

The Overall Score

Most criteria provide a method of weighting the score for each item in the criteria and combining these to arrive at an overall score. This overall score is the most easily communicated (and misused) output from the assessment process. Giving this score too much prominence, or communicating it too widely without explanation, can cause problems. For example:

- It can trivialize the assessment by reducing the richness of the findings to a single number.
- In a large corporation, it can encourage an atmosphere of "one-upmanship" between divisions (based upon scores), which may divert attention from the substance of the report and the opportunities for improvement.
- It can send a very negative message to people who do not understand the criteria or the scoring system, like the board, customers, competitors, even the public. You can just hear the comment, "Only 50 percent? They must be totally incompetent!"

Exhibit 7.4. *A format for presenting scores.*

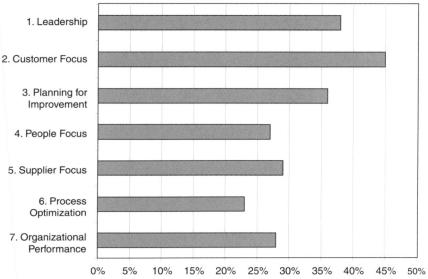

Example: Pattern of Assessment Scores

In contrast, the *distribution* of scores is valuable information that helps to identify the strongest and weakest areas of the management system. Exhibit 7.4 illustrates a presentation format that focuses on the comparison between categories. A similar, more detailed chart could portray the relative strengths of all the individual criteria items.

So it is a good idea to think carefully about how to communicate scoring information, and how much to reveal to the world (at least initially). A good compromise during a first assessment may be full disclosure of category or item scores, but no mention of an overall score in the written report. On subsequent cycles, the overall score can be provided in trend-chart form, showing the year-to-year improvement.

It is also important for people to understand that while these scores are reliable and fairly repeatable, they are not *precise*. For example, if division A obtains an overall score of 515, this simply indicates that they are "somewhere close to 500." If division B obtains an overall score of 530, they have no reason to feel superior. The assessors would consider these two scores to be essentially the same.

Not every organization feels the need to work out overall scores. It is interesting to note that Xerox's highly sophisticated assessment system provides ratings for each element of the criteria, but no method for combining these ratings—there is no overall score.

THE RESULTS CATEGORY

Most awards criteria have a category with a title like "business results" or "organizational performance." This category calls for data on levels of performance, trends over time, and comparisons with competitors or benchmarks. The information in this category helps to confirm that the methods described in the other categories are effective (or not) and that the management system is effective overall (or not). This is a very important category in the sense that it demonstrates whether or not the management system is leading to improved performance.

There are two types of observations that may come out of studying the results:

- findings regarding the completeness and adequacy of the data available
- the story that these numbers tell.

It is helpful to differentiate between these two types of observations, since they are different in nature and should be treated differently.

If the data available are lacking in some way—for example, there is a lack of customer-related data, or few competitive comparisons, or data are not analyzed to show trends—then these are findings related to the *approach* and/or *deployment* of the organization's information system. You may even consider placing these findings elsewhere in a part of the assessment report that deals with the information system.

On the other hand, the story that the numbers tell is the *results* part of the *approach* × *deployment* = *results* equation. For these observations, all that's required is a brief summary of the results, with the aim of confirming that the team has properly understood the performance data. For example, your report might say the following about customer satisfaction results: "Customer satisfaction improved steadily between 1990 and 1997, and is now stable at 95 percent."

When the results category has been completed, the assessment team will usually be able to conclude that *these are the types of performance results that are to be expected from the current management system.* In other words, the *approach* × *deployment* = *results* relationship is evident. For example, inadequate methods for understanding and responding to customer requirements will usually lead to poor scores on customer satisfaction and loyalty. If this type of relationship does not seem to exist—that is, if there are good results in areas that seem to have weak methods—then there is something going on that the assessment team does not yet understand. It's important to develop an understanding of these relationships over time, since these provide the key to improving organizational performance. The organization's strategy may depend upon achieving improvements in specific results areas, such as customer loyalty, productivity, or employee retention. If management can understand the cause-and-effect relationships, they can pinpoint which parts of the system to work on in order to achieve the desired results.

● ● ● ● ●

THE OVERALL SUMMARY

Now that the findings are complete, it is time to write your overall summary.

A good summary is invaluable, because the volume of information contained in the detailed findings can be overwhelming. And the assessment will be a failure if it produces an encyclopedia of detailed observations but does not make clear to the leadership team what is going on.

What is a good summary? It is one that paints the "big picture" in a few well-chosen words, putting the entire report into perspective and bringing out the main themes. A good summary synthesizes and interprets the mass of detailed findings, and thus provides additional insights. It is *not* just a list of the most significant strengths and opportunities, although it must recognize and encompass these.

A method sometimes used is to create the summary by copying the most significant findings from each category. This is an easy, mechanical procedure, and it may seem thorough and precise, but it's a poor method. It often produces a summary that is factually correct but shallow—it does not add value to the report. This method falls short for the following reasons:

- It does not help the team to identify cross-cutting issues— that is, issues that don't really fit in any one single category, but can be identified only by examining several categories. In fact, it hinders the discovery of these issues.
- It does not provide room for the team to "paint a picture" that captures the essence of what they've learned about the organization.

Examples of Cross-Cutting Issues

- There is a wealth of well-designed approaches, but deployment of these is very patchy.
- There are very few examples of evaluation and improvement cycles.
- The results data gathered and presented—although these look good—do not match the most important areas where results data are needed, such as the performance of key processes.
- The actions being taken, such as those related to customers, employees, and processes, do not match the priorities indicated in the strategic plan.

What is the best way for the team to create a good summary? The human mind has a remarkable ability to integrate lots of information, and at this point the team is saturated with information about the organization. So the following simple method works well:

1. After the detailed findings are complete, the team members discuss what the "big picture" looks like, list the main points that emerge, prioritize, and prune this list.
2. The team reviews the report, as well as the initial impressions captured at the start, to make sure that nothing vital has been

overlooked. During this review, the team looks for common threads beyond those that they have already identified, as well as any contradictions. It's important to ensure that the summary is consistent with, and supported by, the detailed findings.

3. The team expresses the chosen points concisely in carefully chosen language.

That's it. It's really that simple.

THE ASSESSMENT TEAM'S VITAL FEW

Having completed the findings and the scores, it is time to capture the team's view of the vital few priorities for improvement. Later, during the planning workshop, the leadership team will finalize these priorities as a basis for the improvement plan.

There are many possible methods of identifying the vital few. This section describes one in detail, the Affinity Diagram, and discusses a number of alternative methods.

The Affinity Diagram Method

The Affinity Diagram is a powerful technique for organizing ideas or information; it reveals the natural structure contained within the information itself. When you've used it once, you will find yourself using it again and again for many other purposes.

Here is how this technique can be used to identify the assessment team's vital few.

1. Each member of the assessment team takes about fifteen minutes to review the entire assessment report and to develop a list of the five most important actions that they feel should be taken to make the organization more successful.
2. Each team member is given five blank sheets of Post-It® notes on which to write their ideas. Each idea is printed legibly in the form of a single, action-oriented sentence (for example, "Establish a regular customer satisfaction survey").

3. The team members stick their notes at random on a convenient surface, such as a whiteboard or a wall.
4. The team members gather around, read all of the notes, and begin to move them around so that similar ideas are clustered together. This step must be done in silence, because premature discussion may influence the clusters that emerge. The aim is to let the clusters be determined by the ideas on the notes, not by the preconceptions of the participants.
5. After a few minutes, the movement of notes dies down as the team becomes satisfied with the placement. There are now typically five to seven clusters of notes, plus a few "outliers"— ideas that seem unique and unrelated to the others.

   The facilitator now leads a discussion of each cluster, to identify the central issue and to give it a suitable descriptive title. Each of these clusters is potentially one of the "vital few" priorities for improvement.
6. The final step is to discuss relative importance and relationships between the issues. The aim is to identify the highest-leverage issues and to understand how these relate to each other. The outliers are usually (though not always) discarded at this stage—the final decision is based upon the leverage of each issue, *not* the number of people who suggested it.

   There are often clear relationships between the clusters: for example, there may be several distinct issues that are people-related. Or there may be a natural implementation sequence: one particular issue needs to be tackled first, and the others can then follow in a logical order.

This entire process typically takes about forty-five minutes. When it's done, the team has a skeleton for the improvement plan that they would come up with if it were their decision alone. They have identified their top priorities for improvement and a number of ideas to support implementation.

The assessment team is usually surprised and pleased at the degree of consensus and alignment that this process reveals. The team members are reassured to discover that their colleagues have arrived at very similar conclusions about the priorities for improvement. And this raises the team's confidence that the leadership team will also come to similar conclusions.

Exhibit 7.5 illustrates the progression through this process, from individual ideas to clusters and then to named improvement priorities.

This concludes the team's group work on the vital few. The outputs of this exercise will be cleaned up later and added to the presentation package.

Exhibit 7.5.   *Affinity diagram steps 3–6.*

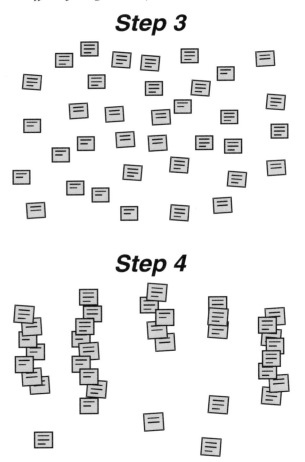

(continued)

Exhibit 7.5.   *(Continued)*

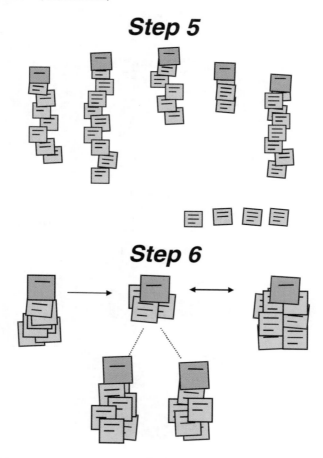

PLANNING THE PRESENTATION

The team is almost ready for the feedback session. The assessment report is now substantially complete, apart from some cleanup that is better done off-line rather than in a group setting. All that remains to be done now, while the team is still together, is to review and agree on the following:

- the proposed agenda for the feedback session
- responsibility for such roles as opening the session, managing the overall flow, and presenting different parts of the report

- techniques for delivering the presentation, encouraging discussion and responding to questions
- the examples and quotes that will be used to support key points
- any other supporting materials that need to be available.

Preparing Examples

The team members should have examples at their fingertips to reinforce any findings that may cause difficulties during the presentation. You can easily tell which findings fall into this category. They are:

- the findings that the assessment team had to discuss at length before everyone understood and agreed
- findings that the leaders may find difficult to believe or to accept, even though the team has been convinced by the weight of evidence revealed during the data gathering.

For these findings in particular, you need to think about:

- Data or other evidence that can be presented as hard facts, to clarify and quantify the problem.
- Recent, memorable incidents that illustrate the issue.
- Striking quotes: memorable things that people said to you during the interviews, or quoted others as saying.
- Examples of recent decisions or behaviors that demonstrate what you are commenting on. These may be drawn from the experience of the assessment team or interviewees.

These examples also bring the report alive by illustrating the findings—which are often rather dry—in terms of real-life events in the workplace, or the impact on the organization's performance. These are more likely to capture the leaders' attention. (See Exhibit 7.6.)

It is usually impractical to include examples in the body of your formal report. Instead, the team should be prepared to talk about these at the appropriate moments during the feedback session. Each assessment team member can add personal reminders to their presentation notes: "mention XYZ project," "ABC client incident," "PQR policy."

Exhibit 7.6.   *Providing examples.*

The Point	The Example
After fixing a problem, there is rarely any kind of root cause analysis to determine why it happened, or to figure out how to prevent recurrences.	After losing $10 million on project XYZ, there *was* a proper analysis of the causes, and preventive measures were taken. However, this is the *exception*—this particular incident got attention only because it was such a huge loss. Past losses amount to much more than this, but because these were caused by a string of smaller problems, none got enough attention to trigger a proper investigation.
There is not a culture of recognizing achievements.	When the assessors asked, "How are people thanked for doing a good job around here?" the most common response was ironic laughter.
There is no means of obtaining input or ideas for improvement from employees.	The call center operators have developed a 'secret' list of workarounds to overcome design problems in their information system. Originally a new trainee created a reference list for her own use, which was then copied by others. It is now kept up to date by one of the operators, who types it at home. The supervisors haven't been told about this document because it is company policy to confiscate "unofficial procedures."

When choosing examples or quotes, you must also remember the promise of confidentiality that was made to the interviewees. Many examples that you may use will be common knowledge, or will have come from so many sources that anonymity is not an issue. However, it is sometimes difficult to provide examples or quotes on some important point without some risk of making the sources identifiable. You can make quotes more anonymous by saying something like "a frequent comment was. . . ." You can also counsel the leaders not to take action aimed at a single "data point."

You need to use your own careful best judgment on this issue. There will certainly be a backlash if you inadvertently identify someone who is then victimized—or if the word goes out that the assessment team leaked information that was given in confidence. However, you also promised the interviewees that you would get the messages across and not pull any punches in the report. That is why you need good examples, and that is why people offered them.

• • • • •

Examples may also be valuable to help get across some concepts that the leaders are not familiar with. For example, people who are not trained in quality management invariably struggle to grasp the distinctions between the following:

- the "fix" for a problem, which simply repairs the damage done (for example, through rework)
- the "corrective action" for a problem, which puts right the direct cause of this specific problem (for example, by modifying a faulty procedure or tool)
- "preventive action," in which root causes are identified and process changes made to prevent an entire *class* of potential problems from ever occurring.

Yet these distinctions might be key to understanding some part of the report. How can managers understand that they need not spend all of their time firefighting, if they don't understand root cause analysis and preventive action?

Mini-Tutorials

When the assessment team thinks about how the report will be received, it may realize that some findings will not make sense to the leaders without a *lot* of explanation—and providing a few examples won't do the trick. In this situation, a good approach is to include a mini-tutorial in the presentation.

Some parts of the criteria assume an understanding of complex topics. In these areas, the leaders may be confused by the findings through lack of understanding of what the criteria are "looking for." After all, the leaders are not supposed to be experts in the interpretation of the criteria—the leadership briefing was designed just to give them the basic idea.

So, rather than presenting findings that will cause endless debate (because the criteria are not understood), it is often better to include a mini-tutorial in the presentation, just before these findings. Process management is a topic that often requires this approach because so few people have been taught anything about this subject during either their formal education or their working careers.

After this mini-tutorial, the leaders will usually grasp the findings immediately. If the assessment team feels that a mini-tutorial of some sort is needed, the process expert—who has already explained this topic to the assessment team—can provide suitable material and add it to the report.

FINAL CLEANUP OF THE REPORT

The assessment team's final group session is done, and the substantive content of the report is complete. But there is still some final cleanup required to make the content complete and presentable. This will be done off-line, probably by the team leader and the process expert.

Assessment Process Overview

The first part of the report is a reminder to the leaders of the steps in the assessment, and a summary of the work done by the team. This section typically includes some tables of statistics summarizing the interviews by level in the organization, department or function, and location if necessary. A well-designed interview-planning spreadsheet can generate these statistics automatically from your interview master list.

Setting out the Assessment Team's Vital Few

The assessment team's vital few are intended to provide a convenient starting point for developing an improvement plan, rather than a final package ready for approval by the leadership team. There is a good reason for this: in order to own the improvement plan, the leaders need to take responsibility for developing it.

So the report should not aim to provide a complete, packaged, and final set of recommendations. It should simply provide a summary of the assessment team's view of the vital few and some of their ideas related to implementation. For the leadership team, this part of the report is a work in process, not the final product.

There's also another important reason for limiting the assessment team's report in this way: The assessment process clarifies and prioritizes the key issues beautifully—but it does not necessarily identify the best solutions for each of these. Some issues will require considerably more work—data gathering, measurements, and root cause analysis—to figure out the precise causes and devise suitable countermeasures. Others will require the development and implementation of systems or processes that currently do not exist. The assessment team's vital few are designed to help clarify *what* needs be done—not *how* to do it.

OTHER REPORT-WRITING ISSUES

Here are some of the issues that sometimes arise in deciding how to go about creating the assessment report.

Category Ownership

Rather than writing all of the report as a single team, an alternative is to assign each category to one or two people and to have these "category authors" draft the different parts of the report. The entire assessment team can then review these drafts and make adjustments. This approach will work best when:

- The team has held effective debriefing sessions during the data gathering, so that the category authors have already gleaned most of the information that they need from other team members.
- The people assigned have a sound grasp of the criteria, particularly their assigned categories.
- The authors have the ability to express their points clearly in writing, and a model presentation style has been agreed upon.
- Pride of authorship is waived. During the team review, the category owners should not become protective of the findings that they wrote.

If these conditions are not present, a category ownership approach will not work well, because the "final adjustments" will prove to be major and contentious. Under these circumstances it will be quicker and more effective to complete the report as one group, under the guidance of an experienced assessor.

There is also a trap to be avoided when using any kind of category ownership approach. During the data gathering phase, *everyone* on the team must gather the information required by the *whole* team, and not just focus on their own assigned categories. For this reason, it may be wise not to assign category responsibilities until late in the data gathering process.

To Create a Presentation or a Standalone Report?

Sometimes it may not be clear whether the assessment team is trying to create a presentation or a standalone report that can be read and understood on its own. At this stage it is usually best to focus strictly on creating a presentation. There are two compelling reasons for this:

1. The feedback session *must* be interactive to allow the leaders to understand and absorb what the assessment team has learned. This works best if the assessment report is set out as a presentation in fairly concise bullet points that are amplified and explained during the session. A report that tries to explain everything in writing is simply not suitable for an interactive presentation.
2. It is extremely difficult—and ineffective—for a team to try to create a full written report by consensus. However, the team leader can easily expand the presentation into such a report later—if such a document is required for communications purposes.

Alternative Techniques for Identifying the Vital Few

The Affinity Diagram method is just one way of identifying the assessment team's vital few priorities for improvement: it is not the only possible approach. This section describes a number of other methods, with their attendant advantages and disadvantages.

1. *Selection of criteria items, determined by scores*
   In this type of process, the vital few might be selected simply by selecting the lowest-scoring criteria items.
2. *Selection of criteria items, determined by judgment*
   In this type of process, the frame of reference is again the criteria items, but the selection is done in a more subjective and less mechanical fashion, such as weighted voting by the team.
3. *Selection of criteria items, determined by a formula*
   Some organizations have devised formulae for selecting the vital few, based upon the relative importance of each criteria item to the organization's objectives, as well as the scores. Using this type of formula, low-scoring items that are important to the organization bubble to the top of the priority list.
4. *Selection of issues independent of the criteria, determined by the assessors' collective judgment*
   This is the approach already described—using the Affinity Diagram technique to crystallize the team's collective view. This could also have been done in other ways: through a structured discussion process or a brainstorming session followed by voting, to achieve a similar result.

Method 4 is the most powerful in the hands of a capable assessment team that has been well prepared and has done a good job of data gathering. Under these conditions it will work well even on a first assessment. This method has the advantages that:

- It is quick and simple to apply.
- It takes full advantage of the team's powers of judgement, based on all the information that they have gleaned.
- It will always lead to improvement issues that make sense to the assessment team (and hence the leadership team), expressed in language that they can relate to.
- It is not constrained in any way, such as by the structure of the criteria.

However, this method can lead to unsatisfactory results in the following situations:

- The team members lack management experience or the ability to take in an organization-wide perspective, or they don't have the intellectual capacity to see the organization in terms of a system comprised of many processes.

- The data gathering has been essentially a checklist exercise—gathering scraps of information but not looking for linkages and relationships.
- There has been inadequate sharing of information—during the team debriefing sessions and during the report-writing process—so that the team members still have different sets of facts, different views of what's going on, and therefore different views about what needs to be done.
- The assessment has been somewhat superficial (perhaps intentionally).

In these situations, some or all of the following problems may appear:

- The team's ideas for improvement may be at too low a level—too tactical and detail-oriented—and thus miss some of the meaty, high-leverage opportunities.
- Efforts to prioritize may be inconclusive, for example, because there are too many "priorities" and little consensus about which are the most important.

The other methods described (1–3) are more mechanical and less powerful in some ways. However, these methods will almost always lead quickly to a set of priorities, even after a superficial or flawed assessment. The chief limitation of methods 1–3 is that they are constrained by the criteria—that is, the improvement priorities are defined as elements of the criteria. This has the following drawbacks:

- Cross-cutting issues may not emerge as clearly or as well defined as they should, or they may not emerge as high priorities. For example, suppose that the organization's process improvement efforts are failing for several reasons, including insufficient training for the teams, poor process improvement methodology, and lack of monitoring and support by the leadership team. This issue may not emerge if the team simply votes on elements of the criteria, because it is partly a leadership problem, partly a human resources problem, and partly a process management problem.
- The scope of the criteria elements may be too broad or too narrow to fit the issue. For example, suppose that inadequate communication of the organization's direction is a serious problem. This is a very specific aspect of leadership, proba-

bly narrower than any single element of the criteria. Or suppose that the organization has virtually no understanding or experience of process management. This issue is broader than the entire process management category.

Thus the structure of the criteria, although highly effective in guiding the investigations, may not always provide the best structure for defining the issues that need to be tackled. (See Exhibit 7.7.)

Having said all of this, there is no perfect process, no single "correct" set of improvement priorities. Any method will work if it leads to plans that respond to the findings and the participants buy into the outcome.

Exhibit 7.7. *Methods of identifying the vital few—pros and cons.*

Family of Methods	Pros	Cons
Selection of criteria elements, determined by scores, voting, or a formula	• Simple, straightforward process • Always leads to answers (a set of priorities) • Helps ensure a focus on methods (provided that the results category is considered off-limits)	• May give poor answers, e.g., if there are problems with the assessment process or the team • May tend to overlook cross-cutting issues • May result in priorities that are too narrowly or too broadly defined • May not define the problem or what success will look like • May lead to priorities that do not "feel right" to the participants or that clash with their own judgment
Selection of issues independent of the criteria, based upon the team's judgment	• Issues can be more precisely defined and scoped • Issues are stated in the language of the organization • Issues usually "feel right" to the participants	• More dependent upon the capabilities of the team and the adequacy of the assessment process • The process may not seem "scientific" enough to some people, due to the element of judgment involved

CHECK POINTS

Here's a list to check whether the team has done a good job of preparing its report and is well prepared to deliver it:

Success	Failure
The report reflects accurately what the team has learned during the data gathering.	Some important messages have been ducked or buried, and there is no plan for dealing with these (e.g. a private session with the senior leader).
The report focuses on what's important.	The report is cluttered by minor details that may obscure the key points.
Findings related to *perceptions* are clearly presented as such (and can be supported by quotes and examples).	Some of the assertions regarding perceptions reflect the views of a few team members rather than what was heard during the interviews.
Findings related to *facts* (rather than perceptions) can be supported by the team using documentation or hard data, as well as quotes and examples.	Some of the 'factual' assertions have not been verified by going back to source documents and data.
All team members understand and support the entire report.	On some important points there are factions or dissident groups within the team.
There is a strong consensus around the vital few recommendations.	The recommendations are a compromise between conflicting camps: some are not supported by all of the team members.
The team is clear about "who does what" during the feedback session, and people are comfortable with their roles.	There is confusion or lack of agreement about "who does what" during the feedback session; or people are being forced into roles that they will find difficult.
The logistics—room layout, handouts, etc.—have been carefully thought out and organized.	The logistics have been left to someone else, or the 'standard' approach has been adopted without discussion.

You now have a great presentation ready that is consistent with what the leaders are expecting. While the team members check their notes and rehearse the examples that they are going to use, you can all look forward to the feedback session with confidence.

• • • • •

^{www}**Companion Website Materials:**

- More tips on report writing
- The seven basic quality tools
- The seven management tools

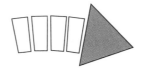 # Chapter 8

Presenting the
Assessment Report

Opinions are made to be changed—or how is truth to be got at?
Lord Byron, English poet

One of the most critical parts of the entire assessment process is the presentation of the assessment report. The team needs to know how to prepare for this session and how to present the report in a fashion that gets across the key messages, wins acceptance of the findings, and sets the stage for planning and implementation.

CHAPTER CONTENTS

- Preparations
- Purpose and agenda
- Opening the presentation
- Summarizing the work done
- The findings
- The scores
- The overall summary
- The vital few
- Wrapping up
- The motivation for change
- Check points

• • • • •

Presenting the assessment report is by far the most critical step in the entire process. It's rather like a moon landing: you anticipate and prepare for it for a long time, it's exciting when it happens, and it's over very quickly. And success depends very largely upon the preparations made beforehand.

In the assessment process, every previous step has been designed to lay the foundations for success during this presentation session. If mistakes have been made earlier in the process (for example, if the leaders have been allowed to build expectations of a glowing report), then the report presentation may be a nail-biting event. But if you have conducted these earlier steps properly, you can look forward to this session with reasonable confidence.

PREPARATIONS

Once its report is completed, the assessment team prepares for this session by discussing and agreeing on the following:

- the agenda for the report presentation
- responsibility for such roles as opening the session, managing the overall flow, and presenting different parts of the report
- techniques for delivering the presentation, encouraging discussion, and responding to questions
- the examples and quotes that will be used to support key points
- any other supporting materials that need to be available.

There are also two other significant decisions that need to be made in advance: what type of venue layout to use, and whether or not to do any advance briefing of the senior leader.

Roles and Responsibilities

The following people will be involved and should be clear about their responsibilities beforehand:

- The *assessment process sponsor* has overall responsibility for the assessment process and so will probably open and close the session.
- This process isn't going to go anywhere unless the *senior leader* is behind it, so this person will likely take the opportu-

nity to make some additional remarks at an appropriate time—perhaps by thanking the team at the end of the session and stressing the importance of taking appropriate action based on the findings.

- It's also important to have someone act as a *facilitator*, to manage the flow of the session and keep the discussions on track. This role may be played by the assessment team leader or the process expert, or it may be shared between them.

Venue Layout

The physical layout of a venue and the seating arrangements have a major impact on the atmosphere that can be created. Think of the differences in ambiance created by the following venues: a church with a pulpit raised high above the congregation; a Broadway-style music hall; or a compact theatre with the seats encircling the stage. This phenomenon also applies to your presentation.

The most obvious way of organizing the presentation is to have one person up front presenting the material to the assembled participants. *"Is there any other way?"* you may ask, since this approach is so ingrained in many organizations. In fact there *are* other ways, and the traditional approach is not necessarily the best for your purpose. Here's an alternative that is much more conducive to the type of open atmosphere that you want to create:

- The seating is a U shape or small groups at separate tables.
- The assessment team and the leaders sit around the same table(s) in such a way that they are interspersed.
- The team members each present their assigned sections of the report from where they sit (with someone else at the front changing the overheads).
- Other team members join in as required, for example to amplify key points, to help answer questions, or to give quotes and examples.

This method helps to avoid a sense of "us and them"—such as you might get if the assessment team sat on one side of the room and the leaders on the other. It also helps to avoid the sense that the messenger is just one person (that is, the person who is standing up front at that moment). It makes it easier for people to join in the discussion of contentious findings—both team members and leaders. In short, the presentation is likely to feel more like an informal discussion among peers than a sermon delivered from the pulpit, or a sales pitch delivered from a soapbox.

This approach may or may not work in your organization. The point is that you need to think about the venue and the presentation style, and decide on an approach that you think will work. This doesn't have to be exactly what people are used to.

Advance Briefing

In some organizations there is a practice of briefing the senior person beforehand—often as a means of "clearing" the content of any report before it is presented. The more hierarchical and political the organization, the more likely that this is the norm. It may even be dangerous not to follow this practice.

However, unless it is necessary for the reasons described, this step adds little value and should be avoided. In a healthy management team, the senior leader is quite content to hear the report at the same time as his or her colleagues, would not want to change or influence the team's findings, and above all doesn't want to waste time by hearing the report twice.

There is one situation where some kind of advance warning is both courteous and prudent. If the assessment has revealed some particularly sensitive problem that could be seen to lie directly at the feet of a senior person, then it may be wise to forewarn that person beforehand. In this situation, you must also remember your promise to the leaders at the start of the process—to focus on the management system, not on the performance of individuals or groups. By maintaining this focus, your report is less likely to victimize anyone, even when serious problems are revealed.

PURPOSE AND AGENDA

The ultimate aim of the report presentation is to enable the senior leaders to see the organization through the eyes of the assessment team members—to describe so clearly and vividly what they saw that the leaders will see it for themselves. Once this level of acceptance of the findings has been achieved, the focus will naturally shift to the need for action.

The formal objectives of the presentation are typically to:

- review how the assessment was conducted
- understand and accept the findings
- understand the assessment team's vital few.

Exhibit 8.1 shows the typical flow of the presentation session.

Exhibit 8.1. *Typical agenda for assessment report presentation session.*

Topic	Duration	Comment
Scene-setting	10 minutes	Led by the assessment process sponsor: welcome, any introductions, and a review of the objectives and agenda.
Overview of the assessment process	5 minutes	A brief summary of the work done (e.g., membership of the team, summary data regarding the number of interviews conducted and documents reviewed).
Findings	2.5 hours	Presented by the entire team, with questions from the leadership team. The aim is to achieve a full discussion of any contentious or ambiguous points.
Scores	10 minutes	Presented in a way that highlights which categories the organization is strong in—and where it is weak.
Overall summary	10 minutes	A broad-brush portrait emphasizing the major points. This may work better at the beginning of the presentation or at the end: there's no one right way.
The vital few	30 minutes	Presentation of the assessment team's vital few priorities for improvement.
Next steps	10 minutes	A reminder to the leaders of the next steps (typically a planning workshop) and any prework required.
Wrap-up	15 minutes	Overall reactions of the participants. Closing remarks by the senior leader.

OPENING THE PRESENTATION

The presentation opens with a welcome—probably by the assessment process sponsor—and a review of the objectives and agenda. The sponsor also makes a few key points about the tone of the meeting, probably in a manner something like this:

- *"The bulk of our time this morning will be spent on the findings, so that we all understand properly what the assessment team discovered. The aim is for us to see the organization through the eyes of the team.*
- *We shouldn't just passively accept **any** findings that we don't understand. We need to probe and discuss anything that doesn't make sense to us, or that seems to contradict our own information and experience. This is where the value of the assessment lies—in understanding why the assessment team sees things differently from some of our current perceptions.*
- *We should avoid jumping to solutions. This session is about understanding the issues. Once we understand these, then we can choose our priorities and start working on solutions. That's what next week's planning workshop is for.*
- *Let's try to avoid 'shooting the messenger' when there are findings in the report that we'd rather not hear. Maybe some of you can help keep **me** honest on this one! Our job is to share all the information that we have available to us, so that we can figure out what's going on and what to do about it."*

Then the team leader begins the presentation.

SUMMARIZING THE WORK DONE

The first part of the report is a brief reminder of the steps in the assessment and a summary of the work done by the assessment team. This reinforces the credibility of the report by demonstrating that the team has done its job thoroughly and in the agreed-upon manner.

This section typically includes:

- a flowchart of the assessment process steps completed
- a list of the team members (internal and external)
- some statistics that demonstrate that the data gathering has been thorough and balanced (see Exhibit 8.2).

Exhibit 8.2. *Example of data gathering statistics.*

Function	Interviews	Interviewees
President	1	1
Operations	9	25
Marketing	7	21
Product Development	6	18
Human Resources	2	5
Finance	3	10
Totals:	**28**	**80**
Level	**Interviews**	**Interviewees**
President	1	1
VPs	5	5
Managers	12	12
Supervisors	3	20
Frontline Staff	7	42
Totals:	**28**	**80**

If the assessment covered more than one facility, the report will also include a table showing the number of interviews by location. If any improvement teams were included, this should also be noted.

Each of the leaders will naturally scrutinize these tables to confirm that their own group and/or location has been adequately covered and to see how many employees at various levels were interviewed. They have all been interviewed quite recently, and they saw that part of the process for themselves. But it may be worth reminding them that the interview format and duration were essentially the same for everyone interviewed.

How do the assessment team members feel about how the process went? Typically they have been impressed by:

- how candid people were in the interviews
- how committed people are to doing a great job, and how strongly they feel about some of the barriers that get in their way
- the number of good ideas that people have for making things work better.

This is a good time for the team members to make some of these observations in their own words. The leaders get the message quickly: It's been a good experience for the team, and they have been able to learn a great deal about the organization. They are pleased with what they've been able to accomplish. It's time to get into the meat of the report.

THE FINDINGS

The findings start with a reminder of what the leadership category of the criteria covers. The first findings presented are the strengths, which go unchallenged, but the opportunities for improvement trigger a lengthy discussion. The leaders want to understand as precisely as they can what the real issue is in each case, and they ask lots of questions, like:

- *What kinds of things did people say?*
- *Is the problem like* **this** *or like* **that?** (giving alternative interpretations)
- *Did you actually see any examples of this happening?*
- *Is this more evident in any particular area or job category?*
- *You said a moment ago* (mentions a strength)—*aren't these points contradictory?*
- *We launched the xyz program last year to address precisely this issue—didn't anyone mention that?*
- *Are you saying that this is a just a perception among many employees, or that this is the reality?*

Sometimes it takes the entire assessment team, working together, to muster enough evidence (and passion) for a particular leader to be convinced of a particular finding. Sometimes other leaders who have already grasped the point will join in to help convince their colleague.

It is normal for the leaders to show some signs of frustration, disbelief, or blaming others (for instance, holding the employees responsible for not having understood leadership messages). But these are usually passing emotions. Once their questions have been answered and you have discussed the findings, there are usually clear signs that the messages have been understood and accepted. For example:

- One of the leaders may summarize wryly, *"It looks like we need to go back to the drawing board on **that** program. "*
- Or they may show signs of wanting to move on.

The rest of the findings are presented and discussed in the same fashion, following the structure of the criteria.

Some findings will be much more significant than others—as indicated by *double*-pluses or *double*-minuses. The presenters highlight these findings and provide more thorough explanations. The examples, quotes, and anecdotes gathered by the team also help to illustrate exactly what is going on.

Handling Questions and Challenges

Maintaining an open, inquiring atmosphere during the report presentation isn't always easy. Sometimes one of the leaders will become upset by a finding or take it personally. The leaders will always push back on many of the findings, asking for more evidence before they are convinced. That's part of their job.

So it is important that the assessment team members avoid slipping into a defensive or confrontational style. They must treat all questions as honest attempts to understand the findings, even if the questioner seems to be hostile.

Key Point

It is essential to treat every question as a genuine attempt to understand, not as an attack—regardless of the demeanor of the questioner.

It is also the responsibility of the process sponsor and the senior leader to help manage the tone of the meeting. If the questions begin to turn into attacks on the team, or attempts to discredit the report by dwelling on minor flaws, this behavior needs to be promptly nipped in the bud.

Providing Examples

The team members have prepared many examples and have these at their fingertips to support findings that require more explanation.

These examples also bring the report alive by illustrating the findings—which are often rather dry or abstract—in terms of real-life events in the workplace, or the impact on the organization's performance. These are more likely to capture the leaders' attention.

Mini-Tutorials

If the assessment team identified any topics that require an in-depth explanation beforehand, they call a "time out" at the appropriate point and switch from the findings to a mini-tutorial. This is introduced as "a more detailed explanation of what the criteria are looking for in this section."

With the benefit of this additional information, the leaders will usually understand the findings quickly. Some people may even anticipate the findings; perhaps someone will say simply, "We don't do anything like that around here." Then much of the controversy is defused, and it's easy to present that part of the report.

• • • • •

The presentation tends to speed up after the first few categories—most of the key points have already come out, and the leadership team has a better feel for the thinking that lies behind the findings. However, it often takes three hours to present all of the findings, even in organizations where the leaders rarely hold long meetings. Why is this? Because the leaders usually won't allow the presentation to go any faster! They need to be convinced that certain findings are accurate, using hard data and other evidence. And they want to understand all the important issues as clearly as possible, because this helps them to see possible courses of action.

THE SCORES

Once all the strengths and opportunities for improvement have been covered, the team leader presents the scores fairly briefly, to avoid diverting attention from the findings that are the substance of the report.

A chart of overall percentage scores by category (or by item) confirms where the organization's main strengths and weaknesses lie, and the overall score confirms roughly where the organization is on its improvement journey. Some discussion of comparisons with others helps the leaders to interpret this number and put it into perspective. For a first assessment, the key messages that come across are typically:

- The scores are not as low as they seem (the scoring system is brutal).
- The scores are reliable indicators of which performance band the organization falls into—but they are not *precise.*
- The scores are fairly typical of an average organization that has been working on continuous improvement for a relatively short time.
- The scores are far short of what's possible and what world-class organizations are achieving.

Although they realize that the scores are not a disgrace, the leaders really don't like their organization being classified as "average." This is definitely a challenge to do better.

That's all the scoring information that's really needed during this session.

THE OVERALL SUMMARY

The overall summary paints a "portrait" of the organization, as seen by the assessment team, in a few broad brush-strokes—it's not detailed, but it's a good likeness. Although the summary does not introduce any new information, it does interpret the findings at a higher level, and so it can provide new insights.

For example, suppose that the organization has lots of good approaches, but deployment is generally weak. In this case, poor deployment has already been flagged several times for *specific practices*. But seeing weak deployment stated as a *pervasive characteristic* of the organization gives it a very different significance.

Sometimes an observation like this will trigger more discussion. But the most common reaction is "Of course, you're absolutely right!" because the supporting evidence has already been discussed and agreed on.

• • • • •

This point in the presentation marks the end of discussions about the current reality, and the transition into discussing what action to take. The team leader draws attention to this, since the nature of the presentation—and the discussions—will now change. Having broadly accepted the findings, it is natural for the leadership team to switch its focus now onto *what should be done*.

THE VITAL FEW

The final decisions about what action to take will be made at the planning workshop, but it is natural for the leaders to want the team's view, as an important input. The next part of the presentation provides this.

Exhibits 8.3 to 8.5 illustrate an effective way of presenting this information. These show:

- A summary of the top priorities for improvement, from the perspective of the assessment team. These may be written as problem statements or as action statements.
- A graphical representation of any relationships between the vital few. Sometimes there is a natural sequence or flow-down from one to another. Sometimes several of the vital few are very closely related—perhaps they are different components of the same issue.
- Some of the ideas that the assessment team put forward for each of the vital few. These are *not* presented as a prescription

Exhibit 8.3. *Setting out the vital few.*

Vital Few: Summary

1. *Strategic Direction:* Clarify the strategic direction within the leadership team and communicate this to all employees.
2. *Process Improvement Strategy:* Devise a rational method of selecting process improvement projects—for example, based on customer feedback, current process capabilities, and the company's future needs.
3. *Improvement Team Support:* Modify the launch process for improvement projects to ensure that teams receive adequate training and facilitation support.
4. *Reward and Recognition:* Implement the current reward and recognition programs fully, especially for completed improvement projects.
5. *Employee Development:* Devise a more systematic process to ensure adequate employee training and development, especially for new employees.

Exhibit 8.4. *Relationships between the vital few.*

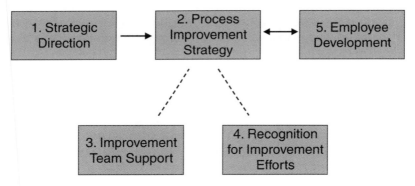

Exhibit 8.5. *Ideas for implementation.*

---

1. Strategic Direction

Clarify the strategic direction within the leadership team and communicate this to all employees.
Some ideas suggested during the assessment:

- Repeat the process used for the 1997 strategy workshop, but provide a more comprehensive and factual prework package.
- Create a revised version of the strategic direction presentation aimed at employees, not the board.
- Set up an annual schedule of town hall meetings with specific topics (rather than have ad hoc meetings arranged at short notice, often with rushed and inadequate preparations).
- Task all managers to discuss the strategy with their people after the town hall meetings, and gather feedback regarding points still not understood.

---

for action, or as a complete game plan. They are provided for two reasons: to help clarify what that "vital few" item is about, and to provide some input to the team that will eventually work on this issue and devise a game plan.

The assessment team presents the vital few as an input to the next step—the planning workshop. The team's mandate was to go only this far, rather than to develop a complete set of recommendations. This was done for a number of reasons:

- For the leaders to take ownership of the vital few and the action plans, they need to participate in creating these.
- It is important that the vital few issues chosen be aligned with the goals of the organization, and the leadership team can judge this better than anyone else. It is the leaders' *responsibility* to make the final decisions about how to respond to the findings. They should not be allowed to abdicate this responsibility—and it should not be taken away from them.

So the leaders are not asked simply to give a "thumbs up" or "thumbs down" to a complete set of recommendations that the team has already created. Instead, they are given a structure and a process that will make it easy for them to arrive at sound plans based on all of the input that they have received. This is what the upcoming planning workshop is for.

WRAPPING UP

As part of the wrap-up, it is helpful to draw out the leaders' overall reactions. A good way to accomplish this is to ask: *how do they feel about the process so far?* The leaders' comments usually reveal a high degree of acceptance of the report, as well as appreciation for the team's commitment and hard work. If there are still doubts about some of the findings even after all the discussion, these will come out again at this point—but in a more thoughtful fashion, and perhaps with some suggestions for resolving them.

The leaders may be curious about the assessment team's perspective, so a similar poll of the team members seems only natural.

At this stage, the team members are usually pretty happy about several things—about receiving a good hearing by the leaders, about the prospect of seeing some action on some of the problems identified, and about the learning opportunity afforded by the assessment itself—and they will say so.

The final task is to remind the leaders about the planning workshop and to ask them to do some prework over the next few days: each member of the leadership team should digest the assessment report, reflect, and then list the five issues that in their judgment should be given the highest priority for action.

This is also a great time for the senior leader to thank the assessment team for their efforts.

THE MOTIVATION FOR CHANGE

A desire for change does not usually spring from a warm, fuzzy feeling. For the leaders it more often springs from a painful contrast between current reality and how they would like things to be.

So, although we aim to maintain a positive tone throughout the assessment process, we should not judge the success of every step simply in terms of how good people feel about it. Sometimes much of the value comes from the shock created by a reality check. The trick is to avoid pushing people into denial by making it too difficult for them to accept the truth.

An Example of How Change Can Get Started

In one branch of a large Canadian government department, the leaders were unwilling to work seriously on improvement because they felt that they were already doing a great job. They were familiar with the management principles, believed that they managed according to these, and felt that an assessment would reveal little that they didn't already know. The turning point came during a session set up to discuss specific management processes used within their groups. It came out that some of the leaders felt that there was no need at all for defined management processes. The others were open-mouthed in astonishment at this view. The shock of realizing how far apart they were in their basic thinking blew away their complacency and provided the stimulus for this group to get serious about improvement.

In this case the impetus for change came, not from a positive experience, but from opening a "can of worms."

CHECK POINTS

Has the report presentation been a success? It's easy to tell. Here is what success (and failure) look like:

Success	Failure
• Everyone participated actively and there was lively and open discussion of the key findings.	• Many of the leaders did not participate in a positive fashion, and the discussion was one-sided or inconclusive.
• The leaders wanted to discuss each point until they understood it properly before moving on to the next one.	• Some leaders became too upset or emotional at certain findings to listen properly to the evidence.
• The leaders stayed focused on "what is going wrong."	• The leaders began to focus on "who is messing up."
• During the discussions the assessment team members were given adequate opportunity to share what they learned and to provide supporting evidence.	• Instead of seeking to understand the findings, the executives attacked the team and/or the process.
• There was explicit acceptance of the key findings by the leaders.	• There was only passive acceptance of the report—the discussion was not open, and some leaders may not really believe or accept key findings.
• The mood of the leaders at the end was one of wanting to start working quickly on solutions.	• The leaders left feeling depressed, angry, or overwhelmed by the findings; or feeling powerless because they cannot see any solutions to the problems presented.

The "moon landing" part is over. Perhaps it was a rough landing, or perhaps it went perfectly. But if the signs are that you got your message across, you should go out with your team and celebrate—things may still *look* the same as before, but you've actually arrived on a different planet, where significant change is about to unfold.

● ● ● ● ●

ʷʷʷCompanion Website Materials:

- Participation in the assessment report presentation

Chapter 9

Developing Improvement Plans

*Unless commitment is made, there are
only promises and hopes . . . but no plans.*
                                    Peter Drucker

After the assessment report has been presented successfully, the next step is a workshop to translate the improvement priorities into action plans. This planning workshop finalizes the vital few priorities for improvement, creates outline improvement plans, and sets the stage for proper implementation and follow-through.

CHAPTER CONTENTS

- The planning workshop
- Opening the workshop
- Selecting the vital few priorities for improvement
- Developing improvement plans
- Reviewing the improvement plans
- Preparing for fail-proof implementation
- Wrap-up
- Check points

• • • • •

THE PLANNING WORKSHOP

Once the assessment report has been presented and the findings accepted by the leaders, the basic foundations for success have been laid. This probably feels like a monumental achievement—obtaining support for the assessment process in the first place, and then winning the leaders' acceptance of some sobering findings. And in most organizations this *is* a great accomplishment. However, the task that lies ahead is equally challenging. The steps that remain are absolutely essential and must be executed well; otherwise all the good work done so far may come to nothing.

The immediate next step is to crystallize a consensus regarding the priorities for improvement, and translate these into practical improvement plans that are owned by the key players. One effective way to accomplish this is to conduct a planning workshop soon after the assessment report presentation. This planning workshop is also the time to be looking farther ahead and making preparations to ensure proper follow-through on the improvement plans.

Workshop Participants

The key participants at this workshop are the leadership team and the assessment team. The leaders will make the final decisions regarding which priorities to tackle, and they will own the improvement plans. The assessment team members take part because of their detailed understanding of the assessment findings, because they can offer ideas for possible courses of action, and because they can ensure that the action plans are focused on the problems actually identified. It may also be helpful to have the process expert participate—perhaps to facilitate parts of the process, or to provide another perspective during the planning discussions.

Preparations for the Workshop

Prior to the workshop, the leaders should:

- Review and digest the assessment report, focusing on the parts that deal with important issues. They may want to dis-

cuss any contentious or complex areas with others, members of the assessment team or other colleagues.
- Reflect on what they consider to be the top priorities for improvement—from the perspective of the entire organization, not just their own departments, and with the strategic objectives of the organization in mind.
- List their chosen vital few priorities for improvement.

All of the participants should also receive the workshop objectives and agenda beforehand.

OPENING THE WORKSHOP

The workshop starts with a brief review of the agenda (see Exhibit 9.1), and the formal objectives, which are:

- to confirm the vital few priorities for improvement
- to develop outline improvement plans
- to make the implementation fail-proof by ensuring close monitoring and excellent support.

The workshop also has some unspoken objectives:

- to achieve ownership of the plan by the leaders—both a collective ownership of the improvement plans, and responsibility assigned to individual leaders for specific parts
- to ensure that the improvement plans are accurately targeting the right issues by tapping into the understanding gained by the assessment team.

Exhibit 9.1. *Typical planning workshop agenda.*

- Review the objectives and agenda.
- Select the vital few priorities for improvement.
- Develop outline improvement plans, one for each of the vital few (small group work).
- Share and review these plans to ensure alignment and avoid overlaps.
- Review the arrangements for monitoring and support of the improvement projects to ensure fail-proof implementation.

SELECTING THE VITAL FEW PRIORITIES FOR IMPROVEMENT

It's good practice at the start of the workshop to make sure that there are no remaining questions or concerns about the assessment report findings. If there are, these should be resolved before going any further. This is to ensure that the participants do not end up debating the assessment findings again during this workshop, but focus on the task at hand.

The leaders have come to the workshop with their own carefully considered lists of the five top priorities for improvement. This input needs to be translated quickly into a final list of the top priorities.

An effective way of doing this is by using the Affinity Diagram process that was described in Chapter 7, but a simplified, fast-track version; the assessment team's vital few should already be posted as headings at the start. Usually, nearly all of the leaders' ideas fit neatly under these same headings, and the exercise confirms quickly (and visually) that everyone is thinking along very similar lines. (Ideas that don't fit can be quickly analyzed to see whether they contain another central theme that should be added to the vital few.) Starting with these predefined headings greatly speeds the process and avoids losing the leaders' attention. Alternatively, you could use one of the other techniques for selecting the vital few, also described in Chapter 7.

Whatever you planned beforehand, it's important to be alert to the leaders' preferences and to avoid wasting any time. They may simply want a brief, unstructured discussion, or they may say "We like the assessment team's vital few. Let's go with those."

DEVELOPING IMPROVEMENT PLANS

Having finalized the vital few, the next task is to create an initial plan for each of these. The workshop participants break into several small groups, each tasked with developing an outline improvement plan for one of the vital few. There should be some logic to how people are assigned to these groups, and each of the

Exhibit 9.2. *Sample template for outline improvement plans.*

1. Name of the project (after one of the vital few)
2. Objective
3. Measurement(s) of success
4. Key deliverables, main tasks and milestones
5. Methodology to be used
6. Participants (sponsor, team members, others to be kept informed)
7. Timetable
8. Dependencies (inputs, tools, support . . .)

leaders should participate in a group where they have a special interest or may become responsible for the task.

These small groups will do a much better job if they are given some guidance on their tasks and a template for the outline plan they are to create (see Exhibit 9.2).

Small Group Work

Once the small groups go into action, they will need at least an hour—perhaps two—to complete their task. Because the nature of the vital few can vary so much, different groups may produce quite different types of output.

A group that is given a complex issue may only create a "plan for a plan"—one that is sufficient to allow a suitable project team to be assigned and given a clear mandate. This group recognizes that the project team, once it is formed, will have to do most of the detailed planning. Another group may be dealing with a less complex task—perhaps a policy change—and can create a fairly complete plan in thirty minutes. A third group may decide that some additional investigation should be carried out before any project is initiated—perhaps an exploration of alternatives, or a cost-benefit analysis. So the groups may all produce quite different-looking plans, yet each of these may be appropriate to the task.

Most of the topics set out in the planning template are fairly self-evident, but two call for further explanation: defining the improvement objectives and choosing a suitable methodology.

Defining the Improvement Objectives   It is vital to define clear, measurable objectives for an improvement project, and it is essential for all of the participants in the planning workshop to understand the difference between a mere fix and a true improvement. This will help them to frame the objectives properly.

Improvement projects should nearly always accomplish a lasting change in the way that something is done, as opposed to just patching up a problem or applying a temporary fix. Unless the project results in a new process or changes to an existing process, then it probably won't create any lasting improvement in "how things happen around here."

Exhibit 9.3 contains some examples to illustrate the point.

The actions shown in the "fix" column will all be beneficial in the short term, but many will have little effect in the long term. In contrast, the actions in the "improvement" column all have the potential to have a lasting effect. Fixes are not bad, they are just insufficient. An improvement plan may often require both aspects:

Exhibit 9.3.   *Examples of improvement versus fixes.*

Issue	Fix	Improvement
The planning process is slow and cumbersome and does not help align departmental plans.	Conduct a workshop to quickly review and realign departmental plans.	Set up a cross-functional team to review and redesign the planning process and associated training.
Many managers lack essential people-management skills.	Identify those currently requiring help and provide training.	Modify the management development system to provide skills-assessment tools and training as necessary for all current and prospective managers.
There is a lack of useful quantitative information about customer satisfaction.	Engage a market research firm to conduct a survey of all current customers.	Establish a system of regular surveys, meetings, and complaint analysis to obtain ongoing feedback from customers.

an immediate Band-Aid,® plus a lasting process change. And applying a fix can often help build momentum by demonstrating an early success.

Another aspect of this fix-versus-improvement distinction is the need for ongoing maintenance of the new way of working. This is typically done by:

- assigning a *process owner* who is responsible for the proper functioning of this process in the future
- establishing *measurements of the effectiveness* of the process.

This is an issue for the improvement project sponsors: they need to decide how to sustain the improvements made. Typically the project sponsor will become the owner of the improved process (or ensure that someone else takes on this role) and will take responsibility for some kind of performance indicator.

Choosing a Suitable Methodology   Another key to developing sound improvement plans is to select an appropriate methodology. Improvement projects can vary greatly in size and complexity. They can range from policy decisions requiring little more than approval at the right level, to major process redesign that will require significant work over an extended period. Some may be relatively straightforward projects that can be expected to unfold predictably according to schedule, while others may be journeys into the unknown, attempts to pin down the root causes of a chronic, hitherto unsolved problem. Some projects only require one or two staff specialists, who will consult with other people as required. Other projects will demand a cross-functional team representing several different departments.

There is no single approach that will encompass all of these projects satisfactorily. But a plan is always required, and it is always feasible to create one. There is no reason to reinvent the wheel. Standard methods exist for dealing with most common situations, such as:

- developing a new process
- improving an existing process
- solving a problem.

These standard approaches provide ideal frameworks for developing improvement plans.

Using an appropriate standard approach not only makes the work itself much simpler and more predictable, it also makes it possible to plan the steps in advance, even for tasks like root cause analysis, where the destination is still unknown. So one of the keys to planning improvement projects effectively is to select a methodology that is appropriate for the project.

For example, if the goal is to establish an effective system for handling customer complaints, a process development methodology may provide a perfect template for the plan. If the goal is to eliminate a certain class of billing error, the problem-solving methodology may be a better choice.

Exhibit 9.4 provides examples of matching a measurable improvement project objective with an appropriate approach,

Exhibit 9.4. *Selecting appropriate methodologies.*

Objective	Primary Methodology	Other Supporting Methods and Tools
Redesign the new product introduction process to reduce cycle times by 30% to 50%.	*Process improvement (generic)*	• Time-based process analysis
Establish a complaint system that categorizes, analyzes, and responds to customer complaints in a controlled, timely manner.	*Process development (generic)*	• Database design
Reduce the frequency of in-service failures for product xyz by an order of magnitude.	*Problem-solving (generic)*	• Root cause analysis • Design of experiments (DOE)
Establish a system to measure overall customer satisfaction and satisfaction with our key products and services.	*Project management (generic)*	• Benchmarking research (into customer measurement systems) • Supplier selection
Revise credit policy for defined categories of customer complaints with emphasis on promoting customer loyalty.	*Policy revision procedure (company-specific)*	• Focus group review of proposed policy

either a standard (generic) methodology or a procedure specific to the organization.

There are a great many proprietary versions of these generic methodologies, and it doesn't matter much which "brand" you choose; any reputable product will do the job. However, it's very helpful to standardize on one brand for each *type* of methodology.

In fact there is only a handful of *types* of methodology in common use. The vast majority of improvement projects can be planned and implemented using one of the generic methodologies listed in the following tables. Exhibit 9.5 contrasts the different capabilities of these methodologies, and Exhibit 9.6 shows how the typical process steps differ.

In world-class organizations, most employees are trained and experienced in a few such methodologies and various supporting tools and techniques, so improvement teams naturally pick an appropriate approach, use this as a template for their planning, and swing into action.

In most organizations this is not the case, and people need some good guidance and support, or they are likely to create ill-conceived plans, which may be worse than no plan at all.

For example, suppose that a team is asked to create an outline plan for eliminating a billing accuracy problem. An experienced team will create an outline plan based on the problem-solving methodology. This plan will have steps such as define the problem, identify possible causes, gather data and determine actual root causes, generate potential solutions, and so on.

A team that lacks experience in formal problem solving is more likely to set out a series of specific actions that it believes will fix the problem, although it does not even know for sure what the root causes are. Furthermore, although this approach is fatally flawed, the team members may be quite comfortable with what they are doing, because this is how they have always tackled problems.

It's easy to see how an organization that doesn't have much experience of continuous improvement can put lots of effort into well-defined improvement priorities, yet still fail to accomplish much. During the planning workshop, firm direction and good coaching may be required to keep inexperienced groups on track. The key at this stage is to insist on plans that are based on a suitable

Exhibit 9.5. *Contrasts between generic methodologies—capabilities.*

Problem Solving	Process Improvement	Process Development
Reactive; starts with an identified or suspected problem	Proactive; starts with a process targeted for improvement	Proactive; starts with a need to create a process where none exists, or to develop a redesigned process
Simple methodology; limited training needs	More complex methodology; builds upon problem-solving skills	Most complex methodology; requires competency in problem solving and basic process improvement methods
Gets results quickly; can accumulate many small gains	Takes longer to complete an improvement cycle and get results, but larger gains are possible	Takes longest to complete, but can achieve breakthrough gains in performance
Risk of fragmentation through many separate, unconnected efforts Risk of sub-optimization; improving part of a process while unintentionally making some other part worse	An integrative approach; pulls together and streamlines activities that are fragmented	Integrative, like process improvement Risk of serious disruption to the organization if too ambitious, done badly, or insufficient attention paid to managing the changes (e.g. the people issues)
Can be done quickly and cheaply; hence, may often be initiated and owned by frontline people	Needs significant time and resources; hence, more likely to be initiated, directed, and owned by management	Requires the most time and resources; hence always initiated, directed, and owned by management

methodology rather than purely ad hoc. If you know in advance that the participants don't have the knowledge to do this, then you need to provide some guidance up front in the planning workshop—and to plan for good training and support afterwards, when the improvement teams are being formed.

Exhibit 9.6. *Contrasts between generic methodologies—steps.*

Problem Solving	Process Improvement	Process Development
Typical steps: • define the problem • identify possible causes • gather data, analyze and determine root causes • generate possible solutions • select, test, and verify best solution(s) • plan for implementation • implement the plan • verify that solutions were effective	Typical steps: • identify process outputs • identify customers • understand customer needs, priorities, and view of performance • understand the current process • select measurements • identify main performance gaps and process shortcomings • devise, test, and implement process improvements (using problem solving) • verify that improvements were effective • monitor ongoing process performance	Typical steps: • define improvement goals (in terms of process performance) • define required process outputs • design a process capable of achieving performance goals • verify feasibility and performance gains (e.g., through pilots, testing) • plan for implementation (typically a major transition) • implement the plan • monitor the transition plan and the performance gains • monitor ongoing process performance
Typically a project or task format: the work is considered done when the solution has been implemented successfully	Requires ongoing effort to hold the gains: a process owner and/or a standing team is responsible for ongoing improvement and maintenance	Requires major effort to effect the changes, then ongoing effort to hold the gains: a process owner and/or a standing team is responsible for ongoing improvement and maintenance
Proprietary example: • Xerox six-step Problem Solving Process	Proprietary examples: • Xerox nine-step Quality Improvement Process • Six-Sigma DMAIC methodology	Proprietary example: • Six-Sigma DMADV methodology

Using a standard methodology as a planning template doesn't always mean that the team can be sure about the size of the task or how long it will take. But the initial plan created from this template is rational, workable, and much more likely to be effective.

REVIEWING THE IMPROVEMENT PLANS

Once the small group work is complete, the participants reassemble and each group presents its outline plan. During the discussion that follows, overlaps and dependencies are identified, and suggestions are made for improving the plans. Most issues can be resolved on the spot, since the decision makers are all present; those issues that cannot be resolved are noted and assigned to someone present.

Eventually there is a consensus that this initial package is adequate as a basis for starting the work. The project teams and their sponsors will be expected to work out the finer details and negotiate any further adjustments.

An essential question to consider at this stage is "Can we do all of this work—and do it well—given all the other work already under way?"

If there are doubts about the answer, these should be dealt with by some combination of the following:

- Pruning the vital few down to a smaller number. There may be no need to eliminate any of them, but it may be wise to delay some in order to achieve a stronger focus on those that are most critical or need to be tackled first.
- Shutting down or delaying some other, less critical initiatives.

This is very hard for management to do, especially when the organization is already under great pressure.

Key Point
A certain recipe for failure is to keep adding new "critical" projects—but removing none—until the vital few becomes the "unachievable many."

This situation resembles the ancient monkey trap made from a narrow-mouthed container: the monkey can just squeeze its hand in to seize some delicious nuts, but it cannot withdraw its hand without letting go of the prize. Sometimes the leaders are unable to accept that they cannot have it all—the organization simply cannot deliver on so many different priorities. By being unable to let go of anything, they overload the organization, obscure the priorities, and seal their fate.

PREPARING FOR FAIL-PROOF IMPLEMENTATION

The most common failure mode for any type of assessment, audit, or external intervention is to reach the point where it is quite clear what needs to be done and then fail to follow through.

The leaders should recognize that improvement projects are especially vulnerable because they are "important but not urgent." If the improvement plans are quietly put aside, no customer is going to complain about this decision, no one is going to sue the company, the shareholders (perhaps even the board) won't know and could probably care less. Yet these plans are essential to get at the root causes of issues that customers and shareholders do care about: faulty products and services, high costs of error and waste, low productivity, and poor profitability.

So although people may be excited right now about getting on with the improvement plans, this work may soon be pushed aside by other more pressing issues, unless the leaders take some steps to ensure that this cannot happen. If the leaders really believe that these actions are vital, they must take steps to make certain that the improvement plans will be implemented, come what may. For these reasons it is usually valuable—and often essential—to spend some time in the planning workshop on the topic of follow-through.

Simply inviting the participants to discuss a few relevant questions can open up this topic. For example:

- What is management's track record for initiatives like this one, in terms of following through to successful completion?
- Where, when, and how should implementation be reviewed, to ensure that the project work is being done?
- Who is responsible for the success of the improvement teams?

This discussion should lead to a better awareness of the pitfalls and agreement to adopt some obvious countermeasures.

A few key actions should be agreed on at this stage:

- The leaders should hold themselves accountable for implementation of the plans—for example, by including the vital few in their personal objectives.
- A reporting format should be established for the improvement projects that will demonstrate progress against the original plans.
- Measurements should be established that demonstrate whether the improvement projects are having the desired effect.
- The leaders should agree on a dependable mechanism for monitoring progress—for example, by incorporating progress checks into an existing regular meeting, or by creating a special review forum.
- A plan should be developed to communicate to all employees the key findings of the assessment and the actions to be taken as a result.

The leaders can also demonstrate their commitment and "nail the flag to the mast" by telling others about their plans: perhaps the board, perhaps some key customers and suppliers who can contribute or may benefit from the plans.

Chapter 10 describes in more detail the challenges of achieving tenacious follow-through. This type of information may be useful to the workshop participants: to help them anticipate and avoid the common pitfalls.

WRAP-UP

It's good practice to have some kind of definitive wrap-up, though you need to use your best judgment at this point; by the end of the workshop, the participants may not have the energy or the inclination to do anything else. However, if it seems appropriate, you can ask for a quick comment from the participants regarding "how you feel about what has been accomplished so far."

CHECK POINTS

When the workshop is over, you will want to compare notes with some of the participants and with your process expert, who may have some additional insights. Here's what a successful planning workshop looks like:

Success	Failure
Everyone participated actively, even though some leaders are more enthusiastic about this process than others.	Those who are not supportive of the approach either mounted an effective rebuttal or kept ominously quiet, saving their ammunition for a better opportunity.
The objective of each project is clear, and each has an outline plan that provides an adequate starting point for the improvement team.	The objectives and outline plans are poorly defined or lack focus.
The plans were discussed openly, and potential problems and overlaps were identified and dealt with.	There was little feedback on the plans because the leaders are focusing only on their own piece of the action— they do not feel responsible for their colleagues' efforts, or for how it all comes together.
Participants express a sense of confidence that the plans are targeting the right issues, and that there will be adequate follow-through.	There is a self-fulfilling cynicism about the chances of success— perhaps because of a history of failing to follow through.
The leaders have clearly defined responsibilities for the success of the improvement projects, perhaps some combination of individual responsibility for specific projects and collective responsibility for the entire process.	The leaders have delegated most of the responsibility for the projects to lower levels in such a way that they will not personally feel accountable for success or failure.
It is clear how the project teams will be staffed, supported, and their progress monitored through to completion.	No effective arrangements have been made for monitoring, reviewing, and supporting the project teams through to completion.

Success	Failure
The leaders have agreed on some process ownership responsibilities, to ensure that the improvements are sustained after the projects are completed.	No-one is thinking this far ahead: Perhaps no-one really expects the projects to be completed.
Participants show a strong desire to "get on with it."	There is a sense of "here we go again": having to go through the motions without a real chance of bringing about changes and improvement.

Postscript

You may not have accomplished all of this perfectly—there may even be some gaping holes. For example, it may be increasingly clear at this stage that some leaders are only paying lip service to the process. Some of the initial plans may seem seriously flawed. Perhaps the senior leader was called out of the planning workshop to attend to a crisis and didn't return.

None of this need be fatal if you have accomplished the essentials. These are:

- a reasonably clear definition of the vital few
- a collective commitment by the leaders to take action
- an agreed-upon method of monitoring progress.

If these are in place, most other shortcomings can be resolved over time. And you have some powerful forces on your side. Many people within the leadership team—and the assessment team—now see the daily problems of the organization in a completely different light. None of these people will be satisfied until they achieve some tangible success in changing the management system.

• • • • •

ᵂᵂᵂ**Companion Website Materials:**

More thoughts on planning for improvement:

- Establishing suitable measurements of success
- How improvement objectives change and progress over time

Chapter 10

Implementation and Follow-Through

Champions keep playing till they get it right.
Billie Jean King

In order to see the improvement plans through to completion, the organization must have a system to support implementation. This includes tasks such as formalizing the improvement objectives and responsibilities, getting the improvement teams into action and monitoring progress. It is also essential to support each improvement team throughout its complete life cycle, from initial start-up to wrap-up, and finally to ensure that the gains are made permanent.

CHAPTER CONTENTS

- Creating a system to support implementation
- Formalizing and assigning improvement objectives
- Conducting formal progress reviews
- Establishing suitable measurements
- Communicating the outcomes of the assessment
- Providing technical and moral support
- Managing change
- The life cycle of an improvement team
- Check points

• • • • •

If you've read this far, congratulations! You may be just the right type of person for this task—someone who has the staying power to stick with it right through the implementation phase.

You now have outline plans that target some carefully selected issues: plans that senior management have committed themselves to executing. You might think that implementation *ought* to be a breeze. Unfortunately, in many organizations, this is not the case; you may need to do a lot more fancy footwork to ensure that these carefully crafted plans are actually executed.

This chapter looks at the task of implementation from two different points of view:

- how to maintain the focus and create a climate of support for all improvement efforts
- how to support the individual team efforts through their entire life cycle, from start-up to wrap-up.

CREATING A SYSTEM TO SUPPORT IMPLEMENTATION

Many organizations are not very good at following through to ensure proper implementation of leadership decisions—whether these decisions are improvement-related or not. This is often because there is not a systematic or reliable way of monitoring and supporting implementation.

How good is your organization at follow-through? You may already know from the track record that there are problems, but it may not be clear what is going wrong. One way to gain some insight into this is to look at the methods used to ensure implementation.

Exhibit 10.1 shows some of the activities required for effective follow-through, plus some methods that work well, and others that don't.

Let's examine each of these activities in more detail.

Exhibit 10.1. *Follow-through: Methods of ensuring implementation.*

Activity	Effective Methods	Ineffective Methods
Formalization of objectives and responsibilities	• Measurable objectives are included in sponsors' personal objectives and in the business plan. • Objectives are integrated and reviewed for alignment. • Key processes have assigned process owners, who have end-to-end responsibility for key cross-functional processes.	• Objectives are ill-defined and not measurable. • Objectives are not formalized or integrated into one set of documents. • Responsibilities are defined entirely within departmental boundaries.
Use of measurement	• Reliable in-process and outcome measurements are established, gathered regularly, and made readily available. • Projects include measurable milestones.	• Projects and processes lack measurements of progress or performance. • Measurements that do exist are often lacking in such areas as timeliness, accuracy, and integrity.
Use of reviews	• Reviews occur frequently, following a regular schedule. • A core of predefined performance measurements and progress reports is presented every time. • Additional measurements may be presented for apparent problem areas. • New projects are registered and tracked to completion.	• Reviews occur infrequently and/or at irregular intervals. • Review format allows for considerable discretion regarding content presented—i.e., "dog-and-pony show." • There is little use of non-financial measurements during reviews. • There is no guarantee that any project, once started, will ever be reviewed for progress or completion.

(continued)

Exhibit 10.1.   *(Continued)*

Activity	Effective Methods	Ineffective Methods
Response to out-of-line situations in reviews	• Problems are analyzed for systemic causes— *"What is going wrong"* • Responsibilities for action are decided by management in review meetings—e.g., to conduct analysis off-line and identify possible solutions. • Management action is focused on both recovery and prevention of recurrences. • The atmosphere encourages early disclosure and open discussion of problems.	• Problems are often blamed on individuals— *"Who messed up?"* • "Solutions" are chosen by management during review meetings. • Management action is focused entirely on immediate recovery (i.e., firefighting). • An atmosphere of confrontation and blaming encourages concealment of problems.
Follow-up after reviews	• Decisions and actions assigned are recorded for follow-up in the next review meeting. • Measurements provide indications of whether actions were effective.	• Decisions and actions assigned are not recorded. • No check is made during the next meeting to determine whether "solutions" were effective.
Technical and moral support	• Teams are systematically provided with facilitation and technical guidance according to their needs. • Early successes are planned for and publicized. • Teams are visibly recognized upon completion of their tasks.	• Teams are expected to get the job done without outside help, regardless of their level of knowledge and experience. • Projects are not designed with early successes in mind. • Team accomplishments are taken for granted and not publicized; team members are assigned to new projects before the first ones are completed.

(continued)

Exhibit 10.1.   *(Continued)*

Activity	Effective Methods	Ineffective Methods
Managing change	• The impact of decisions on employees is always considered. • Changes that affect employees are widely communicated in advance and the rationale explained. • Communications are two-way: there are opportunities for discussion and feedback. • Responsibility for detailed planning and implementation of changes is pushed down to the lowest level possible.	• Only financial/technical impacts of change are considered. • Changes that affect employees may or may not be communicated in advance. • Communications are one-way broadcasts of messages from management. • Planning and decision-making authority is guarded by senior levels; employees receive instructions but not explanations.

FORMALIZING AND ASSIGNING IMPROVEMENT OBJECTIVES

The improvement objectives need to be formalized and incorporated into the few key documents that the leaders use to capture their commitments: typically their own personal objectives and the business plan. Anything less than this is typically a recipe for failure.

When people are under pressure, they will always focus on the few objectives that seem the most important, and they will pay less attention to those that seem secondary. To avoid this fate, the *improvement* priorities need to be given their proper place by documenting them among the other key priorities.

CONDUCTING FORMAL PROGRESS REVIEWS

One of the keys to successful implementation of any plan is to have some kind of regular, disciplined review process that *never allows attention to stray from the plan.* A regular, formal review serves as a kind of corporate memory, so the organization doesn't forget its intentions.

Have you ever walked to another room and then realized that you've forgotten why you went? This is a failure of short-term memory—you acted on a decision to do something, but then forgot what your intentions were. When this happens, your decision to act is thwarted, just as surely as if you were physically immobilized.

Key Point

Organizations that don't have an effective review process are like people who are constantly forgetting their intentions—they are unable to act consistently on their own decisions.

Some organizations set up a special steering committee to oversee any kind of major initiative. Others systematically incorporate important initiatives into the agenda of an existing standing committee.

Another practice that is valuable for the vital few plans is to schedule a more thorough "mid-point review" halfway through the year, in addition to any monthly reporting. At this session, each of the project teams—with their sponsors—presents an in-depth report on progress to date against the planned milestones.

Common Failings of the Review Process

Almost every organization has regular management meetings of some sort, but these are often deeply flawed. Typical problems are:

- A reactive mode of operation, in which attention is focused on reacting to current problems rather than on executing according to the plan or taking preventive action to eliminate chronic problems.
- A relentless focus on recent financial results, but little or no scrutiny of leading indicators that predict future results, or the actions that are required to ensure future results.
- A threatening, adversarial atmosphere that makes people reluctant to reveal problems—until these have grown too big to hide.
- A format that determines who will present during reviews, but not what they will cover. This tends to lead to a "dog-

and-pony show" style of review, in which each person presents a potpourri of recent "successes" but does not necessarily show how they are doing in meeting specific commitments to the organization.

- A lack of understanding of variation (see sidebar). This leads to repeated attempts to solve nonexistent problems, while significant real problems go unnoticed and unaddressed.

Variation

One of the most pervasive and costly problems of management is a lack of understanding of variation. Numerical results will always exhibit some random variation from one period to the next, regardless of how consistently and effectively people are doing their jobs. For example, sales will always vary somewhat from month to month for no particular reason. By failing to recognize or allow for this, management ends up treating people as heroes one month and bums the next for no reason at all. It just depends upon whether random variation causes the results to come in above or below target. By treating random variations as if they had real causes, managers are constantly seeing "problems" or "trends" that are in fact illusions—like faces in the clouds. And while they are busy attacking nonexistent problems, they often fail to spot real problems and real trends, which are masked by random "noise" in the measurement system.

Smart organizations overcome this by teaching people about variation and by giving them statistical tools. For example, adding control limits to run charts allows people to distinguish between random variation that is inherent in the system and variation that is due to a change or event of some sort. This technique works just as well for charts used in the boardroom or on the shop floor—provided that people understand how to interpret them.

www For more in-depth information on this important subject, a good place to start is with the literature on statistical process control (SPC) and the teachings of Dr. W. Edwards Deming.

Thus, in many organizations, the management review process is a monthly ritual of questionable value, which only serves to drive successive waves of reactive, unfocused fire fighting. This activity burns up a great deal of time and creates the mere illusion of being in control and doing something useful. Such reviews always try to answer the question, "What went wrong this month?" However, they rarely address questions such as, "Are we on track in executing our plan?" or "Are our actions having the expected effect?" or "Is our basic strategy still working?"

Such reviews rarely even examine whether the fire-fighting actions initiated last month have been carried out or were effective. If the numbers look better, it's assumed that these actions worked. If the numbers look worse, it's assumed that they didn't. It is hard to imagine a style of management further removed from a closed-loop improvement cycle! This is corporate "memory loss" run rampant.

Minimum Requirements for an Effective Review Process

If the organization's review process exhibits some of these problems, these are likely to get in the way of implementing the improvement plan. If the current review process is really badly broken, it may be necessary to attempt some changes immediately, or to create some better way of reviewing the improvement plans.

The minimum requirements to aim for are:

- A regular forum for reviewing improvement plans that won't be delayed or hijacked by the "crisis of the month."
- A format for the review that doesn't do an end-run around the plan by looking for results before the plan has been implemented. For example, the agenda may be sequenced to focus first on execution of the plan according to the milestones, then on leading indicators, and finally on outcomes and bottom-line results.
- An open atmosphere in which people are not punished for revealing problems, but are assisted—for example, by offers of expert help, careful analysis of problem causes, or the removal of barriers.

ESTABLISHING SUITABLE MEASUREMENTS

Review meetings will work much better with a set of suitable and reliable measurements to examine. In the case of improvement teams, these measurements are essential to demonstrate that the teams are having the desired impact, as well as completing the actions agreed on in their plans. These measurements will also be essential for ongoing monitoring after each team has completed its task, to ensure that the improvements are not lost.

In the process that we have described, the issue of measurement is first raised at the planning workshop, and the participants define what they believe will be suitable measurements of success. It is then up to the improvement teams to refine and implement these in order to establish workable measurement procedures. Selecting measurements often involves trade-offs between the "ideal" measurement and what can actually be measured reliably without incurring excessive costs. If the initial ideas from the planning workshop prove to be impractical, the team will propose alternatives to the project sponsor.

COMMUNICATING THE OUTCOMES OF THE ASSESSMENT

A lot of the implementation support described so far is focused on keeping the improvement teams alive long enough to do their job. However, the assessment interview process has directly touched many people and raised awareness throughout the organization. Now people are looking for action, and they need to be told what will be done as a result of the assessment.

One of the great benefits of quickly completing the assessment and the initial planning is that the employees can be told about the findings and the vital few soon after the interviews. Prompt communications demonstrate that management is serious about the process and is acting on the information gathered during the interviews.

A Communication Event

It is possible to communicate the plans and obtain widespread involvement using conference-style events that can reach large numbers of people very quickly. Exhibit 10.2 shows a type of communication workshop used by one division of an international telecommunications company.

Exhibit 10.2. *Agenda for an all-managers forum.*

- The division president presents the company's strategy and the goals for the coming year.
- The assessment process sponsor presents a description of the assessment process.
- The participants break into smaller groups of people from different functions. Each group receives a presentation of the complete assessment report with time allowed for questions and discussion.
- Back in the plenary session, each of the leaders presents the vital few item that he or she is responsible for and outlines the action plan.
- There is a poll of all the participants to determine whether they agree that the vital few are appropriate and to find out if there is anything important that they feel has been missed.
- The participants form into natural work groups and discuss how they will support these plans—for example, by providing resources for the improvement teams or by modifying some of their departmental plans.

Who should present the findings and vital few plans to the employees? It's a great idea for the leadership team members to take on this task. By doing so they will demonstrate their ownership of the assessment process and the action plans. And by explaining the report findings to others they will further internalize the management concepts upon which the assessment is based.

Hoshin Planning

Some high-performing organizations routinely deploy their annual business plans (including the improvement components) by sharing and refining them systematically at successive levels in the organization. At each level, people provide input and agree to the goals that they are prepared to accept in support of the overall plan. They may negotiate some modifications to make the plan feasible, and they in turn cascade it to the next level, focusing on the goals that they have accepted. This so-called "catchball" process is part of Hoshin Planning, an advanced system of planning and implementation that embodies closed-loop improvement cycles throughout.

This methodology neatly complements the assessment process, and any organization that is struggling with planning (or implementation of plans) should learn about Hoshin Planning as an ideal to work toward. The companion website provides more information on this topic.[www]

PROVIDING TECHNICAL AND MORAL SUPPORT

The improvement teams need a kind of "life support system" to help keep them going: facilitation and technical guidance, publicity for early successes, and visibility and recognition when the job is done.

Facilitation and Technical Guidance

As already pointed out, improvement teams need to use appropriate methodologies, which should be identified during the planning workshop. If the organization is short of people who are experienced in using formal methodologies, then it's essential to provide some combination of training and facilitator support to the teams. And this support should err on the generous side.

Key Point
It's crazy to cut corners when providing support for new improvement teams—you may never again get such a good opportunity to start improving performance in a systematic, repeatable fashion. Don't blow it!

In the short term you may need to go outside for expert help, but smart organizations develop a strong cadre of internal trainers and facilitators, often combining this role with another job. These people can provide support as required to newly formed teams. Smart organizations also value this role, recognize the contribution of the people who do this type of work, and place a high premium on the skills that they develop.

Publicity for Early Successes

In any process that involves change, it is valuable to achieve some early wins and to give these a high profile. Some of the vital few may be tasks that can be completed quickly, or that include significant early milestones. It's smart to communicate these early successes widely and well. These communications will be more credible if they:

- explain the value of what has been accomplished
- avoid hype—such as overstating the accomplishment or presenting the team as super-heroes
- acknowledge the challenges that still exist and the work still to be done.

This treatment shouldn't be reserved only for the early successes or the glamorous projects; the teams that take on more lengthy, complex or mundane projects should also be recognized in the same way.

Visibility and Recognition

It is a good practice to schedule a presentation by each improvement team to the senior leadership upon completion of the project. This practice accomplishes several things:

- It helps to maintain a high profile for the improvement projects.
- It reinforces the accountability of the team for the completion of their task—and the accountability of the sponsor for supporting them adequately.
- It provides recognition for the teams.
- It gives senior management a better insight into the projects: the challenges involved and the commitment and motivation of the team members. This type of interaction with the teams will also help senior management to become more effective in their role as sponsors.

MANAGING CHANGE

This book sets out to show how to use assessments as a vehicle for organizational change. With this aim in mind, every step in the assessment process has been designed to support purposeful change, for example: by engaging the key players, by establishing a sharp focus for action, by involving appropriate people in the planning phases, and by communicating clearly to the organization what is about to happen. This groundwork is a vital part of launching any change process, but what happens next as the plans unfold may not be quite what is expected. Anyone who is involved in improving organizational performance needs some knowledge of how to manage change.

Most of the changes proposed should be easy to accept. Some will be welcomed because they address concerns raised by employees, and others will be welcomed because they are clearly the right thing to do and will help the organization to succeed. However, even minor actions that affect people's lives in the workplace will cause some level of stress and concern. And actions that have a significant impact will trigger strong reactions—including serious opposition from some people—even though the end result is beneficial to all.

So people who are involved in leading change—"change agents"—need to understand organizational change as a *social process.* They need to know what reactions to expect from participants and how to help people through a period of transition that is often difficult for everyone involved.

Here are a few basic principles and pointers on how to manage change.

Change is stressful, and it takes time to adjust.

The major challenges in bringing about organizational change have to do with people, not equipment or technology. Here's why:

- Changes that affect people's lives at work are always stressful to those affected.
- The impact of any change on the participants depends upon the extent to which it disrupts their habits, routines, and expectations. Changes that seem minor to management—such as altering the workplace layout, timetables, or team assignments—can feel like major upheavals to those on the receiving end. On the other hand, some changes that seem major to management—perhaps because they involve major technical risks and/or capital investment—may have little impact on people if these do not change how the work is done.

- Both positive and negative changes cause stress and take time to adjust to. For example, being given a lot more responsibility is stressful at first for most people—even those who are actively seeking this type of challenge.
- Each person has to work through a process of adjustment in order to come to terms with the new circumstances and new ways of working. For a change that is negative, typical reactions are denial, then anger, even depression, before finally reaching acceptance. This is a personal, internal process—it can be helped along, but the pace cannot be dictated by others.

The leaders can speed the changes by helping people make this adjustment.

People need support—not confrontation, threats, or exhortations—to help them adjust, and to enable them to contribute to the organizational change. There are many ways for management to provide appropriate support:

- Set up various additional communication channels, including face-to-face dialog, to meet people's greater need for information during times of change.
- Provide timely and honest information about what is going to happen, and especially why. People need to know the rationale and understand why the changes are necessary rather than arbitrary.
- Encourage openness about concerns, and treat these as legitimate issues rather than as "resistance" to the changes.
- Acknowledge the downsides and the losses for certain people, and if possible take steps to recognize and mitigate these.
- Involve people (at every level) in planning their own part of the journey. This involvement helps by fleshing out the overall plan and filling in the essential practical details, as well as giving people some sense of control over the changes within their own areas.

With groups of people, change happens in phases.

When a significant change is proposed, those involved will usually fall into one of three distinct camps: proponents, opponents, and those who don't care very much either way. This is a normal—almost universal—pattern of behavior, since a few people immediately see the benefits to themselves, and a few others immediately feel threatened. The change then unfolds in phases.

During the first phase, the top priority for those leading the change is to support the proponents so they succeed with the changes, and thus provide role models for others. It is vital to ensure that these early adopters succeed, because if they fail no one else will step forward to take their place. At the same time it may be necessary to protect the early efforts from sabotage by entrenched opponents. However, it is a trap for change agents to spend their limited time and energy trying to convert people who will never be persuaded.

The second phase begins once the proponents have achieved some success and no longer need so much support. Now the main task of the change agents is to encourage the undecided. By this time any concerns about the feasibility of the changes, or about management's commitment, should have been overcome. So people who have been sitting on the fence can now see that this new way is not a flavor of the month that is going to disappear soon. Now they want to catch up with the early adopters, and they may need some help to do so.

Often, a few people hold out to the very end and never get on board. If the change is very significant or important to the organization, the final phase is to neutralize entrenched opponents in some appropriate way. This may sound draconian, but it is often essential to ensure that the changes are not undermined by malicious compliance or simply dismantled later. Fortunately this task is often relatively painless: those who are opposed to the changes may actively seek a way out because they feel that they cannot be comfortable working within the new status quo. As these final holdouts leave for other pastures, their places can be taken by people whose thinking is more in tune with the new direction. The transition is now essentially complete.

• • • • •

These are a few of the basics of managing change. However, this topic is too large to do justice to in a few paragraphs, or even in a complete chapter. This is an area for further study, and the website provides more information on this topic.[www]

THE LIFE CYCLE OF AN IMPROVEMENT TEAM

The activities described so far are required to support improvement efforts in general. This section looks at the complete life cycle of a team-based project and shows how the support system just described, focused through the project sponsor, can ensure a successful team effort.

The phases described here apply to any team-based project, regardless of what task the team is undertaking or what methodology it is using. This chapter does *not* go into the detail of how to apply different methodologies; this is a large topic and well beyond the scope of this book.

The typical phases in the life cycle of a successful improvement team are *formation, preparation, execution, completion,* and *holding the gains.* Exhibit 10.3 summarizes the requirements for success during each of these phases.

Formation

When a team is formed to tackle a task, most of the factors that will determine its success or failure are not in the hands of the team members; they are the responsibility of the leaders who initiate the project. Check this list:

- a clear, measurable objective, linked to the organization's goals
- an appropriate mandate for the team
- assignment of a senior person as the sponsor
- selection of a suitable team leader, and then team members with the required capabilities
- allocation of sufficient time and resources
- establishment of a mechanism for regular monitoring of progress through to completion.

All of these decisions should have been made by the leaders—during the planning workshop or shortly afterwards—before the team is even formed.

Exhibit 10.3. *The life cycle of a successful improvement team.*

Phase	Requirements for Success
Formation	• a clear, measurable objective, linked to the organization's goals • an appropriate mandate for the team • assignment of a high-level sponsor • selection of people with the required capabilities • allocation of sufficient time and resources • establishment of a mechanism for regular monitoring and review of progress to completion
Preparation	• choice of suitable methodology and tools • timely provision of training and guidance • development by the team of a game plan
Execution	• access to support resources • effective application of methodology and tools • regular communication, monitoring, and review of progress • removal of barriers by the sponsor • intervention by the sponsor to recover from setbacks
Completion	• recognition of the team's efforts • debriefing, to learn from the team's experience • acknowledgement of the personal development gained
Holding the gains	• assignment of responsibility for ongoing maintenance • regular performance reporting and review

Once the team members have been recruited and signed up, the first step is a briefing meeting for the entire team, including the team leader, with the project sponsor. This is to review the team's formal objectives and mandate. The project sponsor leads the briefing to ensure that everyone understands the objectives, and to establish a link to the team that will remain until the task is complete. The team leader will be reporting to the sponsor on progress and will call for help if the team runs into barriers that it cannot overcome. Everyone involved carries a share of the responsibility, but the project sponsor is accountable for the success of the team.

This meeting is not a one-way conversation; it includes discussions and negotiations. For example, the team may be concerned about objectives that seem unclear, or about the achievability of the time frame, or about workload conflicts with their regular jobs. These concerns need to be resolved. It is the sponsor's responsibility to ensure that the team members go into action clear about their objective and mandate and believing that they have a good chance of success. They also need to be confident that the sponsor will be there for them if they should need help further down the road.

Preparation

Before it can go into action, the team needs to be equipped for the task and to develop a more detailed game plan for the immediate next steps. The team's first working sessions are typically spent:

- receiving training in the approach to be used, if this is new to the team members
- developing their plan.

If the team members are not experienced in the methodology, classroom training at the start is often not sufficient—it may be wise to make a facilitator available to help them stay on track as they work through the process for the first time.

Execution

Once these initial steps have been taken, it is up to the team to get on with it and complete the task. This may take weeks, months, or even longer, and many things can go wrong during this time. The team may run into barriers that it cannot overcome on its own, or it may become stalled due to internal problems or technical difficulties. It is the team leader's responsibility to keep the project sponsor informed, and the sponsor's responsibility to take action when required— for example, to remove barriers.

A good way to ensure that this happens is to ensure that the status of the project is reported regularly to the sponsor in a standard format, for inclusion in the leadership team's formal review meetings.

For a major, long-term project it is also valuable to recognize the accomplishment of intermediate objectives, such as positive identification of the problem or completion of the design for a solution.

Completion

At some point the team will report that it has accomplished its task, and this triggers a new set of actions. The leaders must verify what has been accomplished, recognize the contribution of the team, and formally wind up the project. The leaders will know that the team has been successful, not just because the project milestones have been completed, but because the measurements of success are beginning to demonstrate this. For example, error rates have been slashed, costs and cycle times have been reduced, or customers have stopped complaining about a particular issue.

It is also invaluable at this stage to debrief the team on its experience (lessons learned), and to capture this information for improvement purposes.

A presentation to the leadership team upon completion of the project is a good way of accomplishing many of these tasks: verifying successful completion, recognizing the team, and getting feedback about their experience.

Sometimes the team members have been assigned more or less full time to the project, in which case there may be a reentry issue. The value of the experience gained by team members should be recognized, for example, in future career-development decisions. The leaders must strive to ensure that participation in improvement projects is seen as an opportunity, not a punishment. It will be much easier to sign up capable people for future projects if employees view this as beneficial to their careers as well as their job satisfaction.

Holding the Gains

The team's task may be complete—and the problem solved for the moment—but leadership's task is not over.

Key Point
In order to hold the gains, it is essential to ensure that the solutions that the team has put in place are not lost over time.

The most effective way of achieving this is to ensure proper integration of the improvements into an existing system of process management—for example, by:

- Confirming who is the "process owner—the person who has an ongoing responsibility for the performance of a process.
- Cementing the arrangements for ongoing measurements of process performance and regular reporting of these measurements.

Process ownership cannot be applied effectively in an ad hoc fashion or as an afterthought. It is a key component of an organization-wide *process management* strategy. Process management typically requires significant changes to the way that the leadership team operates—for example, coordinating efforts across departmental and functional boundaries in a way that is very different from traditional management practice.

If your leadership team has not yet started down the path toward process management, the concept of a "process owner" may not be of much help. But it's essential to assign ongoing maintenance responsibilities somehow—regardless of how you organize this—so that the gains that have been won through so much diligent effort will not be lost again through simple neglect.

CHECK POINTS

You will know that implementation is succeeding if your situation looks more like "success" than "failure" as described in the following table:

Success	Failure
The improvement teams get off to a good start, with appropriate team members assigned, proper briefing of the teams, and work started quickly.	The improvement teams are formed in a haphazard fashion, are not clear about their objectives, and many of the team members assigned lack the necessary skills or motivation.
The improvement project sponsors continue to take a close interest in "their" teams.	The improvement project sponsors are preoccupied by new priorities, forget about the teams, and assume that "no news is good news."
Formal reviews of progress are conducted as planned, track achievement against the milestones, and stay focused on the original intent of the plans.	Progress reviews are sporadic, focused only on certain teams, and are comprised of upbeat presentations, often without reference to the original objective.
Implementation problems are brought forward readily, during the formal reviews as well as off-line with the project sponsors.	The leaders are aware of few implementation problems, perhaps because they have little solid information about the progress of the teams.
When problems occur, the leaders offer constructive support and help to remove barriers for the teams.	When problems are discovered, the team is blamed for the lack of progress and criticized for not seeking help earlier.
Most of the improvement teams are making good progress and expect to achieve their goals.	Some of the improvement teams appear to be making good progress, but it is not clear whether these teams will achieve the stated goals. Some teams seem to have quit or "gone into hiding."
There is a general awareness throughout the organization of what is being done and why. People can see that "something is happening" as a result of their input.	A lack of visible follow-through seems to have proven the skeptics right again: "nothing ever changes around here."

• • • • •

^{www}Companion Website Materials:

- Managing change: recommended reading
- Dr. W. Edwards Deming: recommended reading
- Statistical Process Control (SPC)
- More on measurement
- An Introduction to Hoshin Planning

 **Chapter 11**

Closing the Loop

Visitor to New York: "Excuse me, how can I get to Carnegie Hall?"
Reply: "Practice, practice, practice!"

Based upon the results of a successful first assessment, the leaders will usually give serious consideration to repeating the process at some time in the future. Some will go further than this, by making a long-term commitment to integrate assessment into the annual planning cycle and to link it to the achievement of the organization's vision.

CHAPTER CONTENTS

- The closed-loop improvement cycle
- Steps in closing the loop
- Debriefing after the first assessment cycle
- Developing a vision
- Planning the next assessment
- Check points
- The journey ahead

• • • • •

THE CLOSED-LOOP IMPROVEMENT CYCLE

With the first assessment successfully completed and the improvement teams setting about their work, there will soon be some tangible results to celebrate. However, this is just a promising start, like going once to the gym. It takes more than one workout to become fit and healthy, and it takes a sustained training regime to become a winner.

World-class athletes don't just go to the gym frequently; they are constantly studying and refining their fitness regime and everything else that contributes to their performance. In order to find that extra centimeter or hundredth of a second, they study everything: mental preparation, diet, and equipment, understanding what the best competitors are doing. During the past several decades, athletic world records have been broken again and again as new generations of athletes improve on past performances. This isn't because the human body has changed; it's mainly because so much more is known about all of the factors that make for high performance, and athletes have much better methods, techniques, and equipment available to them.

A well-conducted assessment, followed by effective action, is a valuable step forward. But there is much to be gained by repeating the process, perhaps at regular intervals. Although it is a major step to take, committing to an *annual* assessment cycle has some valuable benefits. This commitment:

- guarantees that the annual operating plan will always contain an improvement component
- provides greater assurance of effective action on the vital few, because the next assessment acts as a milestone and a progress check
- creates more opportunity for refreshing and fine-tuning the assessment process itself, and integrating it seamlessly into the business planning process.

Not every organization that conducts an assessment decides to make such a commitment. Some choose the flexibility of deciding whether and when to repeat the assessment process and some choose to drive their improvement efforts in other ways. However, this chapter is for organizations that choose to "close the loop" by establishing a regular cycle of assessments, in order to drive ongoing change and improvement year after year.

What does "closing the loop" mean? It means studying closely the effects of our actions, and using this feedback to learn and improve so that we can do better next time. This concept can and should be applied to all management actions, from simple tasks such as developing a presentation to complex ones like developing a strategic plan. It should be applied to the implementation of the vital few action plans. (See Exhibit 11.1.)

This concept can also be applied to the entire management system by using the assessment process to reexamine the "big picture" periodically, to gauge the effectiveness of efforts to improve, and to identify the levers for further improvement.

By using the assessment process in this way, the leaders can:

- Verify that the business plans and the improvement plans have been implemented.
- Study the results these actions produce.
- Learn from this experience what worked well and what did not.
- Identify ways to build on what has already been accomplished.
- Develop plans to achieve further performance gains through incremental improvement or breakthroughs.

Exhibit 11.1. *The closed-loop improvement cycle.*

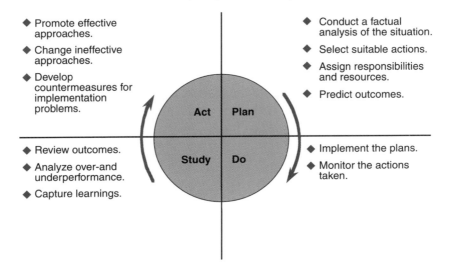

STEPS IN CLOSING THE LOOP

If the decision is made to move from a one-time assessment into a cyclical process, the following steps need to be taken:

- *Debrief after the first assessment cycle,* to understand what worked well and what didn't within the assessment process itself, so that the next cycle can be even better organized and more effective.
- *Develop a vision for the assessment process, linked to the organization's vision.* The leaders will only commit themselves to using the assessment process if this will help them to achieve their vision for the organization.
- *Plan for the second (and future) assessments.* The second assessment may be more streamlined and better integrated than the first one, and future assessments will need to become more rigorous as the organization's approach to improvement becomes more mature.

The following sections describe what's involved in each of these steps.

DEBRIEFING AFTER THE FIRST ASSESSMENT CYCLE

It is essential to debrief the key participants in the assessment to find out how well the process worked from their perspective. You can do this at a suitable juncture—for example, at the end of the planning workshop—simply by taking a few moments to discuss as a group what worked well and what didn't, while capturing the main points on a flipchart. The key output from this feedback is positive identification of *what do we need to do differently next time.*

These conclusions—as well as the assessment process design—should be documented for the benefit of the process sponsor and the next assessment team, so that they can understand the original process and the rationale for changes. Without such documentation, this valuable knowledge is easily lost when key players move on; a new assessment process sponsor may introduce changes that seem like good ideas, unaware that these changes reverse some carefully-designed improvements.

DEVELOPING A VISION

For the assessment process to be *useful,* it has to support the leaders' vision for the organization. For the assessment process to remain *effective,* there must be a shared understanding of this linkage and of how the assessment process will evolve to meet future needs.

Here are some areas to explore in order to make these connections:

- The relationship between the organization's vision, the management principles, and the criteria. There should be some clear linkages. For example, the vision may call for increasing market share. Improving customer satisfaction and loyalty would surely help.
- The need to define and measure excellence. Many organizations have declared aspirations like "become world-class" or "be the best," but they have no definition of what this means, and no way of measuring whether it is being achieved. The criteria provide an operational definition of what a world-class management system looks like, and the assessment process provides a way to measure progress toward this goal.
- The desire for recognition. This book makes a strong case for avoiding a common pitfall: getting focused on recognition *at the expense of results.* But why not go for both? If the game plan is to become world-class in terms of performance excellence, why not collect the awards and the kudos available to organizations that accomplish this? Winning a local or national award provides a wonderful morale booster, a validation that you are on the right track, and a great marketing tool.

By exploring these issues with the leadership team, you may end up with something like this:

- a vision for the organization that incorporates the idea of world-class performance (as defined by the criteria)

- measurements of progress that include assessment scores and receipt of certain awards (internal, then state/provincial, then perhaps even national)
- a long-term strategy that includes using the assessment process to plot a course and to measure progress.

Of course, this will require making the assessment process more searching as the organization becomes more mature. This is like adding iron to the barbell: you will never become really strong by lifting the same puny weights. Fortunately, you already know exactly how to beef up the assessment.

PLANNING THE NEXT ASSESSMENT

When the first assessment is complete, discussions and plans for the next one should begin right away, including both the short and longer term. This discussion and planning accomplishes the following:

- It flushes out any as-yet-unspoken concerns among the leaders about the process. These concerns can be surfaced while they are fresh in people's minds and addressed in the plan.
- It reveals where converts have been gained—leaders who were skeptics but are now convinced that this is the way to go.
- It sends a signal to anyone who is sitting on their hands, waiting for the assessment process to go away. A second assessment suggests that this may be more than just a passing fad.
- It puts a stake in the ground and creates a sense of urgency for the improvement teams and their sponsors. The next assessment (when these projects will be scrutinized) is no longer a distant possibility, but a certainty that is not too far off.

• • • • •

The Second Assessment

It is important to *plan* the next assessment thoughtfully, not just to switch onto autopilot and perform a rerun of the first one. Even if the first assessment seemed to work perfectly, some changes will be essential the second time around. For example, the method of engaging and preparing the leaders at the start needs to change—you cannot simply repeat the executive briefing session in the same format.

Consider some of the following changes that may be desirable for a second or subsequent assessment:

Acting Visibly on the Debriefing Feedback   It's important for the assessment process owner to act visibly on the feedback obtained from participants in the first assessment. This not only leads to worthwhile improvements in the process—it also provides a role model for the owners of other management processes to emulate.

Doing this "visibly" simply means telling people what changes have been made, and explaining how these respond to the feedback that they provided.

Using a Progressively More Thorough Approach   A more in-depth assessment may be needed, especially if the first assessment was rather superficial, or if the management system is significantly more mature. A more thorough approach will enable the participants to continue learning from the process and to generate opportunities for improvement that are more precisely defined.

Testing Implementation of the Previous Vital Few   During a second or subsequent assessment, the assessment team's mandate clearly allows it to examine the implementation of the previous vital few. However, this should not be done just in passing. It is valuable to give these improvement projects special emphasis and scrutiny: to look at *all* of them, to find out *in detail* what has been done, to examine the results obtained, and to compare them with the original objectives.

Scrutinizing the previous vital few is important for the following reasons:

- They are important issues; so important that they were identified as the top priorities for improvement during the previous assessment. If the improvement plans have not been implemented, or have not been effective, then these issues are probably still the top priorities.

- Management decided to act on them. If the leadership team has not been able to maintain a focus on these priorities, what have they been doing instead for the past year? Are the mechanisms to support follow-through weak, have they become distracted by other events, or is it simply a lack of resolve?
- Assessments without action are worthless. To continue in this way is like repeatedly checking the temperature in a cold room, hoping for more warmth—but not lighting the fire. In fact, it's worse than that.

Key Point

Assessments that do not lead to action are damaging. Not only do they consume valuable time and energy for no purpose; the lack of any visible outcome damages management's credibility and demoralizes employees.

One way of scrutinizing the vital few—in addition to asking the leaders about what has been done—is to perform group interviews with some of the teams assigned to these projects.

Reengaging the Leaders The leadership team must be reengaged and prepared specifically for each assessment—but in an appropriate way. Clearly, it would be a mistake simply to repeat the initial executive briefing workshop in the same format. However, it would also be a mistake to assume that the leaders all understand and are fully committed because most of them have been through the process a year ago.

This reengagement is not just about preparing people for the assessment process. The entire improvement journey is a learning process: when the learning stops, so do the performance improvements. So senior management need to demonstrate leadership by setting the pace as learners.

Here are some ideas on how to help them accomplish this:

- Promote the idea of ongoing education of the leadership team (and others) in continuous improvement principles and methods.

- Maximize the learning opportunities available during the assessment process itself—for example, the leaders may conduct their own self-assessment (for comparison with the findings of external experts) and may personally explain the assessment findings to the organization.
- Consistently use the criteria categories—leadership, planning, customer focus, and so on—as the overall context for learning. Virtually everything that there is to know about managing an organization can fit into this type of framework.
- Choose learning topics that provide different perspectives, going deeply into specific categories, and making comparisons with certain best practices used by others.
- Study specific award-winning organizations, perhaps establishing a relationship and meeting with some of their management.

If this type of broad-based learning is going on, the preparation required by the leaders before each assessment may be quite simple:

- a reminder of the assessment schedule and process steps, highlighting any changes made since last year (and the reasons why)
- a reminder of their roles and responsibilities.

Using Documentation from Previous Assessments   After the first assessment, there is always documentation available from the previous cycle. This can be used to advantage in a number of ways:

- A previous application report can be used as a basis for assessor training, as an alternative to a hypothetical case study. This will only work if the organization has put in place some of the fundamental mechanisms of a management system. Until it reaches this stage, the application report will not have enough substance to serve as a useful case study.
- The previous assessment report can also be used during training to illustrate the types of findings that emerged before.

- The previous assessment report can be used as an input to the assessment—with some care to avoid creating a bias. For example, after the preliminary assessment is done, it may be useful to review the previous year's assessment report as a sanity check, to ensure that nothing major has been overlooked, and to identify any apparent contradictions.

What to Do When Follow-Through Has Been Weak

Sometimes there is inadequate follow-through after an assessment, and the vital few are never fully implemented. This lack of follow-through may be due to major events that have radically changed the situation and management's priorities. However, such inaction is more often caused by problems in the way that the leadership team functions. Perhaps the leaders have been too superficial in their monitoring of progress; perhaps they have allowed their attention to be diverted onto other priorities. The assessment team must try to understand what has been going on and paint this picture in its assessment report.

If it is clear even before the assessment begins that little work has been done on the vital few, it may not make sense to continue as originally planned. Here are some ideas for other possible approaches:

- Ask the leadership team to reconfirm its decision to use the assessment process. If the leaders' actions suggest that they have changed their minds, it would be better to call a halt now than to continue with a process that will become a charade.
- If the leaders want to continue, discuss some preconditions that need to be met in order to make this a worthwhile exercise—for example, some degree of visible progress on the previous vital few—and consider rescheduling the assessment.

- Narrow the scope of the assessment drastically, to investigate only certain management processes—for example, the operational review process and leadership decision-making—that are supposed to ensure the implementation of the plans.

Two final points about weak follow-through:

Key Point
A lack of action on the vital few should never come as a surprise late in the cycle.

If the assessment process sponsor is alert, and if the planning workshop addressed the follow-through issues properly, then the leaders should have been tracking progress on the vital few improvement plans from the start, to identify any problems or delays promptly.

Key Point
Some leadership teams just don't have what it takes to pull this off.

Regardless of how good their tools are, these teams will not succeed in using the assessment process properly—or in implementing any form of continuous improvement. The reasons for this usually have less to do with ability or management processes, and more to do with attitude and character.

As explained in Chapter 3, it is foolish and irresponsible to encourage leaders to use this process at all if they seem unlikely to succeed, since this will only cause damage to the organization. One of the unspoken aims of the leadership briefing workshop should be to help such organizations screen themselves out—by giving senior management a very realistic view of the magnitude of the task and the commitment required.

Other Issues

There are two other issues that need to be considered in a different light after the first assessment:

- *Integration with the normal planning process.* The assessment process is much more likely to become a routine—and the findings used effectively—if it is integrated into the normal planning cycle. This is partly a timing issue. Suitable timing will enable the vital few objectives to be routinely incorporated into the business plan and the leadership team's personal objectives. This timing may not have been the most important consideration when planning the first assessment. However, for subsequent assessments, achieving this linkage with the planning process becomes critical; without it, the assessment process will be less effective and less likely to endure.

- *Assignment of assessment team members.* It is good practice to include in the next assessment team some members of the previous team. The team leader in particular should have previous experience of the process. It is also desirable to have some "new blood"—in order to provide a fresh perspective, and to include people who can benefit from this development experience.

CHECK POINTS

You will know that you are closing the loop with an integrated assessment process when you begin to see the following signs of success:

Success	Failure
People discuss how the assessment can be improved and the best timing for the process.	People are still debating whether the assessment should be done at all.
The assessment is seen as a feature of how the organization operates and an integral part of the planning cycle.	The assessment is seen as a distinct event, separate from normal planning and budgeting.
The vital few improvement projects are a routine feature of the business plan.	The vital few improvement projects are a novel add-on and are not viewed as part of the business plan.
The assessment process continues to evolve to meet the changing needs of the organization.	The assessment process is static, and the design is considered a "given" rather than a topic for decision-making.

• • • • •

THE JOURNEY AHEAD

For any organization to come this far is a major accomplishment, and cause for celebration. But the assessment process is just a means of striving toward an end: sustainable improvements in organizational performance. Are you succeeding by this ultimate measure? You will know that you are making progress on the improvement journey when:

- Strong mechanisms are being established that make for a more effective management system: effective processes for understanding and retaining customers, systems for developing and empowering employees, methods of developing business processes that are streamlined and robust.

- These improvements are beginning to drive improved performance, perhaps in pockets at first—small operations that are visibly improved—then flowing through into a few important but small-scale performance improvements, and then into improvements on a scale large enough that the overall results begin to take off.
- Management reviews continually reveal progress: measurable results exhibit favorable trends, customer satisfaction, employee morale. Bottom line performance—whether this is profit-oriented or the achievement of a social mandate—is improving steadily.
- A sense of self-confidence is developing, flowing from the year-on-year performance gains being achieved. People begin to realize that they can make changes that result in different outcomes—that they are in control of their own destiny rather than at the mercy of circumstances.
- Striving to be the best is no longer just a vague ideal, but a tangible goal, pursued by means of well-defined work practices. Working toward excellence—and improving the bottom-line results—is just a normal part of "how we do things around here."

If you have accomplished all of this, well done! You can take the rest of the day off.

• • • • •

The vision described here is not a pipe dream—it has been accomplished by many organizations. The case studies that follow provide some inspirational examples.

• • • • •

ᵂᵂᵂCompanion Website Materials:

- Additional case studies

 # Chapter 12

Case Studies

The purpose of this chapter is to provide some insight into the real-life experience of a variety of organizations and to share the perspectives of people who are using the assessment process. Many outstanding organizations could be profiled here. We have selected just a few that represent a slice of the North American economy:

- Xerox Corporation
- TELUS Mobility
- Medrad
- Cargill
- Pinellas County School District

They all have two things in common. All are highly successful organizations. And all are pioneers in the use of the assessment process—they adopted this approach long before most of their peers. We should be grateful that they were prepared to take this initial risk, because they have beaten a trail that is now well defined and safe for others to follow.

These organizations are not perfect: they do not "walk on water", and like their peers, they are affected by many external factors beyond their control. Although their management systems have served them well, there is no formula that can guarantee future success or even survival. As the research studies indicate, the benefit of effective management practices is to improve the odds significantly.

XEROX CORPORATION

Profile

Xerox Corporation provides a wide range of products and services related to document processing on paper and in digital form. These include copiers, printers, and enterprise document management systems, as well as outsourcing of the document management function. Xerox Corporation operates in North America; its affiliate companies operate on every continent. Sales revenues in 1998 were $19.4 billion, and the number of employees worldwide exceeds 90,000.

THE XEROX STORY

Everyone knows about Xerox (the photocopier company), and most people are familiar with the new face of Xerox as "The Document Company." Many people are aware that Xerox had some bad years back in the 1980s and then bounced back. What most people don't know is that in the field of quality management, Xerox is a legend and a role model for others to emulate. Everyone who begins to study quality management soon learns about the Xerox story. It's a great story and well worth retelling, so here it is again in a nutshell.

The Rise and Fall

The emergence of Xerox during the 1960s resembled in some ways that of Microsoft in the 1990s: here was a tiny outfit that sprang out of nowhere and grew rapidly to become a huge, highly profitable corporation and a household name.

In 1959 Xerox launched a revolutionary plain-paper copier based on xerography, a new technology that it had developed. This unique product took off and created a new market that Xerox owned by virtue of its strong patents. This new market seemed limitless: sales reached $1 billion in 1968 and kept growing to $9 billion. In 1981 the company made record *profits* of more than $1 billion. Given this stunning success story, it was natural that Xerox came to be admired as an icon representing the best of corporate America.

However, the seeds of the company's downfall had already been sown. During most of its early existence, Xerox had no effective competition. Management was very successful in managing rapid, sustained growth, fueled by insatiable demand. But the company's monopoly position provided little incentive to focus on satisfying customers, or to find ways of running the business more efficiently. High profit margins were sustained simply by raising prices, and captive customers had little alternative but to pay up. This situation couldn't last forever.

During the 1970s the tide slowly began to turn against Xerox. Its patent protection was lost, and competition began to spring up. This came from IBM and from Kodak—two corporate giants that Xerox feared—but also from an unexpected quarter. Barely noticed by Xerox at first, Japanese companies began to sell low-end photocopiers in the U.S. at bargain basement prices—lower than Xerox's manufacturing cost for comparable machines.

The financial impact of competition and of Xerox's inefficiency was not evident at first, but in spite of the rosy financial results, the company was actually losing ground throughout the 1970s. Market share steadily declined, and competition also drove down prices, eating into Xerox's margins. For a while the company managed to maintain profitability by selling off its vast base of leased machines. Propped up in this way, profits soared to a record high in 1981, although the company was by then in a very serious situation.

By 1982 the lease base was largely sold off, the façade collapsed, and profits fell by almost 50 percent. By then the company's market share of shipments in the U.S. had fallen to a meager 15 percent. This was an astonishing downfall for a proud industry leader.

This situation was not unique in the U.S. at that time; foreign competitors were grabbing market share in many industries. After decades of operating in a booming seller's market, many segments of U.S. industry had become bloated, inefficient and complacent, and they were easy targets for smart, efficient competitors.

What set Xerox apart was the way in which the company responded to this threat: not by running for government subsidies or seeking trade barriers, not by panicking or giving up. Instead Xerox faced up to its own shortcomings and set out to beat its competitors through skill and competence.

The Awakening

Xerox management had already known for some time that the company was in serious trouble. After a period of denial and blaming "unfair" competition, the company began to study its foreign competitors seriously in 1979. The results were terrifying.

Detailed comparative studies revealed that:

- In the USA, Xerox's ratio of indirect to direct workers was twice that of its best Japanese competitor.
- Xerox used almost double the number of workers to develop a new product, and it took nearly three times as long to bring new products to the marketplace.
- Xerox product defect levels were seven to ten times higher than those of its Japanese competitors.

The Japanese companies' finely tuned design and production methods resulted in excellent product quality *and* remarkably low costs—a combination that seemed contradictory according to conventional wisdom. In fact, the Japanese were making solid profits on the low-price copiers that Xerox thought were being "dumped." And although inexpensive, these copiers were not shoddy junk that customers would soon tire of, but well-designed and well-built products that would help build customer confidence and loyalty.

Although Xerox didn't know this at the time, the problem was even greater than these huge performance gaps indicated. The Japanese were increasing their lead rapidly: Their methods of continuous improvement were creating productivity gains of about 12 percent per annum. Xerox would need to improve at an even faster rate in order to catch up.

During 1982, Xerox's newly appointed CEO David Kearns spent considerable time in Japan, learning first-hand about the competition and their methods. Much of this learning came from Xerox's Japanese affiliate, Fuji-Xerox, which had faced this new competition much earlier and had already accomplished a remarkable turnaround using similar methods. Kearns became convinced that the entire Xerox Corporation had to travel this same journey in order to survive. David Kearns' leadership—and his unwavering conviction and persistence—were to be essential to Xerox's successful renewal over the next decade.

The Plan

Ironically, just as spectacular success had sown the seed of Xerox's failure, catastrophic decline sowed the seeds of the company's rebirth. Through a process of studying itself and its competitors, Xerox had come to understand in detail how its approach to doing business was failing, and why the huge performance gaps existed. Some key people now understood that this was largely due to the superior methods that others were using. Through good fortune, a few potential "change agents" had been exposed to quality management, and they had gained experience through their early stumbling efforts to apply these new methods. And the visible decline of the company eventually drove home the compelling need for change, even to the most complacent. David Kearns, convinced of the destination but unsure how to get there, commissioned a team to develop a quality-based vision and improvement strategy. These were set out in the now famous "Green Book."

Thus Xerox embarked in 1983 on *"Leadership Through Quality."* This was one of the most ambitious corporate renewals ever attempted—and one of the most carefully planned. The Green Book, which documents *Leadership Through Quality*, served as the foundation of Xerox's improvement efforts for the next decade and beyond.

Although the plan was sound, execution was a great struggle. The Green Book called for the transformation to take place in phases and to be completed within five years. It took much longer. David Kearns later observed, "On paper the plan seemed well-paced and eminently appealing. We would never come close to matching that timetable." But although progress seemed slow, the plan did work. As early as 1987 the slide toward oblivion had been reversed. There was still a tremendous amount of work to be done, but it became clear that Xerox was at last on a path that could lead eventually to a full recovery. The challenge now was to stick with it, to keep the improvement process alive, and to step up the pace.

The Development of the Assessment Process at Xerox

Hungry for ways to intensify its efforts, Xerox began to use the assessment process in some parts of the company and to apply for quality awards in order to obtain external validation and feedback. In this way Xerox divisions won several quality awards in Europe: the Netherlands in 1984, the U.K. in 1985, and France in 1987. Then in 1989 the U.S. corporation applied for and won the recently established Baldrige award. Based on experience acquired in this way, Xerox embraced the assessment process and designed its own assessment model and methodology. It did this brilliantly, in a way that would support the continuance and the vitality of its improvement efforts.

The steps leading up to this were a series of learning experiences:

- The team that prepared Xerox's submission for the Baldrige award in 1989 discovered a large number of areas for improvement (513 so-called warts). These were later distilled into a few key issues that became the basis for an "intensification" effort. This assessment far surpassed previous efforts to obtain a reading on the progress of *Leadership Through Quality,* and the findings were a real wake-up call. Thus management discovered that this type of structured, comprehensive self-examination was an excellent way to reveal what was really going on, identify new opportunities for improvement, and reinforce their improvement efforts.

- Although the original principles and plan were well designed and structured, many initiatives had been added since as overlays. So the improvement efforts began to look like a laundry list of separate programs rather than the components of an integrated strategy.

- During the late '80s and early '90s, many new senior managers were hired from other companies. These people, who had not lived through the early part of the journey, found it very difficult to understand *Leadership Through Quality,* and the "old hands" struggled to find a good way of explaining it to these newcomers.

So the following inspired decisions were made:

1. To develop an operational definition of Leadership Through Quality—a model that would describe Xerox's approach and make it clear to anyone.
2. To use this model as a diagnostic tool for examining how well Leadership Through Quality was being implemented.
3. To incorporate this diagnosis into the annual business planning cycle. (Xerox was at that time developing a comprehensive, company-wide business planning system based on Hoshin Planning.)

The Assessment Process at Xerox

Since our focus here is on the assessment process, we will take a much closer look at Xerox's methodology. Here is how it works.

Every year, each business entity within Xerox uses the assessment process during the early stages of its business planning process. The assessment results are used to identify improvement priorities, and the resulting improvement plans become part of the business plan for that group. This process is applied worldwide and at several levels—from major divisions down to individual departments.

The assessment is guided by the Xerox Management Model (see Exhibit 12.1).

This model reflects Xerox's experience with various external criteria such as Baldrige and EFQM, but it is unique and very much geared to Xerox's approach. The model depicts Xerox's management system as five groups of management practices, plus a group of desired business results.

The individual practices are usually defined quite specifically in terms of Xerox's own processes, methodologies, and tools. For example, the Leadership category contains a practice called "Managing for Results"—Xerox's name for its own Hoshin Planning methodology. This methodology has a special feature built in: it specifies that the planning cycle is to include an assessment using the Xerox Management Model. For each practice, the model also

Exhibit 12.1.   *The Xerox Management Model.*

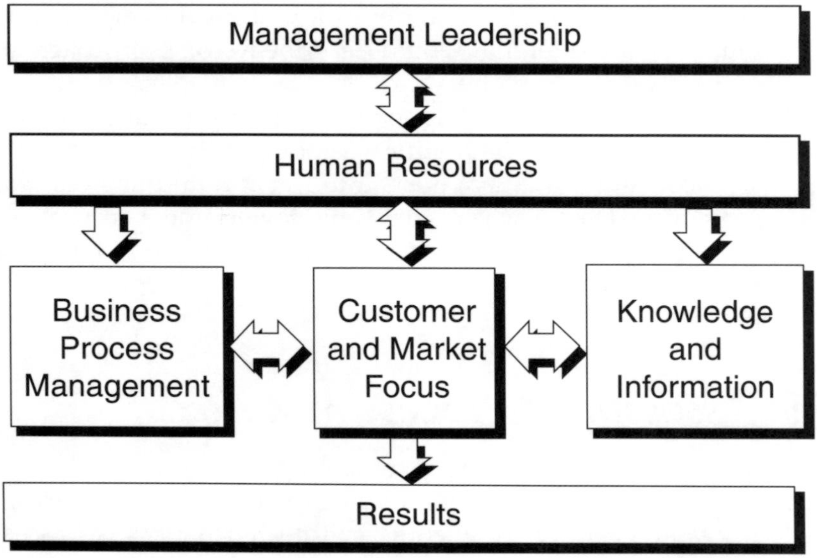

defines a desired state and identifies the relevant processes and measurements of performance.

The planning cycle begins with self-assessment, and it is conducted within a business entity as follows:

1. Information about each management practice in the model is summarized in a predefined storyboard format (see Exhibit 12.2). The storyboard shows how the business entity is implementing and improving this practice, what's working well and what isn't, where the causes lie, and a performance measurement for the practice.

2. The assembled information is reviewed by the management team of the business entity, and a consensus score is arrived at for each element of the model. This process generates discussion where there are significant differences of opinion, so that additional information can be shared.

3. A small number of these practices are selected as the vital few for improvement, based upon which will have the greatest impact on the objectives of the business entity.

Exhibit 12.2.   *Xerox Assessment Summary format.*

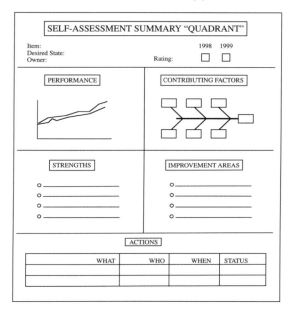

4. A systematic root cause analysis is conducted to determine the main reasons for the gap between desired and actual performance. This is done using the standard Xerox problem-solving methodology, with its supporting tools and techniques.

5. Fact-based analysis and investigation are used to determine how best to close the gap and to prioritize the actions selected. Improvement goals are also set, based upon the predicted effect of these actions.

6. The resulting plans and improvement goals are incorporated into the business plan. The business plan goals are then "cascaded" within the business entity, so that everyone learns about them, and people take on personal goals that are linked to the business goals.

7. As the plans are implemented, regular management reviews are used to examine progress toward the goals, and this information is widely communicated.

8. The cycle repeats.

There is also a validation step to confirm that the assessment process is being implemented properly. Typically, two senior managers from other entities visit after the assessment is complete and conduct a review of the results.

Features of Xerox's Approach to Assessment

Here are some of the notable features of the Xerox system:

- *Customized criteria*
  The Xerox Management Model is highly customized to Xerox's own approach and is therefore more detailed and much more prescriptive than frameworks such as Baldrige or the European Quality Award.
- *Controlled evolution of the criteria*
  Having developed its own model, Xerox can refine and develop it over time to meet its own needs—thus the model is considered "evergreen." In practice it has only required occasional changes. Baldrige is also frequently refined (usually annually), but for a much more diverse audience.
- *Universal application*
  Virtually all of the major initiatives that Xerox launched during its improvement journey were applied first by senior management and then across the entire company, worldwide. The same has been true for the Managing for Results process and the Xerox Management Model. Every major business entity is expected and required to use the process, although they have flexibility in how to go about it. Over 100 business entities within Xerox have used the assessment process.
- *Role-modeling and participation by the leaders*
  Senior management, starting with Xerox top management, are not simply spectators or recipients of the reports, but participate actively in the process and provide role models for other levels of management. In 1999 the assessment process

had been conducted by the senior management team (comprising the CEO and his direct reports) for six consecutive years. Paul Allaire, chairman of Xerox Corporation, describes the Xerox Management Model very simply: "This is how we run our business."

- *Strong use of measurements*
  There is at least one performance measurement associated with each of the elements of the Xerox Management Model. By virtue of using this model, Xerox has dozens of nonfinancial measurements that predict financial results. Although there is extensive use of measurements in the model, the main purpose of the assessment is not measurement but planning. The measurements help to pinpoint practices that are not working well, and they are invaluable for examining whether the improvement plans are having the desired effect.

  Unlike the various national quality awards, there is no overall score, only scores for individual elements. The "real" score may be thought of as the business results achieved.

- *Action planning based upon thorough analysis and use of tools*
  Once the vital few have been identified, the owner of each must conduct a thorough root cause analysis, prioritize possible solutions, establish a plan, and project the expected results of the improvement plan. This is all done using standardized Xerox methods and tools.

- *Process ownership*
  Typically, each of the management practices identified in the Xerox Management Model has an owner, usually a senior manager. Thus the Xerox Management Model is also used as a template for assigning responsibilities for the components of the management system. Since these are nearly all highly cross-functional processes, these responsibilities reinforce cross-functional cooperation among senior management.

- *Closed-loop planning system*
  By integrating the assessment into the annual planning cycle, Xerox has created and institutionalized a powerful closed-loop system of planning and implementation, which embraces the entire management system.

The Results

The results of Xerox's efforts are easy to summarize: after more than 15 years of sustained, systematic improvement, Xerox is now a very different company. It is a formidable competitor: agile, efficient, and close to its customers. It has regained much of the market share that it originally lost. It is staying ahead in an era of rapid change. It is profitable and growing. Instead of struggling just to stay alive, it is now stretching itself to fulfill great ambitions. As Xerox's own management describes it, the company has moved from a crisis of survival to a crisis of opportunity.

References

Several excellent books and many articles have been written about Xerox's transformation. The following is some suggested reading.

Recommended Xerox References	
Prophets in the Dark: How Xerox Reinvented Itself And Beat Back The Japanese David T. Kearns and David A. Nadler. Harper Business	An engaging and candid account of the Xerox story, from the creation of xerography by an eccentric kitchen-table inventor to the company's battle for survival during the 1980s. An insider's view from the cockpit during the most critical years, and a good read.
A World of Quality: The Timeless Passport Xerox Quality Services	Written by a team of Xerox people, this book provides a technically oriented account of Xerox's journey, complete with descriptions of the methodologies and tools, and excerpts from Xerox's 1989 submission for the Baldrige award.
Xerox 2000: From Survival to Opportunity Article from *Quality Progress,* March 1996	This article provides a detailed, authoritative description of how the Xerox Management Model and assessment process support the new Xerox 2000 strategy. Written by one of the team that developed the company's assessment system.

Acknowledgements

Our thanks to Xerox Corporation and the following Xerox people who provided valuable input to this case study: Bill Campbell, Brian Cox, Dick Leo, and Bob Osterhoff.

TELUS MOBILITY

Profile
TELUS Mobility is a provider of wireless services—principally cellular and paging—within the Canadian provinces of Alberta and British Columbia. Its main business activities include marketing and sales (through a dealer network), development and maintenance of the wireless network, and customer support (through its call centers). Following a merger with BC Mobility in 1999, TELUS Mobility has about 1500 employees, sales revenues of about CDN $900 million, and more than one million subscribers.   The following case study covers the period up to this merger.

THE TELUS MOBILITY STORY

This is the story of TELUS Mobility, a Canadian success story. Starting from modest beginnings in 1991, TELUS Mobility has come to dominate its primary market in the face of strong competition. It has achieved this through sustained, profitable growth, fueled by high customer satisfaction and loyalty.

In 1991 the company was a tiny division of the Alberta telephone company, employing about 50 people and providing traditional radio services. A new president, Harry Truderung, was appointed with the mandate of refocusing the business to exploit the emerging cellular market.

Truderung's views on how to accomplish this were strongly influenced by some previous experiences. He had taken part in study tours to Japan to visit leading companies practicing what they called Total Quality Control (TQC), and he had been impressed by what he saw. He had also participated in a failed quality improvement initiative with a previous company. This debacle had not detracted from his belief in the approach, but had given him insight into some possible failure modes. He was attracted to the idea of Baldrige-based assessments because he viewed the criteria as an industry-standard yardstick for total quality. From the very first assessment in 1992, he was committed to using this process in the long term to help drive the company's improvement efforts.

The First Assessment

The first assessment took place in 1992. The main strength that emerged from the assessment was a strong focus on customers; the company had already developed a fairly effective system of customer and market listening.

The assessors were also impressed by the strong senior management commitment to a quality-based approach, and by the fact that they had started down this path at such an early stage—the company had only existed since October 1990, and the new management team had only recently been appointed.

However, the assessment also revealed significant shortcomings. The management style was perceived to be top down, with little opportunity for employees to provide input or feedback. The company lacked effective methods for managing business processes and so was managed almost exclusively in departmental or functional "silos." There were many gaps in the information system, and the information that existed was not aggregated or analyzed enough to support fact-based decision-making. In the area of business results, the information available mostly pointed toward industry-average performance.

In summary, TELUS Mobility looked very much like thousands of other respectable but strictly average companies—capable of meeting industry norms but definitely not capable of exceptional performance.

The Journey

Between 1992 and 1998 TELUS Mobility reexamined and overhauled almost every aspect of its management system. For example:

- The leadership team's management style, their approach to communication, and their methods of monitoring progress were all targets for change and improvement.
- The methods of listening to customers and understanding market needs were refined and expanded.
- The information and measurements used to monitor the business were altered to provide a more complete and balanced view.

- A "Key Business Driver" model was developed—a kind of cause-and-effect diagram—in order to understand better what internal factors have the most impact on business results.
- The methods of analysis were changed to provide better support for planning and decision-making.
- The planning process was revamped to achieve a more integrated business plan and to allow more rapid response to external changes in this rapidly changing marketplace.
- A structure and methodology for process management was introduced, and it was applied comprehensively to both operational and support processes.
- Better ways were found to develop people and to get them involved in improving the business.

Some of these changes were simple and procedural, while others required significant changes to technology, computer systems, and software. Many depended upon the involvement and cooperation of suppliers and dealers. Some changes required education to improve people's skills and knowledge, and—most challenging of all—some required significant changes in attitudes and behavior.

The Results

There is no shortage of evidence to demonstrate that the improvement strategy is working. The company's own metrics tell part of the story:

- Employee morale is excellent: According to the annual survey conducted across all TELUS companies, 80 percent of employees feel that TELUS Mobility is a great place to work.
- Customer satisfaction is high, stable, and markedly better than the competition: In 1999, over 90 percent of established customers gave the company a rating of 7 or higher on a 10-point scale, 44 percent gave a rating of 9 or 10, and more than 90 percent indicated that they would repurchase from TELUS Mobility.
- Customer loyalty is high for this industry: During 1999, fewer than 1.3 percent of customers left each month (voluntarily or involuntarily).

TELUS Mobility is also achieving outstanding business results:

- Market share is high: The company currently has about 65 percent of the cellular market in Alberta, and this has been achieved, not by "buying" market share at low margins, but by providing superior service.
- Financial results are excellent: Positive EVA has trebled in the period 1995–1997, and cash flow margin leads the industry.

As a further indication that the company is approaching world-class levels of performance, TELUS Mobility received a Canada Awards for Excellence (CAE) trophy in October 1998, after a rigorous examination by National Quality Institute assessors. Clearly the company's improvement strategy has paid off handsomely.

THE ASSESSMENT PROCESS AT TELUS MOBILITY

TELUS Mobility's assessment process is essentially an external assessment with a few special features. The fundamentals of this have remained almost the same since the outset. The assessment process covers the entire company in one sweep, and it is an integral part of the company's annual planning cycle.

The following are some noteworthy features of the assessment process.

Senior Management Involvement

Based upon his previous experience of a failed improvement initiative, Harry Truderung is insistent on the need for senior management to lead the improvement effort. "Never delegate it," he says, "because this is the kiss of death—you've got to be involved."

This attitude is reflected in a high level of senior management involvement in the assessment process. The senior management team members each take responsibility for creating a part of the descriptive report, with some help from staff trained in the criteria.

The senior management team also conducts its own evaluation, identifying strengths and opportunities for improvement and developing scores. This is done in parallel with the work of the external assessors, but separately and independently. This approach was adopted in order to reinforce senior management ownership of the process and to increase their opportunity for learning.

External and Internal Evaluation

During the first assessment, the external assessors suggested that the company try conducting a *self*-assessment, and this was done the following year—senior management performed an evaluation based on a written description of the management system. This process provided some learning, but it also confirmed the added value of using outside experts. The approach used since then has combined both methods: The external examiners conduct the validation step and create the assessment report; senior management conduct their own evaluation separately, and then learn from the differences.

Internal Participation and Learning

TELUS Mobility has come to value highly the learning opportunity afforded to people who participate directly in the process. These people have consistently provided enthusiastic feedback about this experience, with comments like, "I learned more in the last five days than in the past two years." The knowledge gained through involvement in the process enables people to contribute to better business results.

For this reason, the initial arm's-length relationship between internal participants and the external assessors has been deliberately superseded by a joint-effort approach, which maximizes knowledge transfer. During the validation phase, the external assessors "buddy up" with internal team members, and participate with them throughout the data-gathering and report-writing phases.

This approach was adopted because the learning opportunities seemed more valuable than the clinical objectivity of the assessment report. But this approach has not hampered the ability of the external assessors to identify issues that are invisible to insiders. If anything, it has enabled them to provide more insightful observations, because they have more information and greater understanding of the company.

Planning for Improvement

The assessment process used to end with the presentation of the assessment report, which identified strengths and opportunities for improvement but did not try to specify what should be done next. Since 1994 the assessment report has also included the external assessors' explicit recommendations for action. These provide one input to a formal process for selecting the vital few areas for improvement.

The assessment process has also been extended to include a planning workshop. During this workshop the vital few are selected, and outline plans are developed for each. There is broad participation at this stage—all managers take part (currently more than 40 people), plus the internal assessors and one of the external assessors. This workshop ensures that there is a consensus on the vital few improvement issues selected, and that the plans are grounded in a good understanding of the current reality. Improvement plans are integrated with the overall business plan.

Training Approach

Assessor training was initially intended only to prepare participants in the assessment process. These chosen people attended public sessions, and the training followed a fairly standard case-study-based design developed for training assessors.

This training is now viewed more as an opportunity to build an understanding throughout the company of a quality-oriented management approach. So the training sessions are open to all employees and are focused more on building an understanding of quality principles and how these are supported by appropriate management practices. In other words, it is now a course for a broad audience, which also meets the needs of assessors, rather than a course for assessors that may incidentally benefit others.

Starting in 1997, the "mythical" case studies used in this training have been progressively replaced by the company's own application report from the previous year. This approach has proven to be more effective and more engaging for participants.

Why TELUS Mobility Has Been Successful

Most companies say that they are constantly working to improve; yet many don't seem to make much progress. Even after sweeping changes in staffing and structure, and years of management initiatives that were supposed to cause improvement, they often look, feel, and perform much the same as before. The names and the faces change, but the game is played in the same way.

What is it that has enabled TELUS Mobility to achieve such significant strides? There have been many contributing factors, but some of the most important appear to be:

- the unwavering commitment of senior management to a philosophy of management based on quality principles, and their persistence and energy in pursuing this ideal
- the development of a rational, structured management system with a balanced set of performance measurements, careful analysis to determine what activities and processes drive performance, and the alignment of everyone's efforts to achieve shared goals
- the use of a guiding mechanism—in this case the assessment process—for focusing the improvement efforts, in order to achieve the greatest impact with scarce resources

Acknowledgments

Our thanks to TELUS Mobility and to Harry Truderung and Lori Topp for their assistance in developing this case study.

MEDRAD

Profile

Medrad Inc. is an international provider of innovative devices used to enhance medical diagnostic imaging techniques such as CT and MRI scanning. Its activities include development, manufacturing, marketing, sales, and service. Sales in 1998 were $141 million with a head count of about 950 people worldwide. Medrad has U.S. headquarters in Pittsburgh, Pennsylvania, and European headquarters in Maastricht, The Netherlands.

THE MEDRAD STORY

Dr. Stephen Heilman founded Medrad in 1964, in the classic style of an entrepreneur—he set up in his kitchen. His idea was to automate the process of injecting patients with "contrast media" prior to radiology imaging procedures such as X rays. Contrast media are substances used to enhance the image in order to better reveal the features of specific diseases. Automating the process permitted better control and more consistent results.

This idea proved to be a winner, and a thriving company was born, which grew steadily over the next two decades. By the late '80s it employed 400 people and had sales of $40 million. Medrad has always been preoccupied with the needs of its customers and committed to developing people, so it is not surprising that the company was in good shape. But the growth in its market had attracted serious competitors, and Medrad is fiercely competitive in the marketplace. So senior management was determined to maintain the company's leadership position.

The Medrad Philosophy

The Medrad Philosophy was written and signed in 1983 by the employees and management of Medrad. It is symbolically rededicated and signed every five years to signify that even though the business environment may change, the key principles around which the company has been built remain evergreen.

Why our company exists:

- To improve the quality of healthcare
- To ensure continued growth and profit
- To provide a rewarding and enjoyable place to work

So in 1988 Medrad started to study quality management and to find out what other leading companies were doing. This process included visits by most senior managers to Baldrige winners. What they saw convinced them that, although Medrad was in good shape, the company could do even better. A President's Quality Council was set up to investigate, to decide how to proceed, and to oversee implementation. The two main thrusts during the early years were an IDEASystem program and quality improvement teams (QITs). The IDEASystem program solicits improvement suggestions from frontline people and helps overcome barriers to implementation. This approach has been very successful: By 1998 over 12,000 ideas had been submitted, and about 50 percent of these were implemented.

In contrast to this success, the initial experience with improvement teams was very disappointing: Of 25 teams set up, only two survived the first 12 months. Undaunted, management set out to figure out what was going wrong. The main problem that emerged was inadequate training for the team members—only the team leaders had received formal training, and they were supposed to train the team members "on the job." This had not been effective. A team was set up to develop improved training for QITs, and in 1991 another 25 QITs were set up. This time both the team members and the team leaders received training (32 hours and 40 hours, respectively). This approach worked much better: 23 out of the 25 teams survived the next 12 months and produced results.

During subsequent years Medrad pursued its quality improvement efforts relentlessly and undertook many initiatives, including:

- establishment of an improved system of goals and measurements
- measurement of end-user satisfaction
- extensive training in various aspects of quality improvement
- employee development and competency-based training
- self-directed work teams, and various forms of QITs
- activity-based costing
- development of various organizational structures to drive improvement
- implementation of Hoshin Planning
- benchmarking

THE ASSESSMENT PROCESS AT MEDRAD

It was natural for Medrad to explore the use of the Baldrige criteria because senior management had been so impressed by the Baldrige winners that they had been exposed to. Three senior people conducted the first, fairly informal assessment during 1994 as a learning exercise, and to determine where the company was on its quality journey. Then in 1995 one of the senior managers learned about Xerox's experience with their internal assessment process, and on the basis of this recommended a formal assessment of the entire company. Seven teams (one per Baldrige category) were set up, comprised of senior and middle management. Together these teams created a comprehensive report detailing the strengths and areas for improvement observed, and a gap analysis. Encouraged by the value of this exercise, Medrad decided to apply for the Baldrige award soon after and used this external feedback, together with the internal assessment report, to select the areas to focus on for improvement. These were structured as a "critical five" improvement initiatives plus a larger number of others that are important but not as critical.

Medrad's annual planning and budgeting cycle now includes a process whereby departmental heads provide lists of improvement initiatives that they wish to nominate as corporate priorities, together with fact-based justifications and outline implementation plans. Drawing on this pool of suggestions, the senior staff arrives at a consensus regarding the critical few improvement priorities at a corporate level.

This process has arrived at the same priorities for several years (the same critical five chosen as a result of the first corporate assessment), but the action plans behind each of these have evolved year by year. For example, for the Human Resources Strategic Planning initiative, the first year's action plan was to develop a fully fledged human resources staff. This was followed in subsequent years by the development of a new hiring process, a new internal job bidding process, and a new performance management process.

The Departmental Assessment Process

Medrad's first full corporate level assessment was considered to be a successful and valuable exercise, but the company wanted to engage more people beyond the senior staff level. So the President's Quality Review was set up in 1997. This is a self-administered assessment for a department or process; it is deployed on a voluntary basis. Five departments completed such reviews during 1998, and nine during 1999.

A President's Quality Review is conducted by an internal departmental team that typically comprises the department head and a cross section of other department members. The recommended approach is to include some frontline people as well as managers.

The process starts with a five-hour workshop for the team. In the course of this workshop, the participants learn about the Baldrige core values and the criteria, and they create a first-cut assessment report in note form. The team members are then assigned to subteams, each of which is tasked with completing an assessment report for that category only.

These subteams are allowed to choose how to go about this. Some will simply work together to agree on the content, others will decide that they need to review some documentation or interview some colleagues. Their category reports set out strengths and areas for improvement and may also include ratings for each item.

About two weeks after the initial training workshop, the entire team reassembles for a "self-review" workshop to complete the report and start work on their recommendations. This workshop requires a couple of half-day sessions.

The first step is to review the category reports to agree on any corrections or clarifications and to arrive at consensus ratings. To make it easier to determine the priorities, the team uses a formula to determine the size of the performance gap for each category item. They rate each item in up to four dimensions: approach, deployment (or results only), urgency, and importance. The formula assigns the highest scores to items that have a combination of low ratings for approach and deployment and high ratings for both urgency and importance. Guided by the scores from this formula, the team selects a maximum of three top priority areas for improvement. A new set of subteams is now created, one for each of the critical few, and initial outline plans are developed for each of these. This concludes the self-review workshop.

The subteams now work off-line to develop an initial implementation plan for each of the critical few and to finalize the entire report. This focuses heavily on the critical few identified, and the outline improvement plans.

About two weeks later, the assessment team has a four-hour session to present its report to a group of senior managers, called the President's Quality Review Team. This includes the president, a core group of senior staff, and the vice president to whom the department head reports. This group is not simply an approval body, but aims to operate more like advisors, helping to ensure that the assessment team's plans and goals are realistic.

After this review, the team normally presents its report to its own department. At this stage there may be additional suggestions or changes to the plans. This is also the forum where other people indicate an interest in participating, and the resourcing of the improvement teams is agreed upon. Sometimes resources are needed from other departments (for example, internal customers or suppliers) to complete the improvement teams.

Implementation is monitored at monthly meetings of the President's Quality Council (now called the Performance Excellence Team). A special report is used for reporting the status of the teams, which uses graphic symbols to indicate visually whether a team is on-track, falling behind, or having difficulty in meeting its goals—rather like green, orange, and red color coding. This enables the senior management to see quickly how all of the teams are doing, and to find out whether any intervention or additional support is required.

Some Features of Medrad's Process

Some of the distinguishing features of the Medrad assessment process are:

- *Continuity of staffing from assessment to implementation*
  The members of the assessment team also help to implement the improvement plans. This is part of the commitment that the assessment team members (and their managers) make at the start of the process.

- *A streamlined process*
  The assessment phase is fairly streamlined (an estimated 36 hours of effort is required from each team member), thus conserving time and energy that can be devoted to the implementation phase.
- *The assessment team represents all levels of employees*
  By including people at all levels in the assessment team, there is less need to conduct additional interviews—the perspectives of these different groups have already been captured within the team.
- *A trend toward involvement of internal customers and suppliers*
  Although it is not currently required by the process, one departmental assessment team decided to include members of other departments that were internal customers and suppliers. This proved to be valuable and resulted in a stronger report and good buy-in from other departments (whose support was necessary to implement the improvements).

Early Challenges

Like most companies, Medrad encountered some challenges in getting the assessment process started. Some of these were:

- The company was (and still is) achieving excellent results. Most senior staff believed that other tools needed to be more fully deployed before introducing new ones.
- The company was acquired in 1995, which placed considerable extra demands on the entire management team.

The Results

Medrad's internal indicators suggest that the company's improvement process is working well:

- Monthly customer surveys indicate that the vast majority of end users of Medrad products are satisfied. Overall satisfaction with the company is 95 percent (users rating the company 4 or 5 on a 5-point scale), 99 percent are satisfied with product reliability, and 98 percent are willing to recommend Medrad.

- A quarterly employee satisfaction survey produces ratings that can be compared with other companies using similar surveys administered by Hay. Based on these comparisons, Medrad believes that employee satisfaction is in the top 2 percent of U.S. companies. Employee turnover is in the top quartile of U.S. companies.
- Product quality, reliability, and on-time shipment have improved steadily since the inception of Quality for Life and are at industry-leading levels.

Medrad's business results reflect what one might expect from a company that is doing a lot of things right:

- The company continues to dominate its chosen market: Medrad has 75 percent of the U.S. market, with about six competitors sharing the remaining 25 percent.
- Between 1990 and 1998, annual sales have increased from $49 million to $141 million—an average of more than 15 percent per annum compound growth.
- Margin has been sustained, so profitability has grown in line with sales.

Independent reviews also confirm that Medrad has developed a high-performing management system: In 1993 the company won the Greater Pittsburgh Total Quality Award at the highest level available. In 1996 Medrad applied for the Baldrige award and scored well—in the 450–550 band. This encouraged management to persist and to reapply in 1999, this time receiving a site visit.

Why Medrad Has Been Successful

Medrad's assessment approach is at the heart of the company's improvement process. What have been the keys to the success of this? Medrad senior management identify the following:

- Exposing the senior management to others who were using the process. This was essential to obtain their understanding and commitment, and it was accomplished by arranging visits to Baldrige winners.

- Involving people at all levels in the assessment process. This has tapped a deep source of energy and enthusiasm. The corporate assessment process, although valuable, did not provide much opportunity to engage middle management and frontline people in improvement efforts. The departmental review process has become the primary means of accomplishing this.

• • • • •

Dr. Stephen Heilman, who is still a member of Medrad's board of directors, is justifiably proud of the business success achieved by the little company he started in his kitchen. He is also proud of how the company is using the quality management principles and the self-assessment process to fulfill his original vision: to improve the quality of healthcare, to sustain a healthy and growing company, and to provide an enjoyable and rewarding place for employees to work.

Acknowledgements

Our thanks to Medrad and Bob Stearns for assistance in creating this case study.

CARGILL

Profile
Cargill, Incorporated is a privately owned international agribusiness concern. Its businesses operate in 59 countries on six continents and provide a wide range of products and services including: grain processing and transportation, meat packing, and steel production. Sales revenues in 1999 were $46 billion, and the company employs approximately 82,000 people. Cargill is headquartered in Minneapolis, Minnesota.

THE CARGILL STORY

In 1865 the young W. W. Cargill left the family home in Wisconsin to make his way in the world. He traveled to Iowa with the intention of becoming a farmer but, as the son of thrifty Scottish immigrants, he was shocked at the exorbitant price of farmland: $1.25 per acre. He decided instead to purchase a grain "flat house"—the predecessor of the grain elevator. This was the start of a highly successful business career. Thus began the Cargill legacy.

Today the company is one of the five largest in the food sector. It has diversified into other industries and is still growing rapidly. Cargill has an entrepreneurial culture, a practice of giving young employees broad responsibilities, and a decentralized organizational structure. The business units have a high degree of autonomy, and there are few management levels for a company of this size.

The Improvement Journey

Cargill got started on its improvement journey by spotting an opportunity, rather than being hit by a crisis. In the early 1980s the company was in excellent shape—it had been doubling in size every five to seven years up till then—but some of its customers were becoming much more demanding.

Customers like Coca Cola and Miller Brewing began to require a prevention-oriented quality improvement approach from suppliers of high-fructose syrups, to achieve greater consistency and to reduce inspection and rejection costs. In the auto industry, the Big Three began to place much more stringent requirements on all of their suppliers, including North Star Steel Co., Cargill's steel-producing subsidiary. In both of these industries, some progressive customers took the high road, working with Cargill businesses to help them improve their methods so that required product improvements could be achieved without price hikes.

This type of pressure from customers had a profound effect on the businesses: they learned a lot about quality improvement methods, improved their product quality, reduced their costs, and won more business from their key customers. They also performed better on people-related metrics, such as employee retention, and safety—a "hot button" within Cargill. Soon Cargill senior management noticed, and they took a closer look at these new star performers, with a view to achieving the same results across the entire business. The result of this was a quality improvement methodology that was rolled out across the company during the late 1980s.

First Steps Toward an Assessment System

By 1991, there was considerable evidence of success in some businesses, and Cargill senior management wanted to recognize those that were leading the way. So the Chairman's Quality Award (CQA) was established, modeled on the Baldrige Award.

THE ASSESSMENT PROCESS AT CARGILL

The Cargill assessment process resembles an internal Baldrige awards system, with some features designed to streamline the process so that it can be conducted efficiently on a large scale. It is a voluntary awards program that any business or administrative department can apply for, and it is the most prestigious recognition available within the company. There are two levels of awards and no limit to the number of award recipients each year. The framework used is a slightly modified version of the Baldrige criteria.

The process works as follows:

1. *Submission of applications*
   Applicants prepare a submission of up to 55 pages, responding to the criteria. Corporate Quality will help applicants to prepare their submissions, and about half of the applicants request this support. There are no restrictions on who can apply, and some administrative groups have done so, including a financial processing center (which won an award) and part of the legal department.

2. *Assignment of examiners*
   A team of four examiners is assigned to each application, to evaluate it and write a feedback report. Each team is a mix of new and experienced examiners and includes an executive.

3. *Examiner preparations*
   Examiners are prepared for their task by specific assignments that they must complete during the three weeks prior to "CQA Review Week." During this run-up period, each examiner is required to do individual study of the application and to complete some worksheets. Three large-scale telephone conferences are held—one each week—to help examiners with their preparations. These work rather like a call-in radio program. Most of the participants listen to a discussion by a panel of experts, and the panel takes questions from listeners as well as a live local audience. These conferences last 90 minutes each, and all examiners (typically about 130 people) take part.

4. *CQA Review Week*
   Finally, all of the examiners travel to Minnesota and gather in a large ballroom for the CQA Review Week, where they complete their feedback reports by consensus. This is an intensive process that involves a lot of just-in-time training and on-the-job coaching. Each day, there is an educational presentation covering specific categories. The teams—typically 35 to 40 of them—then complete their feedback reports for those categories and to arrive at consensus scores. Each team includes an examiner with previous experience who leads the consensus process, and each group of four teams also has a coach who reviews their outputs and provides feedback. Over the years Cargill has trained a cadre of internal people who have con-

siderable external experience with the assessment process—as senior examiners for the Baldrige program, or as examiners for state awards—and they act as coaches. In the early days of the program, an outside expert presented these educational sessions. Today, Cargill senior executives give the presentations— thereby demonstrating their commitment and their knowledge of the criteria as a management model for their business.

5. *Selection of finalists*

   At the end of this week of intense activity, the awards steering committee scrutinizes the feedback reports and selects the applicants that warrant a site visit. In 1999, 17 out of 35 applicants received site visits.

6. *Site visits*

   Site visits are similar to those for the Baldrige award, but much shorter. They typically require one to two days of on-site work, another one day of planning and document review beforehand, and one day of consensus building to finalize the feedback report. The style of the site visit is very open—a "no surprises" approach. Applicants are told in advance what the key issues are, what documents will be required, and which key people will need to be interviewed. At a wrap-up meeting with the applicants the site visit team leader shares some of the team's high-level conclusions. Of course it is not known at this stage whether the applicant will win an award, and the site visit team does not make that decision.

7. *Selection of award recipients*

   The awards steering committee scrutinizes the site visit reports and selects the award recipients. Quality Consultants (team coaches) participate in this meeting.

8. *CQA conference*

   Award recipients are presented with their trophies at a one-day conference in October, modeled on the Baldrige Quest for Excellence conference. Award recipients present their best practices across the six approach-deployment categories and the Cargill CFO shares some of the key results that the recipients have achieved in the five results item areas.

Every applicant receives a feedback report. There is no formal requirement to take action based on these reports, but the corporate quality function visits most of the applicant businesses after the adjudication process is complete, to offer support in prioritizing opportunities for improvement.

To fine-tune the process, Cargill holds an annual Improvement Day, during which a sample of people involved in the process review feedback from the previous cycle and decide on improvements for the following year.

During the first few years of the CQA, the adjudication process was not very searching. Once management realized that this was a lost opportunity, the process was strengthened and refined, and it evolved into a rigorous and systematic process, as well as a highly efficient one. The bar has been gradually raised, and a second, higher level of award was introduced, the Spicola Award. Any business unit that achieves this level should be a strong contender for a national-level award.

Evidence of Success

In 1995, Cargill senior managers asked the question, "What are we getting out of all the effort that goes into this program?" They commissioned a study to find out. The study examined the performance of about 100 Cargill plants, looking for differences between businesses that had received awards and those that had not. To ensure validity, the comparisons were made among plants producing similar products. The conclusion was that, regardless of the line of business, award recipients were performing much better than their peers. They demonstrated statistically significant leadership in the areas of:

- earnings per employee
- employee safety
- employee turnover

These findings reaffirmed the value of the program, and led senior managers to renew their commitment to implementing it throughout the company.

Cargill has earned many sole-supplier contracts with major food and industrial customers around the world. These were won by consistently delivering products and services that meet customer expectations and by offering innovative solutions that meet customers' changing needs. Implementation of the quality process has been an integral part of such success.

Cargill businesses units have also received several U.S. state awards—in Florida, Kansas, Missouri, and Minnesota—as well as the Australian Quality Award.

Special Features of the Cargill System

CQA Week   CQA Week is an important feature of the Cargill process, and it is a model of how to streamline the process without sacrificing rigor. By working from the start with the real submissions, and by receiving training and just-in-time coaching throughout the process, assessment teams can learn and accomplish a great deal in a short time. As one of the architects of this system said: "We spend less time on the driving range and more out on the fairways. This is a playing lesson where the intensity helps the learning process."

Deployment   In 1999, 55 percent of the company had participated in the CQA program (measured by the number of employees in the businesses and departments that have applied). It is a major achievement for a voluntary program to achieve such a high level of acceptance in a company where the businesses have so much autonomy. This is largely due to a constant drive to make the CQA process meet the needs of its customers—Cargill's businesses—and hence ongoing innovations and refinements of the process.

The Link to Continuous Improvement   Although there is no formal requirement to act on feedback reports written by assessment teams, the Cargill system is effective in driving improvement among the award applicants, for a number of reasons:

- The support provided by Corporate Quality (to help applicants prioritize areas for improvement) helps ensure that applicants do not stumble for lack of understanding of the findings or expertise in planning the improvement actions.

- The timing of the awards cycle is such that improvement priorities can be taken into account during the formal planning and budgeting process.
- During subsequent site visits, one of the areas of focus is on the actions taken in response to the previous feedback report. This drives home the message that the applicants are expected to use this information to improve.

Leadership Participation and Learning The CQA system is also driving improvement in an equally important, though less direct way: by providing a valuable learning experience for the executives who take part as examiners. By studying the award applications and taking part in site visits, these executives come away with a greater appreciation for the power of an effective management system, and with some ideas and best practices that they will apply in their own business units.

In spite of the resources required to operate the CQA process, there is no sign of Cargill's commitment diminishing. The focus today is on achieving even wider deployment, and a repeat study is planned to examine once more the differences in performance between award recipients and others. Cargill senior managers today continue the founder's practice of savvy business decisions. Cargill's CQA program—like its original grain house—looks to them like a smart and practical investment.

Acknowledgements

Our thanks to Cargill and Phil Forve, Cargill's Quality Team Leader, for help in compiling this case study.

PINELLAS COUNTY SCHOOL DISTRICT

Profile
Pinellas County School District is the seventh largest school district in Florida and the 21st largest in the United States. It serves all of Pinellas county (in the Tampa Bay area) and has an enrollment of 110,000 students in more than 140 schools. Its annual budget in 1999 exceeded $1 billion.

THE PINELLAS STORY

Pinellas County School District is huge and diverse. Its schools serve communities across a full spectrum of local and urban environments, socio-economic groups and ethnic groups. It is a microcosm of the entire U.S. educational system, and whatever challenges any school in the U.S. faces, Pinellas probably faces it too, somewhere within the district.

In spite of the challenges of size and diversity, Pinellas has stayed closely in touch with the needs of its students, parents, and the community. On almost any measure of student achievement, it is one of the highest-performing school districts in the U.S.A. While many school districts struggle to maintain their current levels of performance in the face of mounting challenges to the educational system, Pinellas continues to improve. How has this been accomplished?

The story begins in the early '90s with two events that were particularly significant for the school district:

- John Mitcham, the president of AT&T Paradyne, a locally headquartered division of AT&T, challenged Pinellas management to embrace continuous improvement. The school district already had a fine reputation, but Mitcham was impatient with what he felt was a complacent attitude. He was concerned that the district was losing the opportunity to be the best that it could be. In addition to throwing down the gauntlet, he offered to provide help and expertise from AT&T's resources. This looked like a real opportunity.

- The state of Florida enacted new accountability legislation—as did many states at that time—mandating that the school districts pursue high student achievement for *all* students. This was a major change of philosophy that would drive significant changes to the educational system. This legislation looked all the more intimidating since many school districts—including Pinellas—felt that they were already doing the best they knew how. Yet there would be negative consequences for school districts that could not meet the new standards. This looked like a serious threat.

This combination of threat and opportunity helped drive the early improvement efforts within Pinellas. AT&T paid for an educational retreat for district leadership, the superintendent and his direct reports as well as teacher union leadership. AT&T shared information generously about their practices, and they provided moral support. The state legislation required action, since it called for every school to develop an improvement plan. The Baldrige-based assessment approach that AT&T was using provided an ideal tool for the schools to use in developing these plans. Thus the improvement process got started on a very sound footing, and it has continued and developed from this base.

Here are some of the steps in the journey:

- 1991: *Training of the cabinet and teachers' union*
  This was the start of the process, when senior management began to learn about quality management. The teachers' union was in the learning process and was a part of decision-making from the onset. Beginning the transformation process as partners has proven to be a critical ingredient for success.
- 1991–93: *Developing internal expertise*
  Pinellas made an early decision to internally develop the expertise that was required, rather than obtain some improvement methodology "off the shelf" and rely on outsiders to provide the expertise. So the proponents steeped themselves in learning: about Deming, Juran, quality management principles and techniques, and the Baldrige criteria. At the same time, a few schools whose principals were keen on this approach went into action, trying to apply what they had learned.

One of the breakthroughs made during this time was the Collaborative Bargaining initiative. Union and management met regularly to work together, using quality management principles, to tackle a range of issues in which there was a shared interest. This evolved into a highly effective partnership, which focused on creating a system to address student achievement issues rather than on the fine print of the contract.

- 1993: *The Florida Governor's Sterling Award*
  This was the first year of operation of this Baldrige-based state award. Since there was no education category, Pinellas applied in the business category, and it received the highest level of recognition. The Pinellas County School District was the first educational institution in the U.S. to receive a state-level award. The award was given primarily for the unique Pinellas approach and plan for transformation. Few results were evident in these early stages. The award was a huge breakthrough, since it validated the quality management approach that Pinellas was taking. Virtually no one else in the education system was doing anything similar, so naturally there was huge skepticism, which this recognition largely overcame.

- 1994: *The Quality Academy*
  The management of the transformation at this stage became a full-time enterprise for those school district employees who were involved. The associate superintendent who led the effort was criticized for "meddling" in other parts of the organization that were none of his concern. Recognition that the transformation must be equally addressed across all parts of the organization resulted in restructuring his position to report only to the superintendent and thereby have authority to "meddle" with all parts of the system. Simultaneously, the Sterling award recognition had generated so much external interest that the expertise of the Quality Academy was soon in high demand. The Academy began to sell its expertise to other districts. These monies were reinvested in Pinellas to provide resources for training its 17,000 employees. The availability of these funds has enabled the Quality Academy to have a degree of flexibility that would never have existed by line-item budget allocation or grant funds, and in many instances this

has insulated the Academy from the inertia of the current system and the bureaucracy surrounding policy change.

- 1994–95: *The Superintendent's Quality Challenge (SQC)*
The SQC is Pinellas's own internal Baldrige-based assessment and award system, which was modeled on AT&T's President's Quality Award. This system provided a means for all schools (and departments) to understand quality management (through the model), assess their own management systems, and create improvement plans.
- 1995: *The strategic planning process*
The district comprehensive planning process was revised to align with the Baldrige model, thus moving this from a highly political process to a more fact-based one. This was a very important step forward, because all of the budgeting and resource allocation is based on this plan.
- 1996: *Leadership development and the personnel evaluation systems*
A revised leadership training and development program for principals-to-be was introduced, to provide this critical group of people with the skills and knowledge required to create an effective management system at the school site level and to perform continuous improvement. At the same time the personnel evaluation systems were aligned with the Baldrige model, thus providing an incentive for people to acquire these skills and knowledge. This shifted the appraisal of schools and their principals away from "bugs, buses, and beans" (housekeeping, transportation, and meals) to focus on their ability to achieve high student outcomes.
- 1997: *Decision-making system*
A process for decision-making was introduced, starting at the school board level. Like the strategic planning process, this was another important step in moving toward a more fact based and less politically driven style of management. The decision-making system can be applied to routine operational decisions as well as strategic ones, and it is used at all levels within the district.
- 1998–99: *Classroom Learning System and PDSA Model*
One of the initiatives that has produced the most dramatic improvements in student achievement has been the *Classroom Learning System*. This is essentially the structured use of the quality management principles and the Baldrige frame-

work as a methodology for organizing how work is done in the classroom.

What does this look like in practice? It looks as different from the traditional classroom teaching process as a self-managed team looks different from a command-oriented hierarchical department. Students in every grade take part in discussing and understanding their goals; students take responsibility for achieving these goals and have a lot of discretion in what learning methods they use to do this; students team up and help each other to ensure that *everyone* masters the topic; and there is a constant process of evaluation and feedback that focuses not just on the achievement of the student, but on the learning process. Through this feedback, both teachers and students find out what methods work best, and they can constantly fine-tune their own approaches.

This way of managing the classroom has led to dramatically higher academic achievement, fewer disciplinary problems, and higher morale among students and teachers. Internal studies show that these results are a consequence of the approach, not differences in teaching ability, and that most teachers can learn this approach.

The *PDSA Model* is a fact-oriented problem-solving methodology based on Deming's Plan-Do-Study-Act cycle. This is invaluable as a tool for use within the management system. It provides a consistent framework and expectation at all levels of the system from the school board to the classroom to continuously improve processes. All students use this as the basis of their learning process.

Results Information

Pinellas is achieving outstanding results. Thanks to a variety of standardized state-wide testing programs, reliable measurements show student achievement at various grade levels for reading, writing, and math. These results allow for comparisons between a school district, the state standard, and the average of other districts in the state.

These results also reveal trends over time. Chart after chart, these measurements, almost without exception, tell the same story:

Since the early '90s, Pinellas has improved student achievement significantly at all grade levels, and in all the three core subjects; Pinellas is doing better than the state average (which is also improving) in all of its programs.

Pinellas also surpassed the state averages in both the verbal and math sections on the SAT. Pinellas County Schools' fourth-graders were first in the state on the 1998 Florida Writes test. Eighth-graders were second, and 10th-graders tied for first.

Many of these improvements are evident as sustained trends, which seem likely to continue. Pinellas uses the Statistical Process Control technique of calculating upper and lower control limits and plotting these on the performance charts reviewed by management. On many of these charts the trends have "broken through" and stayed above the upper control limit, indicating that the improvements are due to a real improvement in the system rather than some kind of fluke. Pinellas reports its results on key performance indicators in a District Quarterly Report. This common business practice represents revolutionary change in educational standard operating procedures.

Perhaps the most significant single indicator is that in 1998 Pinellas was identified as the top school district in the state of Florida in terms of overall student achievement. This was based on a scoring system developed at the state level that combines nine student achievement measures. These measures cover reading, writing, and math achievement in various grades and are based on standard statewide tests. In 1998, Rawlings Elementary School became the first *school* in Florida to win the Governor's Sterling Award (the district won this same award in 1993).

The local business community, which helped Pinellas to get started, has also been impressed by the approach that the District has developed. In recent years Pinellas has been asked to assist several local companies with their quality journey, including Honeywell Space Systems, E-Systems Raytheon and Morton Plant Mease Hospital. Both Honeywell and Morton Plant are Florida Sterling Award winners.

Pinellas has conducted studies to collect data comparing classrooms that use the Baldrige-based Classroom Learning System (CLS) to those that do not. The data from these studies reveal remarkable differences. Classrooms using CLS perform 30 to 50 percent better on standardized tests and have half the discipline referrals. These results are the same regardless of the group demographics: "at-risk" students in a CLS classroom consistently outperform their peers who are not. Many students in special education classes that use CLS are catching up to those in normal classes taught using traditional methods. These are exceptional results, yet Pinellas' experience indicates that they can be replicated in any school.

All of this evidence points to the potential for unprecedented levels of improvement in the future, as these more effective methods are applied throughout the district for the benefit of all students.

THE ASSESSMENT PROCESS AT PINELLAS

The assessment process at Pinellas is called the Superintendent's Quality Challenge (SQC), and it was heavily influenced by AT&T's internal award program. However, in spite of the name and the origins, this is very much a planning system rather than an awards program—in fact, there are no internal awards associated with the process. Here is how the process works:

1. By law, every school in Florida has to create an improvement plan every year. Pinellas created the Superintendent's Quality Challenge (SQC) instrument to enable schools to conduct an assessment, which would show them what issues need to be addressed in their improvement plan. The SQC assessment instrument comes in a variety of "levels," which allow schools to use a simpler approach at first and to work up to the more comprehensive one. These levels include:

   - a format very similar to the Baldrige criteria but using terms familiar to people in a school system environment
   - a somewhat simplified version of this
   - a check-the-box rubric that describes what different levels of performance look like for all of the elements of the criteria.

2. All schools (and administrative departments) are strongly encouraged to submit a self-assessment of their management system annually. The schools decide how to go about preparing this document—there is no prescribed process—and what level

of the SQC to use. The more advanced schools may elect to base their self-assessments on external (state or national) criteria.

3. The self-assessment documents are reviewed by trained assessors, who write feedback reports. Pinellas trains more than 100 examiners every year, using a three-day format similar to Baldrige examiner training. These examiners are drawn from a variety of sources—principals, administrators, and other employees of the district, as well as outsiders, mainly from local business partners but also from other sectors such as healthcare. Some teachers participate as examiners, but relatively few thus far because of the constraints on their time. The evaluation process purposely does not include any type of site visit in order to avoid creating concern in the schools about another outside "audit."

4. The feedback reports are sent back to the schools and are used for developing improvement plans. The schools receive outside facilitator support—if they want it—to help them understand the feedback report, identify suitable actions, and create their improvement plans.

Pinellas has also obtained a district-level assessment of the management system a number of times by using the SQC instrument at a District Cabinet level and by submitting applications of the entire school district to state and national awards programs. The SQC-based assessment was conducted in exactly the same way as for the rest of the organization. The District Cabinet's self-assessment was evaluated using what Pinellas considered to be the best of their external assessors.

Features of the Pinellas Approach

Which aspects of the Pinellas approach have been especially beneficial? Here are a few identified by Pinellas senior management.

Pinellas is steadily building a pool of internal people who have received assessor training and participated in the SQC process. This pool is more than 300 strong and is growing each year, both in numbers and in experience. This is a benefit because of the higher caliber of the evaluation work done by assessors: the feedback reports are more valuable to the schools. However, probably an even greater benefit is the influence on the district of having so many people in responsible positions who have this training and mindset. All of these people are now looking at their own jobs, and at the functioning of the organization, in a very different and more productive way. This pool of trained and experienced assessors in positions of influence is a powerful force for change.

Another aspect of the Pinellas approach that has been helpful is the in-house design of the SQC system. Having control over this has allowed the district to provide an easy entry point to the process for schools performing an assessment for the first time and to "raise the bar" as the district as a whole becomes more mature in its approach. The initial entry-level version of the SQC has been dropped (it is now considered too easy), and an additional level has been added to the range of SQC instruments to provide another rung somewhat higher up the ladder.

The Quality Academy has been a great asset, not just to Pinellas's internal efforts, but in enabling Pinellas to spread the word about quality improvement. The Academy has worked with literally hundreds of other school districts in 32 states and with educational institutions in six foreign countries. The total fees from these services during the past six years have exceeded $2 million and enabled the Academy to be largely self-funding. More important, this exposure to others traveling on the same journey has created many opportunities for collaboration and sharing, which have benefited both Pinellas and the other parties.

Today Pinellas is one of three educational institutions that are at the center of a major initiative designed to accelerate the improvement of the U.S. education system, state by state. The Baldrige In Education initiative is supported by a highly credible and well-qualified consortium of business partners and associations who support this goal. The consortium is offering education and support initially to five state education systems, to improve performance by adopting a Baldrige-based approach.

The Future

A question that people in the field of quality improvement always ask at some point—out loud or silently to themselves—is "will this process survive?" There are predictable hazards on the road ahead: external changes that cause disruption and discontinuities, changes of key personnel, and over time the departure of the people who first championed the process. So the acid test of an effective improvement system is whether it can survive these hazards. Pinellas has already weathered such challenges.

During difficult times, any doubts or thoughts of turning back have been quickly extinguished by the external business partners and by the unions. These groups have repeatedly stepped forward to demonstrate their support and to sustain the District leadership's commitment to the process.

Parents have exerted a similar influence in other ways. When students relocate and have to leave a school that is advanced in the process, they may find themselves in an institution that is not using this approach. When this happens they experience intense frustration at being forced back into a less effective learning environment. There have been cases of the parents of such children forming lobby groups to put pressure on other institutions and to ask them, "why aren't you doing this?"

Parents of students from a Baldrige-based middle school put collective pressure on the high school their students would be attending to maintain the momentum and learning environment in which their students had been so successful. This action encouraged changes in the high school that had previously been slow to implement the new approaches. Nowadays, these parents also have access to results data that make it very difficult to argue against their case.

The signs are that this approach will not only survive in Pinellas and within Florida, but will be successfully propagated within the education systems of several other states over the next few years. Will this be in time to benefit our children—or grandchildren? Let's hope so.

Acknowledgements

Our thanks to the staff of the Pinellas County School District for assistance in creating this case study.

• • • • •

> ### ^{www}**Companion Website Materials:**
>
> - Contacting case study organizations
> - Additional case studies

Another Book
from David Hutton

THE CHANGE AGENTS' HANDBOOK

David Hutton's first book, *The Change Agents' Handbook* (published by ASQ Quality Press) is a personal survival guide for anyone striving to create positive change within their organization.

This guide leads you through the process of assessing the situation to gauge your chances of success, getting established in your new role, preparing to launch the process, creating a plan for the transformation, and managing the ensuing changes. It deals with the practical issues and personal needs that surround the change agent's assignment, including the emotional pressures and the types of opposition to be expected.

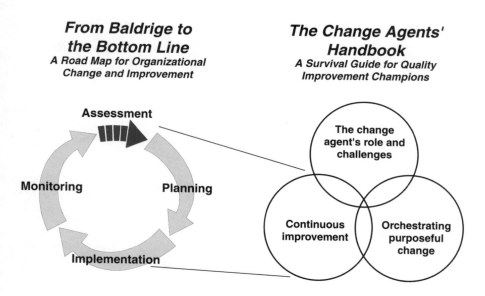

From Baldrige to the Bottom Line
A Road Map for Organizational Change and Improvement

The Change Agents' Handbook
A Survival Guide for Quality Improvement Champions

www.dhutton.com/roadmap

www.dhutton.com/handbook

Index